APOSTOLICITY AND UNITY

APOSTOLICITY AND UNITY

Essays on the Porvoo Common Statement

Edited by

Ola Tjørhom

William B. Eerdmans Publishing Company
Grand Rapids, Michigan / Cambridge, U.K.

WCC Publications
Geneva, Switzerland

Published jointly 2002 by
Wm. B. Eerdmans Publishing Co.
255 Jefferson Ave. S.E., Grand Rapids, Michigan 49503 /
P.O. Box 163, Cambridge CB3 9PU U.K.
www.eerdmans.com
and by
WCC Publications
World Council of Churches
150 route de Ferney, P.O. Box 2100
1211 Geneva 2, Switzerland
website: http://www.wcc-coe.org

Printed in the United States of America

07 06 05 04 03 02   7 6 5 4 3 2 1

Library of Congress Cataloging-in-Publication Data

Apostolicity and unity: essays on the Porvoo common statement /
edited by Ola Tjørhom.
p. cm.
Includes bibliographical references and index.
Eerdmans ISBN 0-8028-0969-3 (pbk.: alk. paper)
1. Porvoo agreement. 2. Anglican Communion — Relations — Lutheran Church. 3. Lutheran Church — Relations — Anglican Communion. I. Tjørhom, Ola.

BX5004.4 A55 2002
280'.042 — dc21

2002033892

WCC ISBN 2-8254-1375-5

Contents

Foreword

The fellowship based on the Porvoo Common Statement has already proved to be a vast enrichment and a blessing to our churches as well as our world communions. As a result of this fellowship a comprehensive sharing of spiritual gifts has been made possible. In addition, our witness to unity in a divided world has become more credible. However, church fellowship is not a static entity. We are committed to a continuous growth in community as well as to efforts to make our unity ever more visible — in order that the world shall see and believe. Moreover, the importance of the Porvoo Common Statement is not limited to fellowship between a limited number of churches or denominations, but must always be evaluated in the perspective of the classical goal of the ecumenical movement: visible unity between all God's people.

Accordingly, Porvoo still represents a challenge to the signatory churches. It commits us to more openness towards each other's spiritual heritage; it challenges us to make our unity ever more visible on all levels of our churches' lives; and it summons us to a better sharing of resources — not the least in our mission in a broken world. This inter alia implies close consultation when crucial decisions are to be made. It requires the establishment of more efficient structures of unity. In this way the Porvoo Common Statement continues to challenge us in our efforts to contribute to the manifestation of visible unity.

Seen against this background, we welcome the present book as an invitation to a constructive discussion of the Porvoo Common Statement as well as the fellowship that is based on this statement — as we approach its tenth anniversary. In this discussion the wider ecumenical implications of Porvoo — vis-à-vis other churches and traditions as well as God's world — call for particular attention. Here Porvoo's emphasis on apostolicity as concrete continuity in the church's ministry, service, and mission represents a vital contribution, together with its proposal on how the different churches' signs of apostolicity may be shared within the framework of communion. We would like to recommend this book to all who are concerned about the Porvoo fellowship as well as those who are committed to visible unity.

K. G. HAMMAR
The Archbishop of Uppsala

DAVID HOPE
The Archbishop of York

Preface

This book has a double purpose. First, it aims at presenting an appropriate introduction to the Porvoo Common Statement (PCS) from the dialogue between the Anglican churches in Great Britain and Ireland and the Lutheran churches in the Nordic and Baltic nations. Second, it is our hope that the book will contribute to a constructive — and critical — debate on PCS ten years after the Porvoo commission finished its work in 1992.

The first part of the present volume includes accounts of Porvoo's background and wider framework as well as some reflections on its reception in the churches. Its second part contains essays on the most central theological concerns of PCS. These essays are written by both "insiders" and "outsiders" — that is, by some who were directly involved in the work of the Porvoo commission and some who did not participate in this work. In the third part of the book PCS is evaluated from the perspective of other churches and ecumenical processes. Even though all authors were given a specific thematic emphasis, there is a certain amount of overlap between their contributions in the sense that several of them focus on what can be labeled as Porvoo's key concern — namely, the role of apostolicity and historic continuity in the episcopal office in building and making visible the unity of the church.

As editor I want to express my deep gratitude to the Thora Ohlsson Foundation in Lund, Sweden — without their generous financial support it would have been difficult to realize this project. I would also like to thank the Church of Norway, the Evangelical Lutheran Church of Finland, and the Evangelical Lutheran Church in Brunswick, Germany, for their contributions. Moreover, I am grateful for the constructive cooperation of our publisher and particularly its President, William B. Eerdmans, Jr. Pamela Mattox has done a marvelous job in making the contributions of those of us who do not have English as our mother tongue readable. Dr. Mickey Mattox, my colleague at the Institute for Ecumenical Research in Strasbourg, has also contributed significantly to the realization of this project. Last but certainly not least, the co-authors of the book deserve a warm word of gratitude. We hope that these essays, which reflect a wide variety of approaches to PCS, will contribute to a constructive exchange on this ecumenical initiative.

In editing the contributions in this collection of essays the aim has not been total standardization or uniformity with regard to notes, references to literature, spelling, etc. Rather, we have chosen to be open to a certain amount of "formal" diversity — reflecting the fact that the authors also come from different scholarly traditions. Our main concern has simply been to ensure that references are basically clear and understandable. We hope that these essays, which reflect a wide variety of approaches to PCS, will contribute to a constructive exchange on this ecumenical initiative.

Obviously, Porvoo is contextual in the sense that it deals with specific churches that are characterized by specific features. Thus, it does not make much sense to try to apply PCS directly in different contexts and to other partners. Still, while drafting the Porvoo statement we never saw our work as exclusively bilateral — let alone in a narrow parochial perspective — but rather as a service to the visible unity of all God's people.

The contributions in the present volume show that there are things in PCS that could and probably should have been expressed differently. At the same time, I dare to read these contributions as indications that the Porvoo Common Statement is of relevance in a wider ecumenical perspective, beyond the Porvoo churches. On this background we invite all readers — ordained and lay, theologians and theological students, professional ecumenists and everyone who is committed to Christian unity — to join us in and contribute to our efforts to identify approaches and "models" that serve the goal of visible church unity.

Ola Tjørhom
Stavanger, Norway, during Lent, 2002

I. The Background and Framework of the Porvoo Common Statement — The Reception and Implementation of the Statement in the Churches

The Background and Genesis of the Porvoo Common Statement

DAVID TUSTIN

1. The Task of the Conversations

The formal conversations that produced the Porvoo Common Statement (PCS) began in 1989 at Sigtuna (Sweden). From the outset it was pretty clear what needed to be accomplished, though the formulation of this task had evolved only gradually and had been expressed in various ways.

a. In 1968 the report of a commission chaired by Bishop Oliver Tomkins (Bristol) on Intercommunion recommended that the terms of the existing sacramental relationship between the Church of England and the Lutheran churches of Sweden, Finland, Latvia, and Estonia should be further clarified "so as to encourage a greater freedom of interchange." It also recommended that "in the case of the other Scandinavian churches, which are in almost all respects identical in faith and order with the churches of Sweden and Finland, it seems desirable to raise again the whole question of movement towards full communion, and the possibility of overcoming the problems raised by the fact that the first episcopal consecrations in Denmark at the time of the Reformation were performed by a priest."[1]

1. See "Intercommunion Today," paragraphs 185 and 221, published 1968 by the Central Board of Finance of the Church of England.

b. In 1970 Anglican-Lutheran dialogue was begun at world level, and the so-called Pullach Report[2] included the recommendation that "the Church of England should no longer make a distinction in the intercommunion arrangements made for various Lutheran churches, but should extend the arrangements for Sweden and Finland to include all Lutheran churches in Europe."[3] Besides recording substantial agreement on many doctrinal matters, the report contained two particular concepts that were to prove fruitful during the Porvoo conversations. The meaning of *apostolic succession* was broadened.[4] Secondly, the *historic episcopate* was regarded not as a necessary condition for interchurch relations, but as something that "those Lutheran churches which have not retained (it) are free to accept where it serves the growing unity of the Church in obedience to the Gospel."[5] The implications of these seminal words were to be drawn out in later years.
c. In 1983 the so-called Cold Ash Report[6] defined the goal of Anglican-Lutheran dialogue as "full communion" — a relationship that was described in broader terms than pulpit and altar fellowship. Being in full communion was seen to carry wider implications, such as "common witness, life and service . . . a commitment to one another in respect of major decisions on questions of faith, order and morals . . . and promotion of justice, peace and love."[7] This began to spell out the potentiality of a far-reaching partnership in mission.
d. In 1988 the Lambeth Conference welcomed the insights of the Niagara Report,[8] and urged that this convergence on the understanding of apostolic ministry should "prompt us to move to-

2. "Anglican-Lutheran International Conversations," published 1973 by SPCK.

3. "Anglican-Lutheran International Conversations," paragraph 97.

4. "Anglican-Lutheran International Conversations," paragraphs 73ff., and the Anglican Chairman's personal note on p. 26.

5. "Anglican-Lutheran International Conversations," paragraph 89 — part of a statement by the Lutheran participants.

6. "Anglican-Lutheran Relations: Report of the Joint Working Group 1983," published 1983 by ACC and LWF.

7. "Anglican-Lutheran Relations," paragraphs 24-27.

8. "The Niagara Report: Anglican-Lutheran Consultation on Episcopé 1987," published 1988 for ACC and LWF by Church House Publishing, London.

wards the fullest possible ecclesial recognition and the goal of full communion."[9]

e. In August 1989 when "Porvoo" delegates arrived in Sigtuna, a useful discussion took place informally on the first evening before official proceedings began. When Prof. Stephen Sykes invited Bishop Tore Furberg to say what outcome Lutherans were hoping for, the latter replied, "That our churches' mutual relations should be able to move forward to the same level, without anyone needing to take a backward step." This tactful and precise way of expressing the aim gained general assent. We later amplified this in our Co-chairmen's Foreword as follows:

> The aim of these Conversations was to move forward from our existing piecemeal agreements towards the goal of visible unity. By harvesting the fruits of previous ecumenical dialogues we hoped to express a greater measure of common understanding, and to resolve the long-standing difficulties between us about episcopacy and succession. We found that we had similar histories and faced similar challenges in contemporary society, and that there were no essential differences between us in the fields of faith, sacramental life or ministry (each church already being episcopal in structure). We became convinced that the way was now open to regard one another's churches, each with its own distinctive character, as sister churches. The time was ripe to move closer together and to implement a practical agreement which would be relevant to laity and clergy alike in carrying out our common mission.[10]

This was how we saw our task at that time. Another way of stating it would be to say that we intended to receive the insights of the Niagara Report, and apply them to our own context of the episcopally ordered churches in Northern Europe.

9. See "The Truth Shall Make You Free" (report of the 1988 Lambeth Conference), p. 204, Resolution 4, published 1988 by ACC.

10. See *Together in Mission and Ministry*, pp. 2-3, paragraph 6, published 1993 by the Council for Christian Unity, London.

2. The Stimulus to Move Ahead

Where did the impulse arise to move beyond the earlier interim Anglican-Lutheran agreements that had been approved in the 1930s and 1950s?[11] God's spirit was moving many hearts, minds, and consciences within the various strands of the one ecumenical movement in the 1970s and '80s. The warmer climate of thought and action was evidenced by the reports of a number of bilateral dialogues and, in particular, by the multilateral Lima text[12] — the culmination of some fifty years' Faith and Order work. These developments were undergirded by much prayer and fellowship across national and confessional boundaries. Specially helpful in preparing for "Porvoo" were the personal acquaintances and mutual understanding built up over many years by two series of Anglo-Scandinavian conferences. The Theological Conferences, begun in 1929 and briefly interrupted during the Second World War, continued to meet every two years and to engage a widening circle of theologians and church leaders. The Pastoral Conferences, begun in 1978 and also held biennially, exercised a similar influence at the level of parochial and sector clergy. Neither of these series were church unity negotiations, but were a valuable means of enabling people from both sides of the North Sea to pray and study together, to share their thoughts and insights on a wide range of topics, and to build up a network of informal contacts. The importance of these growing links in paving the way for formal conversations should not be underestimated.

The Lutheran-Episcopal Agreement on "Interim Eucharistic Sharing" of 1982 in the USA gave a fresh impetus to Anglican-Lutheran relations. So, too, did the publication of the Meissen Common Statement in 1988,[13] which was overwhelmingly accepted in England and both parts of Germany.

Social and political changes in Europe had a marked impact on the climate of thought, as paragraphs 10-13 of PCS briefly indicate.

11. See Christopher Hill's essay "Existing Agreements between Our Churches," in *Together in Mission and Ministry*, pp. 53-58.

12. *Baptism, Eucharist and Ministry*, published 1982 by the World Council of Churches.

13. The fullest documentation is provided in "Die Meissener Erklärung" (EKD-Texte Nr. 47), published 1993 by EKD, Hanover.

Most significant of these were, in the East, the collapse of communist regimes and the re-emergence of the Baltic States as independent republics; and, in the West, the movement to enlarge the membership of the European Union. The Porvoo conversations, though influenced by these events, were nevertheless theologically rather than politically motivated.

These new conversations owed much to the initiative of Archbishop Robert Runcie (Canterbury), who had been greatly stirred by the Luther quincentenary celebrations of 1983. In December 1985 two Church of England emissaries, Canon (later Bishop) Christopher Hill and Canon Martin Reardon, visited Uppsala for informal talks with Archbishop Bertil Werkström and Dr. (later Bishop) Tord Harlin, who keenly supported the proposal for a broader agreement embracing all the Nordic Lutheran churches. Further talks then took place in London and Oslo, involving Bishop Andreas Aarflot (chairman of the Norwegian bishops' conference), Prof. Ola Tjørhom (then of the Nordic Ecumenical Institute), Dr. Mary Tanner, and a few others. Without the vision and determination of those who made these preliminary plans, formal conversations would not have got off the ground.

3. Composition of the Joint Commission

The original members, present at the meeting in Sigtuna, came from only six of the twelve countries that eventually became involved. The Anglicans were all from England, and included the future Archbishop of Canterbury.[14] The English delegates came with the knowledge and goodwill of their sister churches in Ireland, Scotland, and Wales (whose provincial secretaries received all minutes and papers, and were kept informed of future developments). The Lutherans were from Denmark, Estonia, Finland, Norway, and Sweden; delegates from Iceland and Latvia sent their apologies, but came to the three subsequent meetings. These partners were later joined by further delegates: in 1991-92 from Lithuania, and in 1992 from Ireland, Scotland, and Wales. Thus all twelve countries were directly represented at the

14. Dr. George Carey was bishop of Bath & Wells from 1987 to 1991, when he was translated to Canterbury.

final meeting in Finland on 9-13 October 1992, when PCS was adopted and signed unanimously.

An active role was played throughout by the observers, consultants, and staff. Every meeting was attended by observers from the Lutheran Council of Great Britain and the Nordic Roman Catholic Bishops' Conference (through whom the Pontifical Council for Promoting Christian Unity was kept informed). At particular sessions these observers were joined by others from the World Council of Churches (Faith & Order Unit), the Lutheran World Federation, and the Nordic Ecumenical Institute. Consultants attended certain sessions, including Anglican and Lutheran spokesmen from the USA who informed us about the proposed Concordat of Agreement prior to its publication. In addition, minutes and papers were shared with the following parties, who were invited to contribute written comments and were kept informed of progress: the Anglican Consultative Council, the Old Catholic Church in Germany, the Old Catholic Archbishop of Utrecht, the Conference of European Churches, the Roman Catholic Bishops' Conference of England and Wales, the Evangelical Church in Germany, and (until German reunification) the Federation of Evangelical Churches in the German Democratic Republic.

From this it can be seen that considerable efforts were made to conduct these talks in a wide perspective, and to benefit from the comments of ecumenical partners. It was significant that nine of the participants had been involved in the Meissen conversations of 1987-88. The whole body included many talented and experienced ecumenists, several of whom brought a worldwide outlook to this task.[15]

4. How We Approached Our Task

We were conscious that others had labored at this task before us, and that we were entering into their labors. We desired not only to reap the benefit of earlier agreements, but also to combine these with more recent theological insights that might make an ecumenical breakthrough possible. Above all, we wanted to move on from dialogue into a new and changed relationship that could be expressed in common action.

15. See pp. 34-36 of PCS for details of the meetings and participants.

At an early stage we decided to take the Meissen Common Statement as a model framework, and to base our summary of the beliefs and practices held in common on chapter three of the Niagara Report. However, we expressed the intention to go beyond "Meissen" by incorporating insights from the Lima text on "Ministry" and from the Niagara Report as a whole. To shed further light we received two papers on the Goal of Unity and two others on the Episcopal Office. We paid regard both to ecclesiology and to the realities of canon law in our various countries. We set about collating and translating into English the relevant portions of the ordination rites used in all our churches, and commissioned an analysis of what they revealed about our current understandings of the office of bishop.[16]

From the outset we recognized the need to take seriously the past, present, and future of our churches in their diverse contexts. Historical materials were to be assembled about each participating country and church, and about existing agreements between our churches. This information, not otherwise widely available, would be published in the same volume as our report. An opening chapter would set the contemporary scene so as to ground what followed in our actual mission situation. We learned much about the fast-changing scene in the Baltic States, and at our first meeting it was agreed that the Lutheran Church in Lithuania should be given the chance to come "on board" since it shared so much identity and recent history with its sister Baltic churches. As our work developed, we increasingly felt that we faced "a time of unparalleled opportunity, which may properly be called a *kairos*."[17] As to the future, we saw the need for our aspirations to be spelled out in terms of specific commitments. An initial draft of what eventually became paragraph 58b of PCS was made at our first meeting. It was suggested that the Church of England should develop its own direct link with the church in Lithuania; this was initiated in May 1992 by Bishop Stephen Sykes (Ely), and followed up by Archbishop George Carey (Canterbury) in April 1994 and Bishop Brian Smith (Tonbridge) in October 1995.

We were greatly concerned to honor existing links with other

16. See p. 37 of PCS for details of selected papers presented to the conversations. The analysis was made by Canon Dr. John Halliburton.

17. PCS, paragraph 6.

churches, and at our second meeting time was given to hearing about other dialogues in which we were engaged, such as those with the Roman Catholic Church, the Finnish and Russian Orthodox churches, the Methodists, the Swedish Mission Covenant Church, the Free Church of Finland, and the Pentecostals. It was important that any new agreement should not set back these relations, and that our report should be fully consistent with what had already been said to other dialogue partners. The two closing paragraphs of PCS about "Wider Ecumenical Commitment"[18] were no mere afterthought, but rather a statement of general intent.

We made a point of avoiding terminology that could be unhelpful. For example, we refrained from describing ordained ministries as "valid" or "invalid." We did not lay down preconditions, or speak in terms of what was "necessary" or "essential." We held back from using the expression "full communion" owing to difficulties of translation and widely felt misgivings about this terminology, and instead offered our own redefinition of what such a relationship would mean.[19] In place of the ambiguous term "apostolic succession" we carefully differentiated between "the apostolicity of the church," "the apostolic ministry" and "historic episcopal succession."

One topic that did not feature in PCS was the ordination of women to the priesthood or episcopate. Viewpoints *for* and *against* were seen to exist among Anglicans and Lutherans, both worldwide and within our own churches and delegations. These legitimate differences were openly aired, and the need to live with them was recognized. We agreed that this was not an issue around which PCS should hinge, though we all needed to be sensitive to one another's developing situations.[20] In fact, PCS was finalized in October 1992 just one month before the General Synod of the Church of England voted to ordain women to the priesthood; this Anglican-Lutheran agreement was designed to be sustainable whichever way that vote might go.

At an early stage we clarified *for whom* our report was intended. To some extent it could not help being a technical document, especially

18. PCS, paragraphs 60-61.

19. See paragraph 28 of PCS. This may be compared with paragraph 2 of "Called to Common Mission" [USA] and paragraph 7 of the draft "Waterloo Declaration" [Canada] which also attempt to improve on the "Cold Ash" definition of "full communion."

20. See the co-chairmen's Foreword to PCS, p. 4, especially in relation to Chapter V.

on matters of Faith and Order, but we argued that, since its reception would be synodical, at least half of its readers were likely to be lay women and men. We did our best to make it intelligible to them, and trusted that they would take the trouble to grapple with its thinking before making decisions about it.

5. Working Method

Our proceedings were conducted in English, the only language common to all the participants. However, we often paused to consider how translatable a proposed word or phrase might be, knowing that reception would take place in at least nine different languages.

Only twice did we hold a session with Anglicans in one group and Lutherans in another — no more than three hours out of a total of some twenty working days — and even then we had observers with us. For the bulk of the time we tackled our work on a combined basis, with observers, consultants, and staff taking an integral part in plenaries and subgroups. The resulting document was very much a joint effort.

Each church appointed its own delegates. The Lutheran co-chair was appointed by the Lutheran delegates from among their own number; the Anglican co-chair was appointed by the Archbishop of Canterbury. The plenary body set up a small Steering Group, a Drafting Group, an Editorial Group, and several *ad hoc* task groups of differing sizes. The work was conducted in such a way that nobody was idle at any stage! As a general rule each topic was first debated in plenary, after which the Drafting Group worked out a possible text. This was then scrutinized in plenary, but in this body of more than thirty members we followed the principle that, while everyone was welcome to propose amendments, these must be in writing and be submitted via the Drafting Group. This process worked well, and was repeated many times over. Between our main meetings the Drafting Group held five residential sessions, when a great deal of solid groundwork was achieved.

At our first meeting an overall plan was readily agreed upon, and this was later modified in only one major respect. Dr. Günther Gassmann, who had been one of the main drafters of the 1973 Pullach report, wisely suggested that the structure of the document would be improved if the section on "What We Agree in Faith" preceded that on episcopacy, rather than vice versa. Halfway through the project our tenth draft was shared on a confidential basis with senior leaders and ecumenical advisers in each of our churches to test out the acceptability of its general approach. A considerable number of written responses — largely positive — were collated by the Drafting Group, and every point was carefully considered in plenary. The process of refinement then continued as before, up to a fifteenth draft which became the finally agreed text. The outline of the co-chairmen's Foreword was also agreed in plenary. A useful catalyst during our final meeting was a "hearing" held in the presence of Archbishop John Vikström (Turku) and members of the Church of Finland's Council on Foreign Relations and its related committees. The sheer process of presenting our draft report and answering their questions about possible difficulties or obstacles helped to crystallize our corporate mind at this penultimate stage.

On Sunday, 11 October 1992, members of the joint commission were glad to share in the Eucharist at Porvoo (Borgå) cathedral in Finland, and it was a joyful conclusion when the final text of PCS was unanimously agreed on the following Tuesday. It seemed best to name this document after the city in whose cathedral we had worshiped, as the actual venue of our final meeting — the Seurakuntaopisto at Järvenpää — would have presented difficulties of spelling and pronunciation. In making this suggestion most of us, however, were unaware that Borgå had been the scene of a significant Swedish military defeat!

6. Follow-on Process

Public debate on the 1992 Treaty of Maastricht had raised our awareness of the danger of making an agreement conditional on acceptance by all parties. In the case of "Porvoo" we preferred, therefore, to offer a standard Declaration by which each church could *opt in*.[21] This would become effective as soon as one Anglican Church and one Lutheran

21. Paragraph 58.

Church did so, but would not collapse even if not all partners signed. No public celebrations would be held until all potential signatories had had a chance to respond.

Each church took responsibility for translating PCS into other languages, as necessary; for producing any study materials to assist the process of reception; and for handling this process in whatever way best suited their own constituency. Each church appointed one contact person, and Bishop Andreas Aarflot (Oslo) and I became the co-chairmen of a small Porvoo Churches' Contact Group. He undertook to coordinate the translations into Nordic and Baltic languages, and to ensure their mutual consistency. After ten churches had given their synodical approval, public celebrations duly took place in autumn 1996 at three venues: on September 1 at Nidaros Cathedral, Trondheim (Norway), for the Nordic region; on September 8 at Tallinn Cathedral (Estonia) for the Baltic region; and on November 28 at Westminster Abbey (UK) for the British and Irish region.

Although the churches of Denmark and Latvia did not sign, it should be remembered that they were integrally involved in the conversations and their delegates had consented to PCS. In the case of Denmark the main hesitancy sprang perhaps not so much from strictly theological reasons, but from a characteristically Danish sense of independence and an unusual constitutional situation — no synod existed, and only Parliament could take a formal decision. In the absence of broad consent from the "grassroots" the Danish bishops were not in a position to endorse PCS, but their letter of August 1995 was remarkably positive in tone. It stressed that they found no church-dividing differences between the Anglican and Lutheran foundations of faith; that visiting Anglicans could receive communion and, when residing for longer periods, be accepted as full members of the Danish church; that Anglican clergy could serve there without reordination; and that Anglican bishops could be invited to take part in the consecration of Danish bishops. Denmark still sends its representatives — technically as observers — to events involving the "Porvoo" churches, and relations continue to be markedly cordial.

The Church of Latvia, which does have a synod, has postponed putting the question of "Porvoo" to the vote for reasons of internal unity. Conservative influences from the USA and Sweden have played a role in this. As the leadership of the Latvian church faces difficult circumstances and pressing economic needs, this calls for patience and understanding. The interim sharing agreement of 1938 with England is still in force, and there is an active twinning link with the diocese of Salisbury (England). Thus Latvia, like Denmark, is still involved in the Porvoo process.

7. Conclusion

Despite these limitations, PCS has provided the basis on which over 40 million Anglicans and Lutherans in Northern Europe are now in communion, and increasingly share a common mission. This agreement has brought a new understanding of our past histories and present challenges. It has also given a stimulus to Anglican-Lutheran relations in other parts of the globe, and set forth theological insights that are applicable to the wider ecumenical scene.

Porvoo in the Context of the Worldwide Anglican-Lutheran Dialogue

MICHAEL ROOT

The Porvoo Common Statement and the communion among the Northern European Anglican and Lutheran churches it established is not simply a significant event for the churches directly involved. It is all the more significant as part of a much broader ecumenical rapprochement between Lutheran and Anglican churches worldwide. Porvoo[1] was the first to be ratified of a wave of new Anglican-Lutheran agreements proposed during the 1990s. These agreements have changed both the shape of Anglican-Lutheran relations and the ecumenical outlook of the two communions. This essay will place the Porvoo agreement in the context of this broader worldwide dialogue.

I. Earlier History

A. The Dialogue Before 1945

From its beginning, the twentieth-century dialogue between the Anglican and Lutheran churches has benefited from a fruitful interplay between the regional and the global. Initiative and insights have regu-

1. *Together in Mission and Ministry: The Porvoo Common Statement with Essays on Church and Ministry in Northern Europe* (London: Church House Publishing, 1993). I will throughout this essay refer to various Anglican-Lutheran agreements by such shorthand terms as "Porvoo," "Waterloo," or "Pullach."

larly passed back and forth between the two levels. The first modern Lutheran-Anglican dialogue was, in a way, both regional and global. In 1909, representatives of the Church of Sweden met with representatives of the Anglican Communion.[2] While the Anglican group was almost entirely British, one member was American. Commissioned by the Lambeth Conference, the Anglican group's report was entitled *The Church of England and the Church of Sweden.*[3] Thus, while the 1909 dialogue led officially to a new relation only between the churches of Sweden and England, the initial dialogue had a global dimension.

The initial Swedish dialogue was taken up by the next Lambeth Conference (1920, delayed from 1918 due to the First World War) and confirmed in an important correspondence between the Archbishop of Canterbury and the Swedish bishops.[4] The new relation committed each church to engage in mutual eucharistic hospitality, to permit clergy from the other church to preach in its own pulpits, and to invite bishops from the other church to participate in its own episcopal consecrations. While the Swedish bishops used the term "intercommunion" to describe this relation, the place of such a relation on the path to the ultimate ecumenical goal, however understood, was not clear.

The success of the Swedish dialogue led to similar dialogues between Anglican representatives (in these cases, all British) and the Lutheran churches of Finland (1933-34) and Estonia and Latvia (1936-1938).[5] The Finnish discussion led to relations between the churches of England and Finland similar to (although in some symbolic senses more restrictive than) those between the English and Swedish churches. Active fellowship between the English and Baltic churches was effectively blocked by the Second World War and the annexation of the Baltic states by the Soviet Union.

The Swedish and Finnish dialogues were carried out at Anglican

2. All the Anglican-Nordic dialogues, including Porvoo, are discussed in Lars Österlin, *Churches of Northern Europe in Profile: A Thousand Years of Anglo-Nordic Relations* (Norwich: Canterbury Press, 1995).

3. London: Mowbray, 1911.

4. The correspondence can be found in Vilmos Vajta, ed., *Church in Fellowship: Pulpit and Altar Fellowship Among Lutherans* (Minneapolis: Augsburg Publishing House, 1963), pp. 181-88.

5. The reports from both discussions can be found in *Lambeth Occasional Reports 1931-38* (London: SPCK, 1948), pp. 115-87 (Finland), pp. 205-61 (Latvia and Estonia).

initiative (though not without the prodding of Nathan Söderblom, active even before his becoming Archbishop of Uppsala in 1914) and the agenda for the discussion was set by the Lambeth Quadrilateral. At the very beginning of the discussion, one of the Swedish bishops (H. W. Tottie of Kalmar) noted that, of the four articles of the Lambeth Quadrilateral, only the fourth, relating to the historic episcopate, was a matter of dispute between the two churches. While other matters were also briefly discussed (confirmation, the diaconate, doctrinal authority), discussion centered on the episcopate as the decisive factor to be addressed. The Finnish and Baltic dialogues followed the same route. The Swedish-Lambeth dialogue thus set a pattern that almost all Anglican-Lutheran dialogues have followed since.

The Swedish and Finnish as well as the Estonian and Latvian Lutheran churches all claimed episcopal succession at the time of their respective dialogues. As a result, internal Anglican debate over these relations centered on the accuracy of these claims and on the understanding of episcopacy in these churches. The dialogue thus forced the Lutherans to clarify and state their attitude to episcopacy. At the 1909 dialogue, the Swedes, led by Söderblom and Professor Einar Billing, drafted a statement that has since been referred to as the Uppsala Confession.[6] While granting that "no particular organization of the church and of its ministry is instituted *jure divino*," it insisted that the Swedish church was not "indifferent" to such matters. The Church of Sweden valued its episcopal order not just as "a venerable legacy of the past," but as "a blessing from the God of history accorded to us." This outlook, with roots in the Swedish Church Ordinance of 1571, was repeated in the 1922 letter of the Swedish bishops to the Archbishop of Canterbury ratifying the new relation and echoed in a similar letter of 1935 to the Archbishop of Canterbury from the Archbishop of Turku, confirming the new relation of the Church of Finland with the English church.[7] This series of Lutheran statements is significant in two respects. On the one hand, it laid out a Lutheran perspective which sought to understand episcopacy neither as a *ius divinum* nor as an adiaphoron in the strict sense of an indifferent matter, but as some-

6. This text is included in *The Church of England and the Church of Sweden*, pp. 17-19.

7. Correspondence in V. Vajta, *Church in Fellowship*, pp. 202-5.

thing requiring some additional theological category. While such a perspective has roots not just in Swedish documents, but in the Lutheran Confessions, it has been a minority outlook in much of modern non-Nordic Lutheranism, and Lutherans have often groped for adequate theological terms to express it. On the other hand, the clear statement of this perspective within the dialogue established the precedent for a differentiated consensus on episcopacy as a sufficient basis for Lutheran-Anglican relations. The movement toward closer relations between the Lutheran and Anglican churches does require a certain degree of consensus on the practice and understanding of episcopacy, but this consensus need not include every detail or aspect of episcopacy. In this sense, the agreement fits the recently enunciated model of an internally differentiated consensus.[8] The Swedish position was not that of many Anglicans, but that difference need not block the new relation. In both respects, this initial dialogue set the pattern for recent Anglican-Lutheran developments, including Porvoo.

B. The Dialogue from 1945 until 1970

The first quarter-century following the Second World War saw a series of Anglican-Lutheran regional dialogues of increasing difficulty. At the urging of the Lambeth Conference, conversations were held in 1952 between a commission appointed by the Archbishop of Canterbury and representatives of the Lutheran churches of Iceland, Norway, and Denmark.[9] Here, while the Lutheran churches had an episcopal order, the direct personal succession had been broken at the time of the Reformation. As with the other Nordic and Baltic dialogues, agreement was quickly reached on all subjects but episcopacy. In this context, however, the succession issue presented difficulties that were not overcome. Recommendations of mutual eucharistic hospitality were more hesitating; during the meeting, then Professor (later Archbishop of Canterbury) Michael Ramsey, chair of the Anglican delegation, said

8. See Harding Meyer, "Ecumenical Consensus: Our Quest for and the Emerging Structures of Consensus," *Gregorianum* 77 (1996): 213-25.

9. *The Church of England and the Churches of Norway, Denmark and Iceland.* Report of the Committee appointed by the Archbishop of Canterbury in 1951 . . . , with Three Appendices (London: SPCK, 1952).

that eucharistic hospitality would be a matter of economy rather than a sign that "all is well." Unlike earlier proposals, there was no recommendation of "interconsecration," which had been urged in the dialogue by Ramsey as an important sign of fellowship that would also be a means of settling the issue over succession. These conversations thus led to a less extensive fellowship than the pre-war dialogues.

Sharper disappointment was experienced during the two immediate post-war decades in the wave of union discussions among churches in Asia and Africa. The goal of these discussions was more ambitious than the European dialogues: full church union rather than mere "intercommunion," as the pre-war discussions had often stated their goal. While these discussions were never strictly Anglican-Lutheran, in two cases Anglicans and Lutherans were prominent and in one case Anglican-Lutheran disagreement over episcopacy was the decisive difficulty.

Extensive discussions between the Church of South India and the Lutheran churches of southern India produced a series of common statements in the 1950s and 1960s and even a proposed constitution for a merged church. For a variety of reasons, these proposals were never acted on.[10]

More important in terms of its consequences was the East Africa Church Union Consultation of the early and mid-1960s. The discussions climaxed in a meeting at Dodoma, Tanzania, in early 1965, at which both the European mission participants and the African participants came to a stalemate over the issue of episcopacy.[11] The Anglicans, Presbyterians, and to a degree, Moravians were willing to enter a union in which all ordained ministers would be newly commissioned by a laying on of hands by, among others, a bishop in episcopal succession; the Lutherans were not willing to enter a union on such terms. The Lutherans here represent a general Lutheran refusal to solve the ministry question by means of a rite that might be interpreted as a supplemental or conditional ordination. (The one exception I know of is

10. An overview of these discussions can be found in Rajaiah D. Paul & J. Kumaresan, *Church of South India–Lutheran Conversations: A Historical Sketch* (Madras: Christian Literature Society, 1970).

11. "Documentation and Comment on the Dodoma Conference, with Commentary from R. Macpherson, G. Jasper, R. E. Kendall, H. Heisler, and E. H. Arblaster," *Lutheran World* 12 (1965): 266-82.

the entrance of the small number of Lutherans in Pakistan into the Church of Pakistan. Here the union agreement was developed without Lutheran involvement; the Lutherans entered the union at the last minute.) Reading between the lines of the published and unpublished reports, there seem to have been a variety of underlying tensions affecting this meeting (e.g., Kenya vs. Tanzania), and at least some observers thought the impact of foreign missionaries was negative.[12]

C. The Dialogue from 1970 until 1986

The failure of the East Africa Consultation was an impetus for the creation of an international Lutheran-Anglican dialogue during the boom period in the creation of bilateral international dialogues of the late 1960s. Meeting between 1970 and 1972, the dialogue produced the so-called Pullach Report.[13] The report discussed a range of issues: Sources of Authority, Church, Word and Sacraments, Apostolic Ministry. As usual, the stumbling block was apostolicity and episcopacy. Significant agreement was reached on a rather general level. Apostolicity "pertains first to the gospel and then to the ministry of Word and sacraments" (§73). "The succession of apostolicity through time is guarded and given contemporary expression in and through a wide variety of means, activities and institutions" (§74; in a list of such expressions, however, episcopal succession is not explicitly mentioned). Lutherans and Anglicans together in the dialogue could say that "we feel ourselves called to recognize that all who have been called and ordained to the ministry of Word and Sacrament in obedience to the apostolic faith stand together in the apostolic succession of office" (§77). They could also affirm together that "'Episcope' or oversight concerning the purity of apostolic doctrine, the ordination of ministries, and pastoral care of the church is inherent in the apostolic character of the church's life, mission and ministry" (§79).

Despite these agreements, however, the concrete question of the

12. On the impact of missionaries, see John S. Mbiti, *Bible and Theology in African Christianity* (Nairobi: Oxford University Press, 1986), pp. 214f.

13. In Harding Meyer and Lukas Vischer, eds., *Growth in Agreement: Reports and Agreed Statements of Ecumenical Conversations on a World Level* (New York: Paulist Press, 1984), pp. 13-34.

place of a common exercise of an episcopal ministry in succession remained problematic. On this subject, the commission had to resort to separate statements by the Anglican and Lutheran participants. The Anglicans stated that, while they did "not believe that the episcopate in historic succession alone constitutes the apostolic succession of the church or its ministry" (§85), they nevertheless believed that it "is a gift of God to the church" and "an outward and visible sign of the church's continuing unity and apostolic life, mission and ministry" (§84). Thus, "the Anglican participants cannot foresee full integration of ministries (full communion) apart from the historic episcopate" (§87). The Lutherans, however, while stating that "those Lutheran churches which have not retained the historic episcopate are free to accept it where it serves the growing unity of the church in obedience to the gospel," nevertheless insisted that "the historic episcopate should not become a necessary condition for interchurch relations or church union" (§89). The dialogue recommended "a greatly increased measure of intercommunion" between the Lutheran and Anglican churches (§96) and endorsed a "more rapid movement towards organic union" in countries where Anglicans and Lutherans live together, especially in Africa and Asia. The integration of ministries within such unions, however, should not "call in question the status of existing ministries as true ministries of Word and Sacrament" (§99).

The Pullach Report is a good representative of the state of Anglican-Lutheran relations prior to the breakthrough of the late 1980s and early 1990s, especially if read together with the "Personal Notes" of the Anglican and Lutheran co-chairs, Ronald Williams, bishop of Leicester (Church of England), and Gunnar Hultgren (Archbishop of Uppsala). Each seems to express a certain irritation with the stance of his own tradition. Williams notes that "Hooker's objection to presbyterian exclusiveness in the sixteenth century can easily be turned on Anglicans, if they press their views of episcopacy with the like rigidity." Hultgren states that the level of agreement reached with the Anglicans "may lead the Lutheran churches to reconsider their traditional conviction that all questions of church order, including the historic episcopate, are 'adiaphora', of secondary importance." Taken together, the report and the attached notes indicate both the problem and the will to overcome it.

In what becomes a typical movement, following the international dialogue a shift of focus occurred toward the regional and national. Such a shift was explicitly recommended by a small 1975 Anglican-Lutheran Working Group appointed by the Lutheran World Federation (LWF) and the Anglican Consultative Council (ACC). An Anglican-Lutheran European Regional Commission was created, meeting between 1980 and 1982. It produced the so-called Helsinki Report, which saw no "serious obstacles on the way to the establishment of full communion," but did not address concretely how to overcome differences on episcopacy.[14] On the whole, Helsinki did not move the issues or the churches beyond Pullach.

In the United States, an Anglican-Lutheran dialogue had already occurred, producing a report in 1973 that recommended new levels of fellowship.[15] Rather than address these recommendations, the churches instead appointed a new dialogue team, which met between 1976 and 1980, and recommended that the two churches enter into a new relation to be called "Interim Eucharistic Sharing." The churches were officially to invite each other's members to receive the Eucharist and invite clergy from the other church to participate in its own eucharistic celebrations as assisting ministers, standing at the altar with the presiding minister. It recommended also that the churches appoint a third dialogue team to seek to overcome whatever obstacles stood in the way of full communion, e.g., the continuing difference over episcopacy.[16] These recommendations were adopted by the churches (with the exception of the Lutheran Church-Missouri Synod) in 1982 with much fanfare. In Canada, a similar proposal was made in 1986 and adopted in 1989.[17] The Meissen Agreement between the Church of England and the Evangelical Church in Germany (then only of West Germany) and the Federation of Evangelical Churches in the

14. Anglican-Lutheran European Regional Commission, *Anglican-Lutheran Dialogue: Report of the Anglican-Lutheran European Regional Commission. Helsinki, August-September 1982* (London: SPCK, 1983), paragraph 62.

15. *Lutheran-Episcopal Dialogue: A Progress Report* (Cincinnati: Forward Movement Publications, 1973).

16. William G. Weinhauer & Robert L. Wietelmann, eds., *The Report of the Lutheran-Episcopal Dialogue: Second Series 1976-1980* (Cincinnati: Forward Movement Publications, 1981).

17. Canadian Anglican-Lutheran Dialogue, *Report and Recommendations: April 1986* (Toronto: Anglican Church of Canada, n.d.).

German Democratic Republic, formulated in 1988, was also along the same lines,[18] as was the Reuilly Common Statement of 2000.[19] None of these agreements moved beyond the impasse represented by the Pullach Report.

II. The Recent Breakthrough

A. The Niagara Report and Its Children

In the course of the 1980s, Anglican-Lutheran bilateral activity again was taken up at the international level, although not at the level of a full-fledged dialogue. Another Anglican-Lutheran International Joint Working Group was appointed by the LWF and ACC and met in Cold Ash, England, in 1983. The most significant content of its report was the elaboration of an understanding of "full communion" as the goal of Anglican-Lutheran ecumenical efforts.[20] "Full communion" is defined as "a relationship between two distinct churches or communions" in which "each maintains its own autonomy" while sharing a genuine "community of life" through "common worship, study, witness, evangelism and promotion of justice, peace and love" (§§25, 27). While the report did not address episcopacy, its listing of mutual participation in episcopal consecrations as one aspect of full communion clearly presumed a common episcopate as one aspect of life together.

Among the report's recommendations was the creation of a "permanent Continuation Committee" at the international level. This Anglican-Lutheran International Continuation Committee (later renamed Anglican-Lutheran International Commission) was not intended to be a doctrinally oriented dialogue of the sort typified by the

18. *The Meissen Agreement: Texts,* Council for Christian Unity Occasional Paper, no. 2 (London: Council for Christian Unity, General Synod, Church of England, 1992). The Porvoo co-chairs themselves (co-chairs' Foreword, §4) group Meissen with the 1982 U.S. agreement.

19. *Called to Witness and Service: The Reuilly Common Statement with Essays on Church, Eucharist and Ministry* (London: Church House Publishing, 1999).

20. Jeffrey Gros, Harding Meyer, and William G. Rusch, eds., *Growth in Agreement II: Reports and Agreed Statements of Ecumenical Conversations on a World Level, 1982-1998* (Geneva: WCC Publications, 2000), pp. 2-10.

Anglican and Lutheran international dialogues with the Roman Catholic Church. It did, however, sponsor a consultation on "Episcopé in Relation to the Mission of the Church Today" at Niagara Falls, Canada, in 1987 and then itself completed the Niagara Report on Episcopé the following year.[21] The Niagara Report presented both an innovative perspective on the question of succession and a concrete proposal for Anglican-Lutheran rapprochement. Neither the Anglican nor the Lutheran communions, however, made binding ecumenical decisions at the international level. The implementation of the perspective and proposals of the Niagara Report could only occur on the national level or on a regional level sufficiently small to allow the careful coordination of individual churches. The three similar proposals for full communion (or what seems to be its equivalent) that came forward in the 1990s — the Porvoo Common Statement, the Concordat of Agreement[22] (revised under the title *Called to Common Mission*)[23] in the United States, and the Waterloo Declaration in Canada[24] — can all be interpreted as regional applications and adaptations of the perspective and proposal of the Niagara Report. (The influence of Niagara on Porvoo and the Concordat was transmitted in part through overlapping personnel. A Lutheran drafter of Niagara was also a drafter of the Concordat, and an Anglican drafter of Niagara was a drafter of Porvoo. While sharing a common root, Porvoo and the Concordat were produced independently of one another, without significant mutual influence. The Concordat was made public in January 1991, prior to the completion of Porvoo, but by that time the drafting process for Porvoo had already produced a text close to its final form. The Waterloo Agreement was made public in its first form only in 1997, well after the publication of the Concordat and Porvoo and clearly bears the marks of both documents.) The continuing dis-

21. *Growth in Agreement II*, pp. 11-37.

22. Lutheran-Episcopal Dialogue — Series III, *"Toward Full Communion" and "Concordat of Agreement,"* ed. William A. Norgren and William G. Rusch (Minneapolis, Cincinnati, Augsburg: Forward Movement Publications, 1991).

23. Evangelical Lutheran Church in America, *Called to Common Mission: A Lutheran Proposal for a Revision of the Concordat of Agreement* (Chicago: Evangelical Lutheran Church in America, 1999), http://www.elca.org/ea/ccmintro.html.

24. The text of *Called to Full Communion: The Waterloo Declaration* can be found at http://www.elcic.ca/docs/waterloo.html.

cussions between the British and Irish Anglican churches and the Evangelical Church in Germany[25] and the dialogue that led to the Reuilly Report of the British and Irish Anglican churches and the Lutheran and Reformed churches of France may be understood as dialogues that have rejected (or at least not been able to accept) the perspective laid out in the Niagara Report.

B. The Theological Perspective of the Niagara Report

The decisive shift between earlier Anglican-Lutheran discussions of episcopacy and Niagara is the far more thoroughgoing placement of the issue of episcopal succession in the wider context of the continuity of the church in its total mission. The identity of the church is tied to its continuity with the apostolic mission to all nations. "Apostolic succession" is above all continuity in this mission and is a characteristic of a church as a whole rather than simply of its ministry or doctrine. Continuity in doctrine (e.g., the continued use of the early church's creeds) or in ministry (e.g., episcopal succession) is bound up with and is to serve this larger continuity in mission.

The ultimate basis of the church's continuity is not its own faithfulness but the faithfulness of God to his promise to be with the church (§28). The church is thankful for the means God uses to hold the church in faithfulness, e.g., canon, creed, and structures of ministry, but recognizes that all such means are open to human abuse.

> God has persevered with the church even when the Scriptures have been mutilated, ignored, traduced or idolized; even when baptism has been administered promiscuously or received frivolously; even when the Lord's Supper has become routine or been neglected; even when the loss of the connection between gospel and dogma has led to inquisition and authoritarianism on the one hand, rejection and apostasy on the other hand. (§30)

25. See *Visible Unity and the Ministry of Oversight,* The Second Theological Conference held under the Meissen Agreement between the Church of England and the Evangelical Church in Germany (London: Church House Publishing, 1997).

The text then adds: "In the context of our study of *episcope* we have been led to trust God's faithfulness also when bishops in historic succession have been unfaithful in an effluvium of evil" (§30).

In the context of this theology of continuity, Niagara takes up episcopacy. Lutherans and Anglicans have always agreed that there exists a divinely instituted ministry to serve the mission of the gospel. Anglicans in their theological reflection and Lutherans in their practical experience have recognized that some form of oversight is a necessity: "Ministries of pastoral leadership, coordination and oversight have continuously been part of the church's witness to the gospel. Indeed we may say that the mission of the church required the coherence of its witness in every aspect of its life, and that this coherence required supervision" (§20). It is this ministry of oversight that is the heart of episcopal ministry (§54). As minister of oversight, the bishop is vitally related to both the unity and continuity of the church.

The symbolic position occupied by the bishop had two dimensions, the spatial and the temporal. The connections between the local and the universal, the present and the past, are both aspects of the one *koinonia* or communion. On the one hand, the bishop "is responsible for preserving and promoting the integrity of the *koinonia* in order to further the church's response to the Lordship of Christ and its commitment to mission" (Anglican-Roman Catholic International Commission, *The Final Report*, Authority I, 5); a *koinonia* which "is realized not only in the local Christian communities, but also in the communion of these communities with one another" (ibid., 8). On the other hand the bishop as confessor of the faith links the church with its foundation in the prophetic and apostolic scriptures (Eph. 2:20) (§52).

Fellowship in a ministry of oversight in continuity with the early ages of the church is thus seen as highly desirable for unity and continuity in the church's apostolic mission. Nevertheless, the report also recognizes that "the New Testament does not entitle us to assert that such supervision was carried out by a uniform structure of government inherited directly from or transmitted by the apostles" (§20). Episcopal succession cannot be presented as essential to the New Testament identity of the church in the sense that, e.g., baptism or the Eucharist are essential: "Study of the life of the early Christian communities reflected in the pages of the New Testament should make it unthinkable for us to isolate ordination at the hands of someone in linear succession to the apostles as the sole criterion of faithfulness to the apostolic commission" (§20). Theological (in distinction from simply historical) grounds for this conclusion are also given: "It is the oversight or presiding ministry which constitutes the heart of the episcopal office, and that oversight is never to be viewed apart from the continuity of apostolic faith. The fact of bishops does not by itself guarantee the continuity of apostolic faith. A material rupture in the succession of presiding ministers does not by itself guarantee a loss of continuity in apostolic faith" (§54).

Niagara explicitly avoids giving a single unambiguous judgment of what such a rupture does mean. It notes that in both the English and Lutheran churches, efforts were made, conditioned by the different ecclesiastical situations in different lands, to maintain forms of continuity with the ancient church and secure dependable means of oversight (§§55-56). In neither case was continuity in episcopal succession realized in a way that all would recognize as canonical.[26] The discussion concludes: "A similar problem faces both Anglicans and Lutherans, namely that the succession in the presiding ministry of their respective churches no longer incontestably links those churches to the *koinonia* of the wider church" (§58).

As a result of broad agreement in the gospel, of a renewed recognition of complex realities that constitute the apostolic succession of both churches, of significant agreement on the role of the ministry of oversight for the unity and continuity of the church, and of a joint confession of the failures of both churches in their faithfulness to the faithfulness of God, the two teams in the dialogue conclude that "neither tradition can, in good conscience, reject the apostolic nature of the other," that "the ordained ministry is no longer an issue which need divide our two churches," and that "the continued isolation, one from another, of those who exercise this office of *episcope* in our two churches is no longer tolerable and must be overcome" (§59). The report thus recommends that the two churches take concrete steps to bring themselves into full communion with each other and into a more faithful relation to the mission of the gospel in their exercise of the

26. "In the English Reformation, it may be argued, the episcopal succession was secured in an uncanonical fashion in that no currently sitting diocesan bishops could be found who were willing to consecrate Matthew Parker" (§55).

ministry of oversight. In the future, each church should install or consecrate bishops with the laying on of hands by at least three other bishops, in accord with the canons of the council of Nicea. At least one of these bishops should be from the other tradition. Lutherans are asked to bring their structures of oversight more into line with classical patterns (all ministers of oversight to be called bishops; bishops to have open-ended terms, similar to pastors; only bishops to preside at ordinations). Anglicans are asked to "recognize the full authenticity of the existing ministries of the Lutheran churches," and to make the related canonical revisions. This reconciliation of ministries should "avoid any suggestion of reordination, mutual recommissioning of ministries, crypto-validation, or any other ambiguity" (§115).

C. Porvoo and Similar Proposals

The Porvoo Common Statement closely follows the theological vision of the Niagara Report and often echoes its wording. The emphasis again falls on the church as the primary bearer of the predicate "apostolic" (§37). The "ultimate ground" of the church's fidelity and continuity is "the promise of the Lord and the presence of the Holy Spirit at work in the whole church" (§46). The central theological judgment is thus whether "each church as a whole has maintained an authentic apostolic succession of witness and service" (§56). "The historic episcopal succession" is understood as a sign that is "a permanent challenge to fidelity and unity," but which guarantees neither "the fidelity of a church to every aspect of the apostolic faith, life and mission" nor "the personal faithfulness of the bishop" (§51). Because apostolic continuity

> is carried by more than one means, . . . a church which has preserved the sign of historic episcopal succession is free to acknowledge an authentic episcopal ministry in a church which has preserved continuity in the episcopal office by an occasional priestly/presbyterial ordination at the time of the Reformation. Similarly a church which has preserved continuity through such a succession is free to enter a relationship of mutual participation in episcopal ordinations with a church which has retained the historical episco-

pal succession, and to embrace this sign, without denying its past apostolic continuity. (§52)

This vision is shared with the U.S. and Canadian proposals. The Waterloo Declaration, in its text and even more in its accompanying Official Commentary, extensively cites both the Niagara Report and the Porvoo Common Statement. *Toward Full Communion,* the extended theological text accompanying the U.S. Concordat, cites Niagara at the decisive point at which it turns to its own concrete suggestion (§76).

While a shared vision unites these three proposals, they are differentiated by how that vision is developed in detail in different settings. These differences are partially accounted for by the differing ecclesial contexts, but are also partially a function of theological differences within a shared vision.[27] I will compare Porvoo with *Called to Common Mission* (CCM), the revision of the earlier Concordat that was finally accepted by the American churches, and then note how Waterloo, written after both of these earlier texts, takes up the theological option presented by Porvoo, while also bearing resemblances to the American scheme.

The three agreements are alike in including an immediate mutual recognition of ministries, implying a mutual availability of ordained clergy, and also a commitment to a shared episcopacy, including mutual participation in the laying on of hands for bishops. They differ, however, in their approach to existing Lutheran bishops not consecrated in succession.

Decisive for Porvoo is the recognition that all the Nordic and Baltic Lutheran churches, including the Danish, Norwegian, and Icelandic churches where a succession of consecrations was broken in the sixteenth century, are essentially episcopal (see especially §§8, 34, 49). The question Porvoo asks is whether the *single* break in the succession of consecrations, suffered in a time of turmoil during which the bishops had radically failed in their calling, means that in a comprehensive judgment about these churches and their ministries one should con-

27. For an analysis of the relation between Porvoo and the original Concordat, see Michael Root, "The Concordat and the Northern European Porvoo Common Statement: Different Paths to the Same Goal," in *A Commentary on "Concordat of Agreement,"* ed. James E. Griffiss and Daniel F. Martensen (Minneapolis: Augsburg, 1994), pp. 138-51. Portions of what follows are adapted from the earlier analysis.

clude that they simply lack a true episcopal ministry, especially if they are demonstrating their willingness to re-enter an unbroken line of consecrations by adopting Porvoo. Porvoo's conclusion is that a straightforward denial that these churches are "episcopal" would rest on an overly narrow emphasis on an unbroken line of consecrations that ignores the wider reality of both the life and mission of these churches and their real and historically continuous episcopal ministries. Episcopal succession cannot be reduced to an unbroken succession of consecrations. In adopting Porvoo, the Norwegian and Icelandic churches have accepted an additional sign of episcopal continuity (§58b[vi]), but they have not "adopted the historic episcopate" as something new in their lives. Thus, Porvoo implies a mutual recognition by all the churches of the episcopal ministries each exercises and, within organizational and practical limits, an interchangeability of episcopal ministry (§58b[v]).

The situation is quite different in the U.S. American Lutheranism has a short history of episcopacy. Unlike Porvoo, CCM did call for the Lutheran participant to accept the historic episcopate for the first time and called for the Episcopal Church to recognize the authenticity of the ordained ministry in all forms *claimed* by the ELCA. Since the Evangelical Lutheran Church in America (ELCA) does not claim the historic episcopate, its present bishops would be recognized simply as "pastors/priests exercising a ministry of oversight *(episkope)* within its synods" (§15). Thus, while Porvoo involves an immediate interchangeability of bishops as bishops, CCM does not. The ELCA and the Episcopal Church will grow into a fully interchangeable episcopal ministry over time (§14).

This rather detailed difference has various consequences. While Porvoo says that mutual participation in episcopal consecrations will occur "normally" (§58b[vi]), implying the possibility of exceptions, CCM states (§12) that such mutual participation will occur "regularly," officially defined as constituting the rule to be followed without planned exceptions. To a degree, this difference reflects the greater geographical proximity of the U.S. churches, but it also reflects a difference in what the Lutheran partner is undertaking in the two cases.

More significantly, because CCM involves no recognition of the ELCA as already episcopal, the Episcopal Church USA, unlike the British and Irish Anglican churches in Porvoo, has suspended in relation to the ELCA its requirement that all clergy be episcopally ordained (§16). Only thus could clergy be interchangeable, a requirement if the mutual recognition of ministries was to be in deed and not just in word. Such a step is unprecedented for Anglicans.

Because the American churches start farther apart than the Northern European churches, each partner has had to take larger steps to meet the other. This difference between CCM and Porvoo casts the Canadian Waterloo Declaration in a particularly interesting light. The history and present situation of the Canadian churches are more like those of the American churches than like those of the Northern European ones. As in the U.S., the title "bishop" has been adopted only recently by Canadian Lutherans. Nevertheless, in relation to the difference just sketched, Waterloo is closer to Porvoo than to CCM. A full recognition and interchangeability of ministries, including a recognition and interchangeability of bishops as bishops, will occur at the beginning of the new relation (B3, D1).

Waterloo takes the argument of Niagara a significant step further than did either Porvoo or CCM. Three elements laid the foundation for this extension: (1) a recognition by each church of the other as apostolic; (2) a recognition of the intent during the Reformation of even the non-episcopal, German Lutheran churches to continue a ministry of oversight, and thus the episcopal function, even when ordinations were conducted by presbyters,[28] and (3) a clear willingness of the Canadian Lutheran Church to enter episcopal succession and to recognize the installation of a bishop as an ordination (Introduction 9, D2). On this basis, the churches each recognize the ordained ministries of the other, including a mutual recognition of episcopal ministries as episcopal. On the one hand, apostolicity of ministry is even more thoroughly made a function of apostolicity of the church and its total mission. On the other hand, the substance of episcopal ministry (of which succession is a sign) is more thoroughly identified with episcopal function, which may be authentically present apart from the sign of the historic episcopate. For Porvoo, a broader continuity in episcopal ministry bore the absence of the specific sign of a succession of consecrations. For CCM, the conti-

28. "The succession of a presiding ministry was preserved, given that the reformers had themselves been episcopally ordained, and the authority of the bishop passed to the presbyters acting collegially" (Commentary B3).

nuity in apostolic mission and ministry is the basis for a mutual recognition of existing ministries, but was not judged itself to bring ELCA bishops within the historic episcopate so that episcopal ministries would be immediately interchangeable. For Waterloo, the three elements listed above lead to the conclusion that the Canadian Lutheran bishops are bishops in a sense that allows immediate interchangeability. Sharing in a succession of consecrations is seen as a consequence of this new relation, rather than as something that must be in place prior to such interchangeability (Commentary D2).

As a result, Waterloo, like Porvoo and unlike CCM, need not require that Anglicans suspend the traditional restriction that only episcopally ordained ministers can function among them as priests. Waterloo can thus avoid the elements of complexity introduced into CCM by its non-recognition of present episcopal ministries. Nevertheless, in at least one respect, Waterloo is similar to CCM: the presence of bishops of one church at the ordinations of bishops in the other is not to occur merely "normally." An earlier draft had said such interconsecration would occur "regularly," but this word was omitted "to indicate unambiguously the unfailing commitment to invite bishops of both churches to participate in each other's installations/ordinations" (Official Commentary, D2).

Is Waterloo a model for the extension of Porvoo's perspective to churches that do not share the Porvoo churches' particular history? Only time will tell. While CCM demanded of the American churches significant shifts of practice (the Episcopal suspension of the restriction related to episcopally ordained clergy, the Lutheran explicit adoption of the historic episcopate as a *novum*), Waterloo demands significant theological judgments that not all might be willing to make (the Anglican recognition of Lutheran bishops without claims to either a personal or a local succession as episcopal in an interchangeable sense; the Lutheran commitment to installation in the episcopal office as an ordination[29]). The willingness of the Canadian Anglicans and Lutherans to make these judgments may be partially a function of their specific situation, history, and character.[30] Rather than Porvoo, CCM, or

29. This latter element had been included in the original U.S. Concordat (§7) but was vigorously criticized by some Lutherans and eliminated in the revision that produced CCM.

Waterloo uniquely providing a model for others, all three can serve as examples to which others can refer as they explore options suited to their own situation and perspective.

III. Conclusion

The Porvoo declaration is one part of a larger ecumenical development between the Lutheran and Anglican communions. Whether this development comes to include other Anglican and Lutheran churches is a question for the future. Other essays in this volume give some idea of the debates in these churches. However those debates turn out, the recent Lutheran-Anglican agreements have already altered the ecumenical landscape. The immediate result is a complexification of the international ecumenical scene. Rather than a Protestant bloc of Lutheran, Reformed, and others confronting a Catholic bloc of Roman Catholic and Orthodox (with Anglicans floating somewhere in between), a complex web of relations is developing. Some Lutherans are in communion with Anglicans, some with Reformed, some with both. The result is confusing, but perhaps more ecumenically flexible and promising than any present alternative.

A larger question goes beyond the ecumenical structures these agreements create and addresses their implications for Anglican and Lutheran self-understanding. Can Anglicans and Lutherans together develop an evangelical and catholic vision of the faith that each can claim as their own and together offer ecumenically to others? That possibility is the larger promise of Anglican-Lutheran rapprochement that is held out by Porvoo, its forebears, and its siblings.

30. See Alyson Barnett-Cowan, "Anglican-Lutheran Relations in Canada," *Ecumenical Trends* 25 (1996): 49-54. She notes that the Anglican Church in Canada recognized the ministry of the Church of South India far more rapidly than did the Church of England or the Episcopal Church USA.

The African Anglican-Lutheran Commission and the Porvoo Common Statement

SEBASTIAN BAKARE

The worldwide Anglican Communion is engaged in bilateral conversations with other churches such as Roman-Catholics, Methodists, Orthodox, Reformed, and Lutherans. These bilateral conversations are aimed at drawing the participating churches towards a better mutual understanding and at seeking together ways to full communion.

The Anglican-Lutheran conversations are at different stages in different parts of the world. In regions such as Europe and North America they have reached a stage where Anglicans and Lutherans have issued communion agreements. One of these is the Porvoo Common Statement (PCS), which was signed in 1996 by the Anglican churches of Great Britain and Ireland and most of the Nordic and Baltic Lutheran churches. All these churches are now engaged in discussions towards full communion.

1. The Porvoo Common Statement

PCS is a regional statement from the Anglican-Lutheran Dialogue in Northern Europe. Although it is a regional statement, it bears some worldwide implications insofar as the concerned churches belong to worldwide communions. It is a statement of faith declaring the intention of the dialogue partners to join hands on the road to visible unity. In its search for closer cooperation PCS has little to say about some issues of major common concern. Apart from being a statement of faith,

PCS seems to lack a more consistent emphasis on the mission of the church in a continent that has become very secularized. From the African perspective, cooperation of the two families without a missionary dimension could be viewed as a weakness. Indeed, Jesus prayed for his disciples that they should be "one" in order to support each other as they carry on his mission. The church is called to mission, and that mission starts from where we are. PCS should therefore contain a regional "common" understanding by the two families committing themselves to the life and mission of the whole church called to proclaim the gospel of salvation to all humanity.

Where the church has understood its mission of reconciliation, it can do so effectively by overcoming ecclesiological barriers that weaken its mission. If the two families believe that they are "called to be one," then PCS is an expression of that belief, an expression shared by all members at different levels. Ordinary men and women who fill our churches matter and have to be conversant with such a "common statement." Every member of the congregation is an agent of the church called to invite others to be one in Christ. On the road towards the visible unity of the church every member of the community of faith, both clergy and laity, are stakeholders. Often the international, regional, and national conversations that have taken place between Anglicans and Lutherans have remained the "preserve" of a minority engaged in such discussions. It is a known fact and experience of many Christians that resolutions passed at Lambeth conferences and Lutheran World Federation (LWF) assemblies rarely filter through to the average Christian in a congregation. The inability of some church leaders to report back to their constituency can be interpreted as indifference. Often they view the issues as irrelevant to their context, or they are even unable to comprehend or make sense of the topics reflected in PCS.

Agenda for Dialogue

In 1988 the Anglican Consultative Council (ACC) and the LWF recom mended establishing an international dialogue commission as well as assisting in the formation of regional and national dialogues to seek a path leading the two churches towards the goal of visible unity, as a response to Jesus' prayer in John 17:21 that we all should be one.

The main challenge on the agenda for these international, national, and regional conversations was to assist the two families in discovering what they share and understand in common, especially in the areas of worship, ministry, doctrine, and mission. The International Anglican-Lutheran Pullach Report (1973) may be viewed as the first serious conversation between the two families. After the Lambeth Conference of 1978, conversations started in various parts of the world, especially in Europe, Canada, and the USA.

In 1984 the international Anglican-Lutheran dialogue came together to discuss the question of *episcope* and how it was understood by the two traditions. And in 1987 a consultation was held in Canada (resulting in the so-called Niagara Report) that dealt with similar ecclesiastical topics: doctrine, worship, structures, ministry, mission, etc.

The Impact of Porvoo

The Porvoo Common Statement signed in 1996 by the British and Irish Anglican churches and most of the Nordic and Baltic Lutheran churches was significant for the two families and their worldwide communions. It is important to stress here, however, that the signatories of PCS did not have a worldwide but a regional intention, covering the jurisdiction only of the churches involved in the process. Yet at the same time, the worldwide implications cannot be ruled out. PCS was a regional initiative set forth in the hope that other regions in the worldwide communions would be moving towards the same goal of visible unity in their own contexts.

Africans often saw this as a European affair in which they had no share. PCS had indeed worldwide consequences for other churches, in the sense that Anglicans and Lutherans elsewhere were implicitly affected and influenced by that historical event. The remark that one hears often about Porvoo by those who feel left out is that PCS had nothing to offer Anglicans and Lutherans in other parts of the world, including those in Africa. However, PCS by its intention was not meant to be inclusive or exclusive but rather contained a regional response emanating from the 1988 Lambeth Conference. The Porvoo signatories should be commended for their quick response to the Lambeth resolution, whereas we in Africa have not come up with a similar statement to this very day. The Porvoo Common Statement should not be viewed as European ecclesiastical block building but rather as a regional initiative emerging from years of theological dialogues and conversations — and as such it has remained virtually unknown in Africa. Many priests or ministers have never heard about it. It may not even be found in some of our theological libraries. This is largely due to our own inability to find out what goes on in other parts of the world in terms of Lutheran and Anglican dialogue.

It is encouraging that Section 4 of the 1998 Lambeth Conference report dealt with the subject of church unity ("Called to be one"). One of the aims of this section was to give bishops an opportunity to share their reflections about what had been taking place in their respective regions with regard to Anglican-Lutheran dialogue. The involvement of bishops in the subject of church unity is vital since no discussion on this issue can take place in any diocese or province without their cooperation and support. In their role as promoters of church unity, bishops should seek ways to help the two communions grow closer to each other.

PCS as a regional initiative is comparable to agreements in the USA and Canada. The formation of a Pan-African Anglican-Lutheran regional committee is an initiative to bring the two families together on the African continent so as to find common ground and enable them to work towards visible unity. There can be no serious steps taken towards such visible unity between Lutherans and Anglicans in Africa without first of all coming up with a common statement.

2. African Regional Meetings and Developments

In 1992 an African Anglican-Lutheran consultation was held in Harare, Zimbabwe. The starting point of this consultation was to affirm the basic ecclesiological position of the two families as spelled out in the Niagara Report and to further work on "authentic African ecclesiastical structures." Later it was agreed that such an authentic African ecclesiology was to be developed "in the context of the universal church" (see the report of the African Anglican-Lutheran Consultation in 1997). The universal context here refers to other ecumenical statements of the two communions (cf. the Pullach and Helsinki Reports as well as the Porvoo Common Statement). The Johannesburg Consultation (1997) reaffirmed the same basic ecclesiology as set out in the Niagara Report but viewed from "Christ's mission to all in the African context."

African Anglicans and Lutherans from Botswana, Kenya, Malawi, Namibia, Nigeria, South Africa, Tanzania, and Zimbabwe have met on several occasions. They have developed a sense of growing together as well as of being called to oneness in Christ, and they are genuinely striving for visible unity. What they yet have to come up with is a common statement similar to the Porvoo declaration.

What Is the Aim and Mission of the African Anglican-Lutheran Dialogue?

In some parts of the region religious pluralism is creating a serious challenge to the mission of the church. In those regions the expansion of Islam and the imposition of *sharia* law to non-adherents is a challenge to the Christian church in its mission and evangelism. Unity or closer cooperation of the two churches could help them find a way of witnessing to the gospel together.

The two families have to understand themselves as doing mission on a continent that is constantly putting humanity at jeopardy. The context of mission of the church in Africa has to go beyond national boundaries in order to find common solidarity. The church's mission is to address socio-economic systems that are unjust, for instance in Zimbabwe where 62 percent of the population live below the poverty line and 45 percent are very poor.

Zimbabwe

When Anglicans and Lutherans met at a national consultation in Njube, Bulawayo (13-15 July 1993), the focus of the consultation was on ecclesiology. The churches were soon to discover that their ecclesiologies largely were formed and shaped by European reformers. To a certain extent these reformers shared a regional common history that transcended their national boundaries. The liturgical structure found in the Anglican Book of Common Prayer is similar to the Lutheran Agendas. The participants discovered that both churches have the tradition of regular celebration of Holy Communion, use similar elements (bread and wine), practice infant baptism, and acknowledge in different ways the authority of bishops. At Njube, Anglicans discovered that Lutherans:

- stand for all Scripture readings, and not just the gospel,
- do not use the westward-facing position for the celebration of Holy Communion, no bells or incense,
- do not permit lay persons to administer bread and wine at the Eucharist,
- do not require confirmation to be carried out by a bishop.

Lutherans on their part discovered that Anglicans:

- have bishops who serve as bishops until they retire,
- have titles such as Archbishop, Archdeacon, Canon, Rector, etc.

While this may appear rather simplistic, some of the participants, who had had previous exposure to the two traditions, soon realized how important these discoveries were. These are the issues that mark our denominational identities and are therefore vital, especially for people at the grassroots level.

A non-Zimbabwean has to appreciate that the traditional historical differences of the Reformation in Europe are not of paramount importance in the African churches. This has to do with the way missionaries planted European churches in Zimbabwe. When the British came to occupy Zimbabwe, denominations like the Lutherans, United Methodists, and United Church of Christ were confined to certain areas. The Lutheran Church was confined to Matebeleland South around Mberengwa. Although the Anglican Church was allowed to plant churches all over the country, except in Mberengwa, you have a situation in which some members of the two church families hardly know one another. Since the churches in Zimbabwe as a whole do not always consider church unity a key priority, members of different churches have remained ignorant of each other. The discoveries at Njube of the things we share were important for further consultation.

At the same conference, minor convergences and divergences became the starting points for a better understanding of our relationship. Different ecclesiological elements helped participants appreciate each other. At the end of the consultation, both delegations agreed that "there was an urgent need for a clear statement on the nature and extent of inter-communion between the Church of the Province of Central Africa and the Evangelical Lutheran Church in Zimbabwe." The respective leaders of the two bodies were to see that this matter was further discussed with the aim of moving towards visible unity. Participants went on to suggest among other things the use of a common liturgy, hymnbook, Sunday School material, and a joint theological training program. Insofar as the local clergy and laity were concerned, "the Spirit" was moving them towards visible unity, but "the flesh" of the leadership was weak.

Tanzania

In Tanzania, where the Germans were the first colonial settlers, the situation is different. The two churches are represented in all provinces of the country, and members of the two families have fair knowledge of each other's ecclesiology. Accordingly, a close cooperation between the two churches has taken place in Tanzania, such as jointly translating the Niagara Report into Swahili. Anglicans and Lutherans have also shared pastoral responsibilities here more than their counterparts in Zimbabwe. Participation at each other's episcopal ordinations has been more regular and visible than in Zimbabwe.

In spite of all these experiences of sharing and growing closer to each other, the churches in Tanzania have not yet come up with a common statement of cooperation at a national level.

Namibia

The Anglican and Lutheran churches in Namibia have largely shared a common ministry, particularly during the political liberation struggle. Anglican or Lutheran chaplains in exile had pastoral responsibilities across denominational boundaries. Unfortunately, this cooperation was primarily politically motivated. Soon after achieving political independence, the two church families went back to their separate existence, and the ecumenical advancement that had been gained prior to independence stagnated. What is important about the Namibian case is that the two churches have a substantial knowledge of each other, as they shared a common experience of unity during the war.

Elsewhere on the Continent

My knowledge of what has taken place elsewhere in Africa with regard to ecumenical cooperation between Anglicans and Lutherans is limited. Information about noticeable steps towards ecumenical cooperation have not yet filtered through in our regional consultations. Our major problem in the region is that communication is poor. Moreover, the disproportionate presence of the two traditions on the continent makes ecumenical links difficult to establish, and the need for such links may not even have been felt. The Pan-African Anglican-Lutheran conversations have, therefore, tended to focus on countries with a substantial presence of the two traditions.

A Challenge to the Africa Region

In his opening remarks at the Anglican-Lutheran joint meeting in Johannesburg (December 1997), Canon John L. Peterson, the ACC General Secretary, challenged African Anglican and Lutheran leaders to work towards unity because the continent and its multifaceted problems can best be faced by a united church. He reminded members of the African region that:

> There are few places in the world where the struggle for human dignity and survival is such a prominent daily feature as in the African continent. There are few places in the world where unity and reconciliation are more needed, between nations, between peoples of different ethnic backgrounds, even between religions. . . . Most Anglican Christians in the world live on this continent. Ours is a predominantly African Church. Ours is a Black church. The time

> has come when ecumenical dialogue, which has often been dismissed as being a "Northern" concern, must become part of the life of our church in Africa. You have the advantage of . . . not being bound by the particular histories of nation states and churches in Europe. The historic divisions, localized in Europe, are not unimportant, and in many cases have been exported. But you are leaders of the African Church, and not merely leaders of a European religion on African soil. And as leaders of the Church you speak for most of our Communion, as Anglicans.

Canon Peterson's remarks are based on observations of the African church leaders and how they have responded to the call for visible unity.

One would wish to have a united church on the continent in order to stand together against those things that divide and destroy Africa. One would wish to have a church that is engaged in programs that try to bring about unity where the Organization for African Unity has failed dismally. Pan-African politicians have at least tried. One would wish to have an African church that is seeking a way to respond to God's plan for the unification of all things in Christ. This would reflect that Africans on the continent share an African culture and its values of communal life.

3. Defining an African Vision

When the Anglican-Lutheran interim committee met for a consultation at the University of Zimbabwe in March 1999, they came up with what they defined as "an African vision." They said:

> The vision which guides our deliberations is that of a united African church with an African identity, in which Anglicans and Lutherans are in full communion and visible unity with one another. We look forward to a unique liturgical unity so that we may worship God as one church. We hope for a spirit of generosity which will accommodate our cultural and regional differences, so that we can celebrate our God-given diversity. We commit ourselves to the proclamation and teaching of the Gospel as our primary task. We

> hope to foster ecumenical fellowship throughout all levels of our churches and to be steadfast in the task of evangelism, mission and social activism as imperatives of the Gospel of our Lord and saviour, Jesus Christ. (March 1999)

The entry point for the African Anglican and Lutheran churches to achieve the goal of visible unity between the two families does not even mention the European reformation or sentiments expressed in the Porvoo Common Statement. The convergent point between Anglicans and Lutherans in Africa and those of the Porvoo churches is the common desire and longing for visible unity, "that they all may be one" (John 17:21). It is this call to unity that has motivated the two traditions in the North — in Europe, the USA, and Canada — to be where they are today.

The vision of the African region is to approach ecumenical cooperation from our own context. Where are we as Anglican and Lutheran Christians today? How do we relate to each other? What are the challenges we face? Facing bad governance on the continent as well as unemployment, refugees, HIV/AIDS, homelessness, and natural disasters, what is the church's mission to the people of God in such a context? The African church needs to be visibly one in its proclamation, diaconal services, and prophetic witness. Yet, Anglicans and Lutherans in the region do not have to work towards unity solely because of insurmountable challenges on the continent. What is required here is an obedient response to Jesus' will that we should all be one.

At its first meeting, held in Nairobi in April 2001, the African Anglican-Lutheran Commission recognized active cooperation already existing between the two church families. The Commission adopted the above cited African Vision recommended by the interim committee as a guideline for future work.

African Community and Its Diaconal Ministry

African community exists for its members, and members in turn for their community. It is this sense of belonging that makes life more purposeful and meaningful to an African. Members sustain each other in times of sorrow, and they also share joyful moments collectively. A funeral service in the community is attended by everybody. Traditionally, people in the community are not invited to a wedding; they just come.

Caregivers undergo training before they exercise their ministry of care and love. Diaconal ministry is a ministry that every member has to be involved in. An African understanding of care in the community should also be considered as the key to what membership in the community of faith entails. The love and care Africans offer one another expresses the sacramental meaning of diaconal ministry. Each individual person understands his/her role in the community as that of a "deacon" without special training.

The basis for African unity lies in the service offered by members to one another. Where such an understanding of community exists, there is unity. The African region should not be afraid to initiate programs that bring people together. To engage in conversations that seek to realize the goal of visible unity should certainly be a priority. In this connection, members of the Anglican and Lutheran churches in Africa should encourage the traditional practice of care in their churches.

4. Weaknesses Contributing to the Slow Pace Towards Unity in the Region

Lack of Structures

The region suffers from a lack of structures. The Anglican Church has no desk for ecumenical relations at diocesan and provincial levels to coordinate ecumenical activities. The absence of an ecumenical officer is also true for the Lutheran churches. If the African vision is to work towards the goal of visible unity, the establishment of an African secretariat should be considered seriously. The establishment of such a desk would improve and consolidate mutual understanding between the two families and develop contacts between bishops, clergy, and laity in the region.

The task of the desk would be to facilitate and coordinate ecumenical activities between the two families, to inform the region of similar ecumenical efforts in progress in the worldwide communions, and to initiate new areas for joint ecumenical ventures. For the desk to succeed, the local and regional leadership on its part will have to support and assist the ecumenical officer(s) by identifying or seconding individuals who have the ability to work with local church groups towards visible unity. Unless all members of the church are involved, the road to unity may be long, cumbersome, and confusing.

In view of the rapid growth of our churches in the region, ecumenical cooperation should be seen as a missionary opportunity to proclaim the gospel in a region ravaged by human misery, and to venture into new areas of mission and evangelism. An ecumenical office would produce material for use in our congregations that would help members understand each other's ecclesiology. The office would also promote and encourage common ecumenical projects for the two families.

Funds for the Secretariat

The scarcity of financial resources in the region is one of the limiting factors in the pursuit of the goal of visible unity. All the consultations held so far have been financed by ACC and LWF offices. Yet, the Pan-African region has to "own" the program. Ownership of a program of this magnitude has to be viewed as a priority by all members of the two families.

For the time being, every effort should be made to encourage the churches in the region to commit themselves to work towards visible unity. But the road to realizing such a goal is a long one, and the process has so far been slow.

The African Commission therefore recommended to all concerned parties to consider ways of raising money for the mentioned ecumenical desk. Furthermore, it is hoped that both churches will develop ideas on how the Commission's proposal can be implemented:

a. that in countries where Anglican-Lutheran cooperation is already experienced this should be intensified and nurtured towards official relationships of communion;
b. that in countries where Anglicans and Lutherans coexist but where there are no bilateral relationships between the two churches, immediate contact be encouraged between the appropriate authorities at the national level;

c. that in both these cases, the following steps be taken by the churches involved:
   i. undertake education at a grassroots level to bring about knowledge and understanding of each church as to history, liturgy, doctrine, and church order and polity;
   ii. exchange visits, extend mutual invitations to each other's synods, hold discussions, and engage in other forms of getting to know each other;
   iii. as a way of deepening cooperation between the two churches, plan and carry out together joint theological education, lay training, and women's and children's programs;
   iv. take action in these matters at a provincial/synodical level at the appropriate time.

Conclusion

A resolution from the Anglican-Lutheran consultation in Bulawayo, calling for the church leadership in Zimbabwe to come up with a clear statement on the nature and extent of communion between the churches of the Province of Central Africa and the Evangelical Lutheran Church in Zimbabwe, together with the Pan-African vision, would form the basis for a common statement comparable to the Porvoo agreement. What the two families need in the region is a bold open confirmation of what is already happening in the churches. A public declaration is vital at this stage if we are to consolidate the aims already achieved. At the same time, the Commission is also of the opinion that in order to realize the African Anglican-Lutheran vision, the discussions between the two communions should not be the privilege of a few specialists but an exercise in which members of the two churches at parish level also participate.

The Commission now waits eagerly for responses to its proposals.

Reflections on the Reception and Implementation of Porvoo in the Churches

The Porvoo Process in the Church of England

CHARLES HILL

The main body concerned with the implementation of Porvoo in the Church of England is the Porvoo Panel. The Panel was constituted in 2000, and meets three times a year under the chairmanship of the Archbishop of York and the vice-chairmanship of the bishop of Portsmouth. Its brief is to serve as a reference, support, and oversight group for the Church of England representation on the Porvoo Contact Group. The Panel monitors and encourages involvement in the Porvoo communion on the part of the central bodies, dioceses, parishes, training institutions, and other bodies. As well as preparing publicity and resource material, it monitors church and general developments in the Nordic and Baltic countries.

The Panel keeps the profile of Porvoo high on the church agenda by reporting back to the House of Bishops and the General Synod, through the Council for Christian Unity. Regular contact is maintained with the ecumenical specialists in the dioceses, through the network of Diocesan Ecumenical Officers and European Links Officers, who in turn report back on work and progress at the local level.

Mapping the reception of Porvoo in the dioceses has been an interesting and inspiring exercise. In 2000, the Council for Christian

Unity asked the dioceses of the Church of England to respond to a questionnaire on specific Porvoo commitments. These (commitments i-iv) related to the practical outworking of Porvoo in diocesan and parish life. The questions posed were open-ended so that the maximum amount of information and evidence could be offered.

The extremely high response rate from the dioceses indicates the seriousness with which the Porvoo agreement has been received in the Church of England. The responses were wide-ranging and the overall picture very encouraging. It is clear that different dioceses are at different stages on their "Porvoo pilgrimage." Some dioceses have not yet had the opportunity or the resources to develop relations with the Porvoo churches, but are committed to the agreement (perhaps through use of the Prayer Diary in local parishes), and are looking forward to opportunities arising in the years ahead. Other dioceses have established formal links with Porvoo churches, with a wide range of contacts, and are enjoying the fruits that these links are providing to share in a common life. Porvoo is, of course, only one possibility for overseas contact open to the dioceses: many have committed their main resources in this area to links, for example, with the German Evangelical Church (Meissen Agreement) or with churches within the worldwide Anglican Communion.

The diocesan links continue to grow, and it is hoped that an information pack on Porvoo will be produced for dioceses and parishes considering new links. Active formal links include the following dioceses: Carlisle, Chelmsford, Derby, Guildford, Lincoln, Newcastle, Norwich, Oxford, Portsmouth, Rochester, Truro, and several cathedrals, including a new covenant between Southwark and Bergen, Norway. Rochester has a longstanding and very active link with Estonia. Most diocesan links are with Sweden and Norway, and ways of extending links to the other Porvoo countries are being actively pursued by the Porvoo Panel.

Almost all dioceses of the Church of England have committed themselves to pray for the other Porvoo churches. *An Invitation to Prayer,* a booklet of prayer requests produced by the Church of England on behalf of the Porvoo Contact Group, provides a useful tool for all the Porvoo churches to pray in turn for each other. Extracts from this booklet are incorporated into diocesan prayer calendars, which are used in many places at the local parish level. It is, therefore, increasingly common to hear the dioceses and bishops of the Porvoo communion mentioned in the general prayers for the church in Church of England worship.

An important aspect of the move towards full visible unity among churches is the opportunity to share in education, training, and resources. Dioceses have been looking at areas such as confirmation preparation in the Nordic countries, the role of churchwardens, and counseling provision. Church musicians and youth leaders have been sharing their experiences. Some recent examples include:

- The Diocese of Derby has assisted the Church of Sweden in setting up a community-based project in Norberg.
- Representatives from the Diocese of Guildford and the linked Diocese of Visby (Church of Sweden) have met to compare best practices in education and training.
- A study day has taken place with the Bishops' Council in Lincoln and the Uppsala Diocesan Board, Church of Sweden.
- The Bishop of Tonbridge (Rochester Diocese) has attended the Pastors' Conference in Estonia.
- The St. Albans Cathedral Education Centre has established links with similar bodies in the Church of Sweden.
- The Diocese of Rochester has provided funding for building two residential huts for a new youth camp in Estonia.

A key aspect of the Porvoo commitments becoming reality in the life of the church is the interchangeability of ministers. Seventeen dioceses report that clergy from the other Porvoo churches have taken up appointments in their diocese or vice-versa, and this has proved very useful at a time of clergy shortage in the Church of England. The Diocese of Lincoln has been in the forefront of such work, hosting seven appointments from Sweden and two from Iceland lasting from six months to seven years. There are some eighteen clergy from the other Porvoo churches who have been given permission to officiate in the Diocese of Europe. In a few instances, clergy from Church of England dioceses are serving short-term appointments in their link diocese, which in turn strengthens the bond between each side. A former canon of York Minster has been serving short-term placements on the staff of a Swedish diocese and cathedral, and several other senior clergy have been able to benefit from similar arrangements.

The most obvious obstacle to the interchangeability of ministers is, of course, language, and both the Contact Group and the Porvoo Panel are concerned that adequate linguistic training and preparation for pastoral work can be provided. The process of induction and continuing ministerial education is important for Porvoo as for any other area of ministry, and the diocesan guidelines point to the need for the provision of this support both before and after appointment.

Building on the success of these pioneering appointments, the Porvoo Panel of the Church of England has drawn up a set of guidelines to inform diocesan bishops of the issues and procedures involved, and to promote a common approach. The guidelines, approved by the House of Bishops in 2001, should encourage more dioceses to consider such appointments and enable parishes and sector ministries to benefit from the gifts of clergy from the Porvoo churches. The guidelines are based on practical experience, and have been put together in consultation with the Diocese of Europe and the Lutheran Co-Secretary of the Porvoo Contact Group. An in-service training course on the Nordic churches, organized by the Church of Sweden, was attended by some twenty-five clergy from the Church of England. The Church of Sweden also holds training courses for Nordic clergy wishing to familiarize themselves with various aspects of Anglicanism, and a number of course members have gone on to successful appointments in the Church of England. The Porvoo Panel is keen to open up such opportunities for clergy at any stage of their career, and to develop interchangeability also in the context of house-for-duty appointments and post-retirement ministry.

The agreement provides for bishops of all the Porvoo churches to participate in consecrations, ordinations, and confirmations, thus providing a further outward sign of the communion we share. Many bishops in the Church of England take up this opportunity, which is coordinated — as far as consecrations are concerned — by the staff of the Archbishops of Canterbury and York, in conjunction with the Council for Christian Unity. Some recent examples:

- The bishop of Bradwell (Diocese of Chelmsford) participated in the Diocese of Karlstad's ordinations (Church of Sweden), and the bishop of Karlstad participated in the Diocese of Chelmsford's ordinations at Petertide 2000.

- The bishop of Grimsby (Lincoln) has had the opportunity to participate in the consecration of six Swedish bishops.
- The bishop of Tonbridge (Rochester) shared in the consecration of the Archbishop of Estonia.

An important dimension of Porvoo is the opportunity to welcome members of the other churches into local congregations, where people have moved abroad to work, study, or retire, or for family reasons. A few dioceses are in the fortunate position of welcoming members of the Nordic and Baltic Lutheran churches into their parishes on a regular or temporary basis. In the Diocese of Europe, some members of these churches regularly worship with local Anglican congregations, often partners of mixed marriages, or people who feel particularly at home with Anglican worship, whether modern or traditional. Equally, there are many members of the Church of England resident in, or visiting, the Porvoo countries who regularly worship in these Lutheran churches, especially when there is no local Anglican congregation. An exciting recent development has been the establishing of a shared Anglican/Lutheran chaplaincy in Tallinn, Estonia.

In some cases, sharing buildings is a further outward sign of the growing relationship between the Porvoo churches. An Icelandic Lutheran congregation use a parish church in Grimsby several times a year, and on some occasions joint Anglican/Lutheran services are held. The Diocese of Newcastle also hosts services for Finnish Lutherans in the cathedral.

The responses to our questionnaire, and the many regular reports from the dioceses, make it clear that the links established at a local level with the Porvoo churches are a growing feature within the life of the Church of England. The response from one diocese specifically mentioned that the provision of sacramental and pastoral hospitality to Christians of other traditions is so much part of diocesan life that each individual case cannot be monitored. In some cases, relationships between the churches build on established civic links, for example, like that linking Grimsby and Reykjavik. Joint eucharistic celebrations are frequently held in many of the dioceses maintaining active links.

The first of a regular series of gatherings of Primates and Presiding Bishops of the Porvoo churches was held at Lambeth Palace in late 1999. The occasion provided a valuable opportunity to consider the issues facing the churches and the particular role of Primates and Presiding Bishops as the focus of unity for their churches. Episcopal visits and contacts between the Church of England and the Porvoo churches take place regularly, including many at the diocesan level with an annual invitation to a bishop or other senior figure to attend the General Synod in York. These visits have proved to be an extremely valuable way of extending Porvoo networks in the areas of church government and national policy-making.

The Church of England was honored to host the first Theological Conference of the Porvoo Communion, in Durham in September 2000. The conference, on the theme *Diversity in Communion*, was the next event in the cycle of conferences and consultations mentioned in paragraph 58 of the Porvoo declaration. The six-day residential conference gathered together a wide range of theologians and church leaders to focus on a possible common understanding of unity and mission. The papers and group discussion covered the main areas of Scripture, human sexuality, ministry, and the contemporary world in which the church exists. A series of key recommendations were drawn up for the Porvoo churches to consider as the framework for collaboration over the coming years. The Church of England will be presenting these recommendations to its central boards and councils, and to the General Synod, through the Council for Christian Unity. The recommendations covered the reshaping of theology to meet current needs, the sharing of theology through a large range of specific initiatives and contacts, a strong commitment to the needs of young people, the promotion of mutual accountability among the Porvoo churches, and a concern to work together in common mission.

The Church of England is keen to involve Porvoo partners in the context of new initiatives in theology and ministry. A number of theologians and others involved in ministry training maintain regular contacts and study/teaching visits with the Porvoo churches. The experience of the Porvoo churches has provided valuable material for the Church of England working party on the renewed Diaconate. It is hoped that the new Church of England theological working party on women and the episcopate will also draw on the experience of our Porvoo partners.

A further important context for theological work with the Porvoo churches is found in the work of the Anglo-Nordic-Baltic Theological

Conference, first held in 1929, and its separate forum for parish clergy, the Anglo-Scandinavian Pastoral Conference. In 1999 the Theological Conference was hosted by the Diocese of Portsmouth on the theme *Christianity Facing the Millennium,* and participants shared in Sunday worship throughout the Diocese. In 2001, the Conference is being held in Denmark on the theme of *Music and Theology.*

Our research shows that a large number of people, throughout the Church of England and in a wide variety of contexts, are involved in links, activities, ministry, training, and study directly deriving from Porvoo. Above all, this is due to the enthusiasm and commitment at the local level, coordinated and disseminated through the national church institutions. Porvoo reflects abundantly the two fundamentals for the church that underpin the work of the Archbishops' Council of the Church of England: *worship* and *the quest for full visible unity.* Porvoo is regarded in our church as one of the greatest achievements in our work on this quest in recent years and, together with our partners, we look for a continued realization of the Porvoo commitments in the years to come.

The Porvoo Process in the Church of Ireland

JOHN NEILL

The Church of Ireland has its roots in the ancient Celtic church, which flourished on the western edges of Europe. This gave way at the beginning of the second millennium to influences from the Anglo-Norman invasion from neighboring Britain. Halfway through the second millennium the Irish church experienced almost at second hand the influence of the English Reformation. It was at the point of Reformation that the Church of Ireland, though retaining both the episcopal sees and church property, perhaps ceased to be a "folk church" and began to be the church of the ruling classes. Such a change in the fortunes of the Church of Ireland was not made explicit until Disestablishment in 1869. History has shown that this was a moment of liberation for the church. It weakened its ties with the political structures that would disappear within fifty years, and so the church was enabled to take its place with fresh confidence in a changing political and religious scene.

The Church of Ireland to this day cherishes its Celtic heritage, and the Irish saints of the first millennium take their place alongside the apostles at the dedication of parish churches throughout the land. There is within the Church of Ireland a determination that while remaining part of the wider Anglican Communion, the Church of Ireland should express this in a distinctively Irish way.

The liturgical practice of the Church of Ireland is within the central and lower traditions of Anglicanism, and the spirituality is influenced to this day by much of the Evangelical revival of the nineteenth century. There also remains a great loyalty to classical Anglicanism as expressed by the Caroline Divines, which has protected the Church of Ireland as a whole from the extremes of either Anglo-Catholicism or rigid Evangelical Fundamentalism.

The Church of Ireland is by its Constitution an episcopal church and a synodical church, having had its own General Synod of Bishops, Priests, and Laity since 1870. There is a deep appreciation of the historic episcopate, which remained unbroken in the Church of Ireland at the period of the Reformation.

There are twelve dioceses in the Church of Ireland (several including at least six of the ancient smaller Celtic and Anglo-Norman dioceses). Each diocese is under the care of a bishop. In each diocese there is a Diocesan Synod, which consists of all the licensed clergy of the diocese and about four or five laity elected from each parochial unit. In Diocesan Synods, any matter may be voted on by orders, with the result that both clergy and laity (and indeed the bishop) have to approve any major matter.

The Diocesan Synod sends representatives of both clergy and laity to the General Synod (twice as many laity as clergy) who form the House of Representatives in the General Synod. The General Synod also has a House of Bishops, which includes the bishop of each diocese (but not retired bishops). Bishops participate in the General Synod, which is presided over by the Primate of All Ireland, though the bishops do not vote as part of the Synod, but separately after the House of Representatives, and that only very seldom.

There remains a certain creative tension between synodical structures and episcopacy. The General Synod is the chief administrative and legislative body in the Church of Ireland. The episcopal nature of the church is expressed in matters of ordination and to a lesser extent in certain matters of faith and order. The pastoral, liturgical (including all confirmations), and leadership role of the episcopate is seen most clearly in the life of the individual dioceses. This creative tension can be expressed as part of the Anglican understanding of "dispersed authority."

The Church of Ireland dioceses are divided into two Provinces. Armagh in the northern part of the island geographically includes seven dioceses and is presided over by the Archbishop of Armagh, who carries the title Primate of All Ireland and is the senior Metropolitan. The Province of Dublin, consisting of five dioceses, is presided over by the Archbishop of Dublin, who carries the title Primate of Ireland. Neither provincial nor diocesan boundaries correspond to the political division of the island, and a substantial portion of the Republic remains in the Province of Armagh. There are about 370,000 members of the Church of Ireland and about three-quarters of these live in Northern Ireland. It is the largest minority church in Ireland as a whole, but of course the Roman Catholic Church accounts for about three-quarters of the members of any church on the island. There are about six hundred serving clergy, of whom about ten percent are women, and about thirteen percent are auxiliary priests who do not draw a stipend from the church. (*Church of Ireland population* [per 1991 census]: Northern Ireland: 279,280; Republic: 89,187; Total: 368,467. *Serving Clergy:* Stipendiary Clergy: 510; Auxiliary Clergy: 78; Total Serving Clergy: 588.)

The Church of Ireland has a long history of ecumenical involvement. The Irish Council of Churches was the first national ecumenical council in Britain or Ireland, and the Church of Ireland was a founder member. The Church of Ireland was involved in the British Council of Churches and now in its successor, Churches Together in Britain and Ireland. It is a member of the Conference of European Churches, and it has been a member of the WCC since its foundation.

The Church of Ireland has been generally enthusiastic in expressing its full communion with united churches in which former Anglicans are involved, and this was apparent specifically in relation to the churches of the Asian subcontinent.

Clergy from churches officially in communion with the Church of England have had no difficulty in ministering on occasions in the

Church of Ireland. Relations with the Old Catholic churches and with the Church of Sweden were taken for granted rather than established by way of formal agreement.

The Church of Ireland was not part of the Meissen process, due mainly to limited resources. However, the House of Bishops did endorse its principles and, as a measure of assent, sent a representative to the signing.

The Church of Ireland was also part of the Porvoo process (though not from the start, as its full significance had not been grasped), and it was involved in the final stages of the discussions. The Church of Ireland formally ratified the agreement, and representative bishops were present at each of the signings and signed the Porvoo declaration with the prior approval of the General Synod. The Church of Ireland has since agreed to sign the Reuilly Agreement. Within Ireland, a process leading to a possible covenant with the Methodist Church is now being explored.

The Reception in Ireland of the Porvoo Agreement

The process of ratification of the Porvoo agreement was fairly simple within the Church of Ireland. In the first instance, the Committee for Christian Unity studied the text of the agreement. The agreement was examined in relation to guidelines issued from time to time by the Lambeth Conference, and in particular against the criteria of the Chicago-Lambeth Quadrilateral. Care was taken that nothing within the agreement contravened the formularies of the Church of Ireland, or its historic documents. The study concentrated on the declaration itself and not on the structures or doctrinal emphases of other churches within the process. The Committee for Christian Unity commended the agreement without reservation to the Standing Committee of the General Synod, which includes all the bishops, as indeed does the Committee for Christian Unity. Once more the agreement was recommended for acceptance, and in due course it was presented to General Synod and approved without dissent.

The Porvoo declaration did not provoke theological debate within the Church of Ireland. Theological debate is often prolonged in issues of Roman Catholic/Anglican relationships, where many factors combine, not of all of them theological, to provide ample scope for such debate. The other issue likely to provoke debate of a theological nature would be any agreement involving interchange with a ministry that was not episcopal. The Porvoo agreement falls into neither category. It might be added that those not directly involved in the process, that is, the vast majority of those voting in General Synod, would have viewed it as a matter of international ecumenical relationships, providing little challenge to change at the local level.

No changes in Canon Law were required in the Church of Ireland. There is no obstacle to a priest of a church in full communion with the Church of Ireland officiating within the Church of Ireland. A license or permission to officiate is required from a diocesan bishop, but this applies to any Anglican priest who comes from another part of the Anglican Communion. In the same way, lay members of churches in full communion with the Church of Ireland possess all the rights and privileges (including marriage rights) that apply to members of the Church of Ireland. All significant church law makes no distinction between clergy/members of the Church of Ireland and clergy/members of a church in communion with the Church of Ireland. The Porvoo agreement brings the Church of Ireland for all practical purposes into the same relationship with the Nordic and Baltic churches as it enjoys with its fellow Anglican churches. Questions of employment might require some further investigation under civil law if the person involved does not come from a country within the European Community.

The Implementation of the Agreement in Ireland

There have been several examples of sharing in the ordinations of bishops between the Church of Ireland and Nordic and Baltic churches. The bishop of Porvoo attended the ordination of an Irish bishop, sharing in the laying on of hands. Irish bishops have twice shared in ordinations of bishops in Sweden, and once in Finland. Bishops from Sweden and Finland have shared in the ordinations of priests in Ireland on several occasions, and likewise an Irish bishop has shared in such in Sweden. During a meeting of the Porvoo Contact Group, priests from Lithuania, Sweden, Finland, and Iceland shared in the laying on of hands in the ordination of priests in Dublin. In this context, a significant part, short of such full participation, was found for priests from Denmark and Latvia who were present. Representation at synods has not yet occurred, though it is about to do so in connection with diocesan links.

The manner in which the Porvoo agreement has overcome differences in the historical experience and continuity of the historic episcopate has given fresh impetus to some ecumenical work, and in particular in relation to Anglican/Methodist conversations. Exact parallels do not exist, but yet hopes for a fresh breakthrough have been raised.

Some of the invitations from Nordic and Baltic churches have presented some practical difficulties for the Church of Ireland. As a church with such limited resources in both finance and numbers, it is simply not possible to accept all invitations to send representatives. This is accentuated by the fact that there are virtually no members of the Church of Ireland who can converse in any Nordic or Baltic languages. Clearly, it is easier to welcome people to Ireland who invariably speak English, than for Irish people to make any real contribution in a Nordic or Baltic context.

Diocesan links are well established between Connor (Northern Ireland) and Linkoping (Sweden). These have involved groups traveling from each diocese to visit the other. They have involved sharing in ordinations, conducting retreats, and youth and parish links. A link between the diocese of Lund (Sweden) and Cashel and Ossory (Republic of Ireland) was established late in 2000 and already each bishop along with others have visited the other diocese. Choral and youth links are also being explored.

In its day-to-day life, the signing of the agreement has had limited impact in the Church of Ireland. There has been some perception among people that the Church of Ireland is now part of something bigger within Europe. Anglicanism has not shared the European links enjoyed by the Reformed and to a lesser extent the Methodist churches. Thus the Porvoo agreement has had particular relevance in a country for which European identity is of some real significance, as is the case in the Republic of Ireland.

There is a growing awareness where nationals from Nordic and Baltic Churches come to live in Ireland that they belong in the Church of Ireland in a very real way.

The signing of the agreement has changed the context for diocesan links. Heretofore Irish links in the developed world would have been with dioceses in the United States or Canada.

The ecumenical impact of Porvoo could yet be quite significant. The concept of being in full communion with a church not too far away that is not Anglican opens up vistas closer to home than with, for instance, united churches in Asia. One great ecumenical issue is how a church enters into full communion with another church existing side by side with it, and yet retains an autonomy and an identity of its own. Porvoo brings this issue that much closer.

The Reception and Implementation of the Porvoo Common Statement in the Evangelical Lutheran Church of Finland

JUHANI FORSBERG

1. Introductory Notes

The Porvoo Common Statement (PCS) is the most significant ecumenical statement ever adopted by the Evangelical Lutheran Church of Finland (ELCF). The significance of its adoption has several dimensions. First, PCS is theologically deep and comprehensive. Second, it seeks and finds ecumenically well-grounded solutions to the problems that previously hindered full communion between the signatory churches, and between churches of Anglican and Lutheran confession and tradition in general. Third, the significance of PCS lies in its ecumenical concretization: the "acknowledgments" and "commitments" embedded in PCS mean that it cannot remain as an expression of general ecumenical hospitality; rather, it demands and encourages the signatory churches to enter into a process where they are willing to grow "towards closer unity." This process also implies a readiness to consider changes in the constitution and spiritual life of the signatory churches. How this process is understood and implemented so far in the ELCF is described on the following pages.

A fruitful ecumenical background made it possible for PCS to come quite rapidly into existence. First, a common doctrinal basis was guaranteed, because there were never any doctrinal condemnations between the churches concerned. Second, there has been, since 1936, an agreement between the Church of England and the ELCF on eucharistic fellowship. Third, during the last decades of the twentieth century, several important ecumenical documents such as Faith and Order's *Baptism, Eucharist, Ministry* (1982) and the Anglican-Lutheran dialogue paper called the "Niagara Report" (1988) were published.

The representatives of the ELCF in the official theological conversations on PCS, and especially our representative in the Drafting Group, Dr. Lorenz Grönvik, were always aware of the theological and ecumenical presuppositions of a successful reception of the planned agreement in the ELCF. The ELCF has underlined the importance of the Ecumenical Creeds and the Lutheran Confessional Books as expressions of apostolic faith and kept keenly to its episcopal constitution. At the same time it has been ecumenically open and constructive. The necessity of the traditional formal interpretation of the apostolic succession as a guarantee for being a true church was never very strongly represented in the ELCF. In fact, there has been one break in the apostolic succession of our bishops since the end of the nineteenth century. One of the most important achievements of PCS is the inclusion of the apostolic succession into the wider context of the whole apostolicity of the church. Thus, PCS was able to combine apostolicity in doctrine — traditionally seen in Lutheranism as the most important dimension of apostolicity — with the apostolic succession in the ministry of oversight.

One of the most crucial prerequisites to assure a successful reception of PCS in the ELCF was the carefully formulated summary of Christian doctrine in §32. For instance, paragraphs 32b and 32c actually express the distinction between "law" and "gospel" — without explicitly using the formula so important for the interpretation of the Holy Scripture according to Lutheran doctrine. Several other important points in §32 became relevant in ELCF's process of adopting Porvoo.

2. Discussion about PCS and Its Adoption by the General Synod

The work in the official theological conversations from 1989 through 1992 proceeded without any controversial discussions in the ELCF. When, in 1992, the final text of PCS was agreed at Järvenpää and celebrated in Porvoo, it was noted in the publicity. The text of PCS was translated into Finnish, and the Bishops' Conference — which has an important role in doctrinal issues — started preparations for the adoption of PCS by the General Synod. The Bishops' Conference was unanimous in its positive attitude towards PCS, and the preparations were made without any controversial debates. The Diocesan Chapters were invited to express their opinions, and all local parishes and deaneries also had an opportunity to do so, even though very few parish councils used this option. There was little discussion about PCS in the press or other media before its handling in the General Synod.

The General Synod discussed the matter in its two sessions in spring and autumn 1995. Even though the final decision was clear, the Synod used a lot of time to debate PCS. Reading the minutes of the Synod, one gets the impression that some members of the Synod were only just beginning to realize how important and far-reaching a matter was put into the agenda and wondered why PCS had so far not been discussed more broadly and deeply on different levels of the ELCF.

The Synod debate concentrated on a few points. First was the question: What is the doctrinal and confessional status of PCS? Is PCS a new confessional document, or is it a new interpretation of the Lutheran Confession? The Synod rejected both these descriptions, and in the final statement the possibility of such misinterpretations was avoided with the wording "the synod decided to adopt *on the basis of the confession of our church* the Porvoo Declaration." The words in italics should be seen as a pastoral concession to the opponents of Porvoo, since it must be self-evident that all decisions of the Synod are based on the confession of the ELCF. The Synod did not describe or determine the doctrinal character of PCS, but when it saw the necessity to decide the matter with a qualified majority (¾ of the votes), that was also an indirect expression of the fact that PCS is a significant doctrinal document.

Second, a couple of points in §32 were also called into question. Some members of the Synod doubted that the sayings of PCS about *justification* were in harmony with the Lutheran doctrine. This accusation was clearly based on the outdated view that the only true expression of the Reformation concept of justification is a *forensic* one. The text of §32c says: "We share a common understanding of God's justifying grace, i.e. that we are accounted righteous and are made righteous before God only by grace through faith because of the merits of our Lord and Savior Jesus Christ, and not on account of our works or merits. . . ." The text clearly reveals both aspects of justification, the *forensic* or *imputative* and the *effective* one. Modern Finnish research on Luther has clearly shown how these aspects are inseparably interwoven, as several speakers at the Synod noted.

Third, some critical voices at the Synod doubted whether the Anglican doctrine on the Eucharist is compatible with the Lutheran doctrine. The main point was that the doctrine on the Eucharist, as it is formulated in the Thirty-Nine Articles, is a Calvinist one and does not sufficiently reflect the real presence of Christ in the eucharistic elements. The real presence is nevertheless clearly expressed in §32: "We believe that the body and blood of Christ are truly present, distributed and received under the forms of bread and wine in *the Lord's Supper (Eucharist)*." This wording is fully compatible with Article X in the Augsburg Confession, which naturally did not remain unnoticed by PCS supporters.

Fourth, some remarks were made in the Synod against the understanding of the ministry, especially of the ministry of oversight, in PCS. The most critical voices maintained that the concept of *episcope* and especially of the historic episcopate in apostolic succession means an alteration in the interpretation of the Lutheran Confession. Some speakers expressed their fear that PCS, with its concept of *episcope*, is leading us into the bosom of the Roman Catholic Church. The majority of the Synod did not see any danger in the concept of apostolic succession in PCS, because it is so well structured into the apostolicity of the whole church.

Fifth, the probably most "propagandistic" accusation made by a few opponents of Porvoo was that the whole PCS actually will place the ELCF under the power of the Pope. "The Porvoo train does not remain in Canterbury, but continues to Rome," was the most glaring metaphor used for opposing PCS. This opinion was nourished by the fact that at the same time, there was a vivid discussion underway in the ELCF about the "Joint Declaration on the Doctrine of Justification," an important consensus document between the Lutheran World Federation and the Vatican.

After the debate in two meetings of the Synod, PCS was adopted on 8 November 1995 by an overwhelming majority: ninety-four yeas, seven nays, and two abstentions.

3. The Implementation of PCS in the ELCF

With the adoption of PCS, the Bishops' Conference, the Church Council, and the Committee for the Service Book were given further measures for implementing PCS in the ELCF. The Bishops' Conference appointed a working group to fulfill this task. The first problem the working group faced was the role of the church act or law and the church order of the ELCF. At the very beginning of its work, the leading church lawyers regretted that they were not consulted during the preparation process of PCS. They maintained that the formulations of PCS need a more exact interpretation before its commitments can be implemented in the church laws and church order of the ELCF. Therefore, by the initiative of the working group, the ELCF asked the Porvoo Contact Group to organize a Porvoo Church Lawyers' Consultation in order to achieve a common interpretation of PCS for its implementation. This consultation was called together in London, 16-17 January 1998. Represented at the consultation were the senior experts in church law from most Porvoo churches. A happy result of this consultation was a unanimous commentary on PCS. With the help of this commentary the working group could finish its task and put it forward through the appropriate church bodies to the General Synod.

The main challenge for the implementation was that the church act and church order of the ELCF contain some obstacles to fulfilling the commitments of PCS. Some changes in the church act and in the church order were needed to remove these obstacles. The goal of the proposed reforms is the full, reciprocal exchange of members and ministers in the Porvoo churches.

To mention one example of need for reform, there is an order in the church act of the ELCF, that the position of a vicar (leading minister in a local congregation), as well as some other ministerial positions, can be held only by Finnish citizens. Because this order belongs to the church act, that part of the church law which finally must be adopted by the Parliament of Finland, a proposal to remove this national prerequisite was adopted by the General Synod in spring 2001 and recently (summer 2001) sent to the Parliament.

A second example is from the realm of the church order that needs only internal church measures to be changed. According to PCS, the full interchangeability of ministers is only possible if a person is *episcopally* ordained (PCS 58b.v). Normally that is the case in the ELCF, but our church order allows that if the office of a bishop is vacant or he/she is prevented from participation by an illness, the cathedral dean or the senior canon of the diocesan chapter can officiate at the ordination. This order, needed in earlier times when there were only a few bishops in the ELCF, was removed by the General Synod in spring 2001. As an echo from earlier debates, a minority of the Synod saw in the maintaining of the presbyterial ordination a question of *status confessionis* in Lutheranism.

The canonical reforms for implementing PCS are thus on their way to becoming adopted in the near future. However, the implementation of PCS is clearly not only a legal question. The ELCF understands PCS as a process "towards closer unity." Therefore, Porvoo must be implemented at all levels of church life. Since the adoption of PCS, contacts and cooperation between the small Anglican congregation in Helsinki and the ELCF have become more regular. The ELCF has strengthened its financial support to the Anglican congregation so that it can employ a full-time Anglican minister. There is a growing number of Finnish ministers who are licensed to officiate according to the Anglican rite, and worship services according to Anglican rite are celebrated in a growing number of Finnish cities.

PCS allows a diversity that stems from different traditions in Porvoo churches. The intention of PCS is not a uniformity in all spheres of the church's life. A single, uniform liturgical order of worship is not intended. Liturgical and spiritual diversities are a richness. There are, nevertheless, situations where specific expressions of the existing and growing communion are welcomed. For instance, when Lutheran and Anglican ministers are serving in a worship according to the rite of one or the other, they are not only guests, assistants, or visiting preachers at the service. The communion should be expressed as deeply as possible at the Lord's table. Therefore, the Bishops' Conference has recently given to the appropriate organs of the ELCF the task to formulate recommendations for *concelebration* in Anglican-Lutheran Eucharist services.

Also, it would be most desirable for PCS to stimulate twinnings between Anglican and Lutheran congregations and dioceses. Due to the barrier caused by the difficult Finnish language, this activity may not become so common as is the case in Scandinavian churches where the exchange of ministers already is a reality. An important task of implementation is to create sufficient resources for this as well as for mutual scholarship programs.

Altogether, PCS has already proved to be a very inspiring and challenging ecumenical concern for the ELCF. I have treated its implementation almost exclusively from the point of view of Anglican-Lutheran relations, because the Lutheran Porvoo churches already have close relations to each other. The most important aspect of the implementation of PCS in all its member churches is expressed in the very first commitment of PCS: "We commit ourselves: (i) to share a common life in mission and service, to pray for and with one another, and to share resources" (PCS §58b.i). As the title of the larger publication of Porvoo, *Together in Mission and Ministry,* indicates, PCS is not only an agreement on the ministry, but also a strong reminder on the need of common witness and service by the churches in a secularized, multireligious, and multicultural Europe.

The Reception and Implementation of the Porvoo Common Statement in Estonia

TIIT PÄDAM

Already from 1989, or in other words from the very beginning of the dialogue process, the Estonian Evangelical Lutheran Church (EELC) participated in the interchurch negotiations that led up to the Porvoo Common Statement (PCS). The subsequent approval of the document by the EELC can be described as a natural step in the wake of this process. When the final statement was presented, however, the Estonian church and the society to which it was sent were no longer the same as they were when the process started. This applies not only to Estonia but also to the other Baltic states.

This contribution does not aim at presenting a solution to the theologically and ecclesiastically extremely complicated problem of reception, but will be restricted to a description of the Estonian situation. Reception should, of course, be viewed as a very diverse process. Starting out from a narrower point of view, this paper contains an account of the instruments by which the Porvoo statement was received in our church. Seen in a broader perspective, however, the participation of the EELC in the preparation of PCS, the approval of the statement, and the implementation of the current text and its results also call for some attention here. I shall in the following try to convey a picture of the approach of the EELC within the wider context of the so-called Porvoo process.

In addition to the negotiations themselves, the participation of the EELC (as the only Lutheran church from the Baltic states to be involved in the process from its beginning) and its role in the Porvoo process were influenced by two external factors. First, parallel to the negotiations considerable changes were underway in the political and legal structure of Estonia, leading to the country's becoming independent. Second, as opposed to the majority of other nations involved in the dialogue, there was no church in Estonia belonging to the Anglican tradition and for this reason the EELC lacked some relevant experience. In one way, these circumstances made the process simpler but they also turned it into something much more than a mere participation in ecumenical negotiations.

The process was initiated in the EELC by a decision of the church government, the Consistory, to participate in the negotiations, despite a certain initial ambiguity as to the goal of the dialogue. The decisive factor here was the invitation received from the Archbishop of the Church of Sweden and from the Nordic Ecumenical Institute to send representatives to the negotiations. The Consistory appointed as its representatives Professor Dr. Toomas Paul and Mr. Tiit Pädam, then secretary general of the Consistory with responsibility for legal and practical issues.

At the starting point, the EELC had limited experience in ecumenical dialogues. During the previous decades, the EELC had only responded officially to Faith and Order's so-called Lima statement *Baptism, Eucharist and Ministry* from 1982. The relevant views and opinions of our church were listed in a proposal by Toomas Paul that was approved at an informational meeting of the EELC deans. At the same time, the EELC also decided to sign the Leuenberg Concord, but this took place without any prior theological debate. The subsequent protests of the deans against this action were not taken into consideration. The Concord was signed on behalf of the church by Archbishop Alfred Tooming. However, as there are no Reformed churches in Estonia, the disagreement may be seen as a more theoretical problem.

It is important to stress the differences in the reception of PCS from what had happened earlier in this field, since the Porvoo process had a significant impact on the development of the EELC. Two factors are particularly important in this connection. First, the proposal needed to be approved theologically at the informational meeting of the deans — a meeting of the predominantly administrative leaders within the church and not representative of the whole church. Second, the church had so far not been free to decide anything when it came to internationally binding agreements, since such agreements also had to be approved and coordinated by a state that officially had declared itself to be atheist.

The reception of the Porvoo declaration was different from previous experiences in two ways: In the new independent Republic, the Estonian church had passed new regulations as to how documents in the field of canon law and theology should be handled. This new approval process consisted of two steps: First, the EELC Pastors' Conference, to which all theologians who have completed their education and have been ordained in the EELC belong, should discuss the contents of such documents and submit its theological evaluation to the Church Synod. Only then can a decision be taken by the Synod, which is the highest legislative body in the church. Contrary to the previous system, the final decision is now taken by a body that is much more competent in theological and ecclesiastical matters and is also representative of the church in the sense that all congregations participate in the Synod through representatives of the deaneries. The second difference is that by the time the Porvoo declaration had been completed, the church had become politically independent and was able to take decisions based on its own religious and theological convictions.

The most important events of the Porvoo process for the EELC took place in 1994, when PCS and the results from the conversations were presented to the church and an official response was given within the framework of the just mentioned procedure.

That year (1994) the Pastors' Conference of the EELC met in Tartu on 25-26 January. A translation of PCS had previously been sent out to all members of the clergy. It was presented to the Conference by Dean Peeter Kaldur. The questions that were raised in the discussion following the presentation focused on the problems of ordination. Moreover, matters concerning the process of ratifying the document were seen as more important than purely legal concerns. Based on both theological and ecclesiastical-political criteria, the Conference voted by a clear majority to approve the document and to pass it on to the Church Council or Synod with the recommendation that it should be ratified.

The highest deciding body of the EELC — the Church Council — dealt with the Porvoo declaration at its regular meeting on 19 April 1994 in Tallinn. A speech outlining the main aspects of the document was given by Jaan Kiivit, chairman of the foreign affairs committee of the church. As the Pastors' Conference had already given a theological assessment of PCS, the debate at the council meeting focused mainly on formal topics, after which the chairman submitted the document to the Synod for action. In the subsequent vote on the ratification of the Porvoo statement, thirty-eight members voted in favor of PCS, two voted against, and three abstained.

If we look back at the beginning of the Porvoo process, we can definitely say that the church has changed both internally and externally during this process. Externally, the decision to sign the declaration has brought the EELC closer to the other signatory churches. While the process was underway, the new regulations of the church and all the necessary accompanying documents and legal acts were being drawn up. Thus the concerns and obligations of PCS could be taken into consideration here as a vital criterion. Internally, the other Porvoo churches have — through their spiritual and religious heritage — assisted the EELC in its task of finding the particular "contextuality" of the gospel that is special to the Estonian church. In this respect the process has been of great significance to the development of the

EELC. First, it marks in a certain way the return of a theological awareness in our church. Second, the process contributed to a recognition of the possibility of contextual theology without disregarding the church's universality. A new ecclesiastical paradigm had been created, and this required a new awareness — on the one hand of being part of the wider ecumenical fellowship and on the other hand of our responsibility to identify the new possibilities and opportunities that were being opened up in Estonia. And third, the process created both the need and the opportunity to give a critical assessment of what our church had achieved up to this point and also to reconsider parts of its previous practices. All of these tasks placed completely new expectations and demands on the shoulders of the EELC.

The Porvoo process coincided with a time when dramatic change was underway in Estonia both at state level and in a spiritual sense. In this particular situation, which was new and special for everyone and not just for the church, the need for completely new forms of self-understanding and determination emerged. Previously, the church had consciously opposed the atheist society and defined its identity more negatively or in terms of what it was not. The unexpected realization of independence forced the EELC to define itself more positively, in terms of what it actively believed. Although the church was not really ready for this, its participation as an equal partner in an ecumenical process involving other churches with more historic traditions, but where there was still room for particular identities, really helped the EELC to find itself in its new surroundings.

At the same time, the process also created a demand for a new type of awareness and for greater competence. In the wake of this, several important EELC tasks and functions for the years to come can be identified — in addition to proclaiming the gospel, our need to find our own identity, and also the requirement of self-realization. As these tasks and functions have not yet been completed, Porvoo is still an ongoing concern and the EELC can be grateful for everything the churches of this new communion have to share with each other.

Entering a New Millennium Together: Porvoo and the Church of Norway

JAN SCHUMACHER

Many years ago I was visiting an old farmstead far up in one of the Norwegian valleys. For my host it seemed to be a unique occasion, having a theologian as a guest. And when, in addition, he was told that I was a church historian, he wanted to pay me special attention. Out of a large cupboard he fetched what he called "the old book." Instead of a Bible printed in black letters, to my big surprise he brought me a book with the words "The Whole Duty of Man" printed on the frontispiece together with the year 1660. Here I was, in a Norwegian valley close to the mountain area, with a classic of English seventeenth-century devotional literature in my hand and heard to my amazement how this book had been in his family, and at the small farmstead, for generations. I soon discovered that it was only the title that had kept the English tongue. In an excellent seventeenth-century Danish, this manual for lay people describes in close details the patterns of churchmanship: how to prepare oneself for Sunday morning, with what the mind and thought should be occupied when going to church, and how to take part in the church services with appropriate reverence and awe.

When, some weeks later, my surprise at finding a classic of Anglicanism in such an unexpected place had been exchanged for curiosity, I discovered that several of my fellow church historians were able to tell me about the so-called "English awakening," which had played a fairly important role during the seventeenth-century consolidation of the Reformation within the realms of the double monarchy of Denmark and Norway.

Already then, the Anglican contribution to a Scandinavian Lutheran mentality could be paraphrased in terms like spirituality, practical devotion, and *praxis pietatis.* But instead of foreboding eighteenth-century pietism, this wave of English influence — embodied in a fairly large amount of devotional texts being translated into Danish — focused upon a devotion being lived in, with, and through the church's liturgical tradition. It was an example among many of the oft-mentioned Anglican ability to balance inward and outward, Scripture and tradition, prophetism and order, Protestantism and Catholicism.

Why have I chosen as my starting point this personal memory of finding an Anglican devotional manual that had strayed onto a small Norwegian farmstead? I am the first to admit that a comparison between this unknown chapter of Anglo-Nordic connection and the present-day Porvoo process is farfetched. Nevertheless, the story is a reminder of the fact that it could be possible to write a history of the connections between English Christian tradition and the Norwegian church over the past centuries. In addition, this brief seventeenth-century "English awakening" conveys some hints and suggestions that I, for my part, find helpful when trying to strike a balance with the present-day relationship agreed upon in the Porvoo declaration. Conscious of such relations and connections in our past, we are reminded to ask for critical evidences that will tell us whether and to what extent the declaration has been substantiated.

The declaration itself is not difficult to pinpoint, and the booklets published for the signing ceremonies are available. But in order to take the next step and speak about the implementation of good intentions, we have to play the part of the critical historian. And the historian will have to move beyond the fair words of official occasions in his or her search for real proofs.

Although responsible church leaders normally will try to do their utmost to minimize the influence from accidental circumstances, one would have to admit that the final stages of the Porvoo process, together with the official signing, took place under a favorable constellation. In 1995, between the completion of the Porvoo agreement in 1992 and the solemn ratification in Nidaros Cathedral in 1996, the Church of Norway celebrated the 1000-year anniversary of the first Christian Eucharistic Service on Norwegian soil. Although a fixed dating of events so far back in the past is highly insecure, this anniversary was chosen for a fairly well-documented — and symbolically rich — event, which in addition brought into focus and celebrated the Anglo-Norwegian connection at the very beginning of Norwegian church history. The Icelandic thirteenth-century historian Snorri Sturluson related the story of King Olafr Tryggvason returning to Norway after having been paid off by the English king to stop his raids on the eastern and southern coast of England. If we are to believe the sagas of the

Norwegian kings, Olafr landed on Moster island near the southwestern coast of Norway in 995 and there put up some tents and had mass celebrated by his English monk-missionaries. According to tradition, this event marked the beginning of the first successful attempt to officially introduce Christianity in Norway, and a millennium later the commemoration of this event gave impetus to the introduction of the first interchurch agreement of its kind in modern Norwegian history. The role played by the late tenth-century English church in the Christianization of Norway was marked by the presence of the then Church of England bishop in Europe John Hind at the large open-air Eucharist Service at Moster on the day of Pentecost 1995. In addition, the "motherhood" of the English church was also marked in several scholarly and popular publications issued as part of the anniversary.

For the future, one link between this event and the Porvoo agreement has turned out to be of great importance. Focus on the historical connections gave rise among Norwegian clergy to a renewed interest in the Church of England and present-day Anglicanism. Traditionally, Norwegian theological education and pastoral training had been strongly oriented towards German theology. During the late 1980s and early '90s a new development was underway. The reason for this was partly due to the decreasing knowledge of German language among the students, and a growing demand for study literature in English. But as the Porvoo process approached an agreement, and the churches of the British Isles and Ireland entered the horizon of the Church of Norway, a growing interest in these churches emerged. Earlier, the Church of England had been little else than a part of the curriculum in church history; from now on, one could detect a genuine interest in this church as a present-day living reality. In hindsight, it was significant when, in 1994, the Norwegian Lutheran School of Theology in Oslo hosted a group of Church of Norway ministers for a study tour, bringing the participants to York "in search for the roots of the Christianization of Norway" as it was stated in the program for the study tour. This trip did not just concentrate on events around the year 1000, but also brought the participants in contact with key representatives from the Church of England who were playing a central part in the Porvoo process.

This form of contact has, since the mid '90s, been an important aspect of the process of implementing the Porvoo agreement in the

Church of Norway. Of great significance in this respect has been the fact that the program for extended vocational training run by the Union of Church of Norway Ministers during the last half of the '90s has included regular study tours to England. Both the study program for Practical Liturgical Training and the program for extended studies in spirituality and retreat have been spending one week out of a four-week study in England, financed by the Union in cooperation with the diocesan councils. As a result, these study programs have brought many active Norwegian ministers into contact with places like Westcott House in Cambridge and Sarum College in Salisbury. And the unanimous response from the participants has been highly appreciative.

These experiences exceed personal pastoral benefit. The opportunity for extended vocational training, which is unique within a European context, represents in itself a highly valuable implementation of the Porvoo agreement on the level of local parishes and deaneries. Here the analogy to the strayed devotional book is less farfetched. In the past several years, the fruits of an increasing knowledge and experience with the Church of England, its life and mission, have been brought back to Norwegian parishes throughout the country. It has been, so far, one of the most promising means of fulfilling the commitment expressed in the Porvoo declaration: ". . . to share a common life in mission and service, to pray for and with one another and to share resources" (§58b.i). Especially within the field of liturgy, there seems to be a widespread understanding among Norwegian ministers that the Church of England, by being herself in the middle of a process of liturgical reform, has resources to share. Two aspects of liturgical life in the Church of England have been a particular challenge to Norwegian ministers: first, the general impression of unity in diversity in contrast to a Norwegian tradition where liturgical uniformity has been the norm; and second, the stress laid on prayer within the liturgy and the way lay members of the congregation in a skillful way take active part and are given responsibility in leading the congregational prayer.

Prayer is a key word for the further implementation of the good intentions in the Porvoo declaration. How should we prevent the Porvoo agreement from being reduced to a field of interest for the clergy only? How are the lay members of the church, the congregations gathering around word and sacrament, to experience the commitment and the fellowship in a common life and mission? Much can and should be done in terms of information. For the Church of Norway, there is a risk that the realities of this important turning point in ecumenical relations enter into oblivion, unless the Porvoo commitment is given a voice within the public and communal prayer of the Norwegian church. It seems to be of utmost importance that the already available booklet "An Invitation to Prayer" should be promoted in local parishes through the dioceses. Mutual prayer creates commitment, a commitment that then should be followed up by the establishing of links within the whole Porvoo communion. While it is of great value that three of the Norwegian dioceses have permanent relationships with dioceses in England, it seems important that similar contacts be established by other dioceses for implementation to be furthered — and that the links on the diocesan level be carried on at the parochial level.

Recently, one of the key theological issues of the Porvoo declaration has again been brought into the internal debate of the Church of Norway. A committee, appointed by the Church Council, has finished a large report on the ecclesiastical ministry of the Church of Norway ("Ministry in the Church of Norway," 2001). The report was occasioned by the relation between, on the one hand, the theological understanding of ministry in the church, and on the other, the differing categories of actual ministries within the church. In our context here, the report is of relevance because the committee was explicitly asked, as part of its task, to reflect "the ecumenical talks which the Church of Norway has taken part in." The committee, for its part, has chosen to concentrate this part of its deliberations on "the ecumenical *agreements* which the Norwegian church has entered." As a result, the committee has contributed to a picture of the Porvoo reception within the Church of Norway.

Over several pages the report gives a detailed account of the key issues from the discussions leading up to the Porvoo declaration: the ministry of oversight *(episcopé)* (paragraphs 46ff.), the historic episcopal succession as sign (paragraphs 50ff.), and the threefold ministry of bishop, presbyter, and deacon (as stated in paragraph 32k, where it is said that "the threefold ministry of bishop, presbyter and deacon may serve today as an expression of the unity we seek and also as a means for achieving it"). One must agree with the committee's opinion that these three issues easily could have formed a major obstacle to the reception of the Porvoo agreement. Nevertheless, these issues are stated in a way that made it possible, after all, to accept the common statement as joining in a process of mutual reflection. The perspective of Porvoo, the committee states, is turned towards the future, and not backward to a certain fixed form of ministry in the past. Within this genuine openness towards the future lies the value of Porvoo as a truly ecumenical agreement, in combination with its fervent call for renewal in faith, life, and mission, which is the tenor of the whole common statement.

Within the limited scope of its report, the committee brings into focus two future issues of crucial importance if one wants to keep the Porvoo agreement from ending up as just another piece of paperwork. First, reflection and deliberations about the ministry of the church should not be pursued further without taking the Porvoo Common statement and the life and mission of the concerned churches into consideration. And second, the Church of Norway should not continue practicing arrangements that are, in light of what we have agreed upon, idiosyncratic. Two concrete arrangements are explicitly mentioned in the report. The practice of allowing the dean to preside at ordinations in case of the bishop's absence should be repealed, and second, the practice of transferring limited sacramental rights to unordained substitutes should be regulated, the committee suggests, to bring it closer to a kind of installment- or presentation-rite.

These recent reflections on the Porvoo reception in Norway suggest that there are still great challenges ahead, challenges in terms of letting the visions from the common statement become a point of reference at a time when the church is constantly being reminded of its calling as a church for the twenty-first century. Even other areas of church reform will need the ecumenical perspective represented by the Porvoo fellowship. Continuous liturgical reform and renewal is one such area. Through its participation in the Porvoo agreement, the Norwegian church has already met the inspiring and promising challenge of the new Revised Common Lectionary — inviting us into a common listening to the Word of God, as "a sign of . . . our joint commitment in the faith and sacramental life of the Church" (PCS §59).

The Danish "No" to Porvoo

PETER LODBERG

The Decision

At a meeting, 28-29 August 1995, the bishops of the Evangelical Lutheran Church of Denmark decided from the responses and the discussion that a consensus about the adoption of the Porvoo Common Statement in Denmark had not emerged. Thus, it was a "No" to Porvoo.

At the same time, the bishops went on to say that the close relationships between the involved churches must be strengthened. They also stated that, seen from the Danish side, there are no differences of a church-dividing character between the faith of the Evangelical Lutheran Church of Denmark and the Anglican churches. Anglicans are invited to participate in the Eucharist in the Danish church and to become members of the Evangelical Lutheran Church of Denmark if they remain for a longer period in Denmark. Anglican pastors are welcome to serve as pastors in the Danish church without reordination, and Anglican bishops are welcome at bishops' consecrations in Denmark. The bishops concluded their statement by stressing two issues: (1) that according to Lutheran understanding of the ministry, the office of bishop is a pastoral ministry that has certain obligations concerning oversight of congregations and pastors; (2) that full equality between male and female pastors is a reality in the Evangelical Lutheran Church of Denmark.

Thus, the bishops' statement contains a "Yes" to the practical content of the Porvoo text. But, importantly, the "No" to the signing of the Porvoo Common Statement came first, not the other way around.

After the bishops' decision, the Council of Interchurch Relationships has taken over the responsibility to follow the work of the Porvoo Continuation Committee and the Porvoo Contact Group as an observer.

The Process

The bishops' statement refers to an important process within the Evangelical Lutheran Church of Denmark. It was started when the two Danish representatives, Bishop Henrik Christiansen of Aalborg and Gerhard Pedersen, director of the church's pastoral institute, sent the text to the bishop of Copenhagen, who has special responsibility for ecumenical contacts with churches abroad. Since there was no established practice of how to deal with ecumenical texts and officially adopt them, the bishop of Copenhagen, Erik Norman Svendsen, decided together with his eleven colleagues to send a Danish translation of the text to all 2,116 parishes and 2,095 pastors on 1 May 1994. In their foreword to the Danish translation of the text the bishops stated: "Herewith the bishops present this statement for open debate and ask for responses before Easter 1995. Thereafter we will decide how to proceed." Since the bishops did not have a plan for the process, they did not pose specific questions about the text but turned it over for a free debate. The result was a long and heated debate about the Porvoo Common Statement in many congregations, in the media, and in meetings around the country. For the first time in Denmark, ecumenical theology and relations with other Christian churches were discussed on a broad scale at the grassroots level. Because the debate was so intense, the bishops had to postpone the deadline for responses. Finally, at the bishops' meeting on 28-29 August 1995, they decided from the responses and the discussion that a consensus about the adoption of the Porvoo Common Statement had not emerged.

The Arguments

An analysis of the responses may help explain the Danish "No." Some of those who opposed signing the Porvoo Common Statement argued that it would make the Anglican understanding of the episcopate in historic apostolic succession the theological and practical norm for understanding the ministry in the Evangelical Lutheran Church of Denmark, and that this would introduce two different kinds of ministries (pastors and bishops) into a church that since the Reformation has understood the bishop as a pastor with responsibilities for the enlarged parish (the diocese) without paying any attention to the issue of historic apostolic succession. To sign Porvoo, the opponents maintained, would in effect be to give up our Danish Evangelical Lutheran identity and to acknowledge that our understanding of the ministry since the Reformation has been wrong.

Behind this argument was an uncertainty concerning the theological status of Danish pastors ordained by a female bishop. Would they be recognized as ordained ministers in their full right by an Anglican church that had decided to ordain female pastors but had not decided to allow for consecration of female bishops? Theologically, if there is no difference between a pastor and a bishop apart from the size of the congregation, the Anglican position pointed towards a kind of discrimination between male and female pastors that was unacceptable to many in the Evangelical Lutheran Church of Denmark. In this connection it is interesting to note that the very important §53 in the Porvoo Common Statement does not play any role in the Danish debate. In §53 it is stated that "the mutual acknowledgement of the churches and ministries is theologically *prior* to the use of the sign of the laying-on of hands in the historic succession" (my italics). Furthermore, §53 states that "resumption of the use of the sign does not imply an adverse judgement on the ministries of those churches which did not previously make use of the sign." The laying on of hands is rather "a means of making more visible the unity and continuity of the Church at all times and in all places." In the Danish debate the suggestion of and the theological weight given to the laying on of hands was regarded as a critique of the Lutheran Church in Denmark for being not as good or fine a church as the churches that already practiced the suggested understanding of the historic succession, e.g., the Lutheran churches in Sweden and Finland together with the Anglican churches.

These very simple observations come from the many responses to the Porvoo Common Statement. The Porvoo discussion offers excellent material for studying the theological and non-doctrinal factors behind the Danish "No." Many congregations welcomed the invitation to respond in writing to the Porvoo Common Statement in order to help the bishops make a decision. As a case study, let us look at the responses from the diocese of Aarhus in the eastern part of the peninsula Jylland.

In the diocese of Aarhus, 40 percent of the congregational councils (133 of 326) responded to the Porvoo statement; 73 percent opposed signing it, 21 percent favored it, and 6 percent did not give a clear response. Besides several individual responses, there was a common (negative) response from twelve deans in the diocese and from seven national church organizations, six of which were positive (YMCA and YWCA, the Danish Diaconal Council, the Danish Missionary Society, Danish Santalmission, the Ecumenical Center in Aarhus, the YMCA scouts) and one negative (Kirkeligt Samfund).

The responses from the congregational councils varied a great deal in form, length, degree of theological content, and church-political point of view. Very few gave a long, theological rationale, though the general impression is that those in favor of signing submitted the longest and most theologically comprehensive responses — perhaps because during the debate they felt they were put on the defensive. It is also likely that those in favor of signing tried to "translate" the theological content of the Porvoo statement into a Danish Lutheran context in order to make it appear less alien.

Many responses — from supporters and opponents alike — mentioned that the Porvoo statement was difficult to read. Both pastors and lay members of congregational councils saw the theological presentation of the problem as strange — because the Danish Lutheran Church differs fundamentally from the Anglican Church — or unnecessary — because the communion of churches is already a reality. The problem behind the Porvoo statement was considered too difficult to solve or too artificial for ordinary churchgoers. Many thought that the issue of historic succession was of interest only to academic, ecumenical theology. Theological language was regarded, especially by the opponents, as pompous and patronizing to the laity, confirming the suspicion that Porvoo was seeking to promote a church governed by bishops at the expense of laity and pastors. Where the respondents' view of what the Church of England or the Danish national church stand for did not correspond to the presentation in the Porvoo statement, no self-critical questions were asked, nor was satisfaction expressed for the opportunity to formulate new theological knowledge. Instead, the gap between one's own opinion and the content of the Porvoo text was seen as evidence that the statement was misleading or disregarded the facts. Most congregational councils were positive about the contacts of the national church with other church communities.

The great disagreement was over whether or not Porvoo serves the participation of the national church in international church cooperation. While only a few of the congregational council members have opposed on principle the national church's signing of the Porvoo Common Statement, the opponents believe there is a "more Danish" way of organizing interchurch work than signing theological common statements that inhibit the freedom of the national church. At the same time, many congregational councils welcomed the discussion on Porvoo as a contribution to a long overdue debate on the identity of the national church. The bishop of Aarhus and his colleagues were called on to involve the congregational councils in this continuing discussion.

All responses from the diocese of Aarhus express general satisfaction with the situation, structure, and theological identity of the national church. Practically no congregational council speaks of a need to change it. Supporters of the Porvoo Common Statement argue for an endorsement within the existing scope of the national church; opponents base part of their resistance on the threat they see it posing to the national church. It has been pointed out that Porvoo can be read in two different ways: in a defensive, destructive, and confessionalistic way, or in an offensive, constructive, and confessional way. This is confirmed by the responses from the diocese of Aarhus. Much of the opposition is based on fear of what Porvoo might lead to: a future national church that has become a political power bloc ruled by the bishops. The supporters on the other hand try to read the text on the basis of the current situation of the national church. It is evident that for some opponents the very existence of the Porvoo statement confirms their negative scenario, and most of the congregational councils that say they have not understood the text respond with a "No." There is little inclination among those having any doubts to refrain from taking a stand and leave the matter to the bishops' judgment. This "hermeneutic of suspicion" was bolstered by a number of statements from national church organizations.

There are parallels here with the political debate in Denmark on the European Union. The Porvoo Common Statement is rejected because it is said to promote a union between the churches that will destroy the local principle that is characteristic for the Danish national church, contrary to the much more "top-controlled" Anglican church. A typical response warns that "Porvoo will transform the Danish national church (the *folk* church) into a bishops' church, governed by officials." Porvoo is seen as a directive from above, conflicting with the nature of the national church which is ruled from below, starting from the parish. "The natural starting-point for the identity of the national church is our parish, in which the neighbor is a concrete living person and it is possible to take responsibility for each other's lives. But the parish does not seem to have any importance in the Porvoo Common Statement. Thus a closer attachment to foreign churches might alienate us from the concrete church we belong to." Just as in the debate on Danish membership in the European Union, the world outside is regarded as a dangerous and hostile place that will alienate the Danes from their true selves. National and confessional identity is one and the same issue, endangered by what is foreign.

Related to this is a rejection of how the Porvoo document uses the expression "visible unity." Thus one parish council writes that "the people are the church and with that the church is visible; therefore, we do not need any Porvoo statement." Here the people of God, the Evangelical Lutheran Church of Denmark, and the national Danish people merge effortlessly into a single identity. The starting point for the critique of Porvoo's use of "visible unity" is that it does not take seriously the existing identity in the parish between people and church or, put in another way, the identity between the national people and the Christian people of God, which is seen as the characteristic sign of the identity of the national church. "We care for our broad and comprehensive national church, which is something unique and well adjusted to our Danish Tradition and understanding of Christianity. We are happy as we are."

Behind this argument is the Danish Constitution from 1849 as amended in 1953, which in §4 states: "The Evangelical Lutheran Church of Denmark is the Established Church of Denmark and that, as such, it shall be supported by the State." An accepted interpretation of this very important paragraph is, that as long as more than 50 percent of the Danish population on a voluntary basis, e.g., through baptism, claims membership in the Evangelical Lutheran Church, the State must support it. The key concept is the concept of *folkekirke (Volkskirche/Established Church),* which comes out of Romanticism in the nineteenth century. The church is governed by the people and not the State, because after 1849 the king (the State) lost his absolute sovereignty to the people, who became the new subject for the sharing of power within the Danish society. It is debated for the time being whether this construction also means that the Evangelical Lutheran Church can be recognized as the fourth power of the State alongside the power to give laws and to judge and execute them. This would mean that it is part of the Constitution that the Evangelical Lutheran Church also supports the State in the form of being the foundation of the value system in Danish society. The point is that the Evangelical Lutheran Church is regarded as one of the pillars of Danish society and as a defender of the close identification between nationhood, confessional identity, and citizenship.

In this connection it is interesting to note that none of the responses reflects on what it means for the theological self-understanding of the national church — or for its idea of the parish as the principal administrative and theological unit — that the identity between people and church is, in fact, disintegrating. Not only are there parishes in which fewer than half the residents are members of the national church, but an ever-smaller part of the Danish population are members in the legal sense. Yet it is still believed in the parish councils of the diocese of Aarhus that the parish church forms the visible unity of the church. This narrow, geocentric perception of the church collides with the ecumenical understanding of the unity of the church, which emphasizes both the unity in the local worshiping parish and the communion in faith, preaching, and sacraments among Christians and their churches across confessional and national borders.

Here, we cannot go into detail about the origins of the particular Danish theology of the parish, but it should be noted that all church groups share this positive theological assessment of the parish. What belongs to the unity of the church, and more broadly, the official views of the national church, is decided from the theology in the parish. Against this background the opponents of Porvoo see it as a sneaking catholicization of the national church, rooted in a theology other than that of the Danish Reformation. It may be noted that in doing so these tend to consider the Porvoo Common Statement as a new confession rather than as a collaboration agreement.

There are differing opinions among the opponents on whether the church in a Lutheran sense is to be described as invisible, visible, or something in between. A few parish councils assert, without further argument, that the church is invisible; others are more nuanced, claiming that "the visible church becomes, in Porvoo, an institution whose Christian character is secured by the bishops' teaching authority. To talk like this about the visible unity of the church was seen as deeply problematic from an Evangelical Lutheran point of view. Of course the church is not invisible, but the true church is hidden, and it is fortunately not possible for any person — lay, pastor or bishop — to point it out or to delineate it." Similar paraphrases of Porvoo, without reference to its own terms, feature in other responses, creating a straw figure only to shoot it down. For example: "We believe that our present office of pastors and bishops is as evangelical as a church institution can be. We are thus concerned about the authority given to the bishops in the document. It is un-Danish, it is un-Lutheran. It is popish. It is making an office divine. This is basically what we have to say about it!"

In short, such responses seek to apply Luther's confrontation with the church of the late middle ages to the Anglican Church of today. The basic point of view is that Catholics (and Anglicans) are guilty of "too much church from above." The office of the bishop is made too divine. What the response forgets, due to its polemic form, is that there is much more to be said about the Lutheran understanding of the ministry and the church. The Danish version of a Lutheran understanding of the church expressed in most of the responses to Porvoo ends up either in a Platonic separation between visible and invisible church or in a one-sided anti-Catholicism that verges on the fanatical. The opponents who accentuate the visible/invisible dichotomy impose a theological framework on the Porvoo document which the text itself does not use and which has been abandoned in modern debate on ecclesiology. It would carry us too far afield here to describe how this visible/invisible framework has come to dominate ecclesiological debate in Denmark and isolate us from ecclesiological discussions in the surrounding European churches, but it is evident that the national church has a theological deficit in this matter.

Finally, I want to point out another theological deficit revealed by the responses to the Porvoo Common Statement. Practically none of the responses are framed in theological terms. The closest one comes from a paraphrase of Luther's claim (in *An den christlichen Adel deutscher nation* from 1520) that anyone who has been baptized is already pastor, bishop, and pope. Luther said this in order to emphasize the dignity of the Christian, not as the theological basis of an ecclesiology of the office of pastor or bishop. This was interpreted by Hieronymus Emser and Henry VIII to mean that Luther would ordain without bishop and taught that all Christians have the same authority concerning the ministry of the word and the sacrament. Both were rebuked by Luther, but they were not the last to misinterpret his views. Thus the opposition to Porvoo uses Luther's statement on the dignity of the Christian as an argument against the attempt by the Porvoo Common Statement to formulate a contemporary understanding of apostolicity. The Danish Lutherans of today understand Luther as Henry VIII did. That is the paradox that makes church history and theology so interesting! The argument was bolstered by a misunderstanding of what Luther said about the common priesthood of all believers as a principle of organization for the church; and this wrong formulation of the problem made the Porvoo statement look like a medieval Catholic text.

But this talk about the ordinary Christian as a critical principle over against the theological content of the office of bishop fits perfectly with the Danish idea of "the church from below," in which there is an identity between people, nation, state, and church. This corresponds to the most fundamental myth undergirding the self-understanding of the national church: that it has been built up from the bottom, parish by parish, by independent Danish farmers. Until recently, theologians and historians have not doubted that the farmers together built the many village churches, sharing the expenses in solidarity with each other. The Danish church is thus supposedly not merely a folk church, but just as much a people's church. The people literally built their own church. Despite the doubts cast on this view — for example by archaeological research — the beautiful myth has persisted that some sort of medieval cooperative created the grounds for a democratic, popularly rooted church. The continued power of this myth is revealed by the overwhelming resistance against the Porvoo Common Statement.

From the responses in the diocese of Aarhus, one must conclude that the Evangelical Lutheran Church of Denmark said "No" to Porvoo on account of national motives, substantiated by theological viewpoints that serve to legitimate the Danish church as a national church living on an allegedly ongoing identity between people, nation, state, and church. A positive response to Porvoo was thus out of the question from the outset, because its intentions were incompatible with the dominant mentality in the Danish national church.

The Future

The discussion about the Porvoo Common Statement helped to solve the problem of authority in the Evangelical Lutheran Church of Denmark. For the first time, a process was put into place in order to make a binding decision concerning an ecumenical text and its intention to formulate a basis for church fellowship. The bishops took responsibility for the process and spoke on behalf of the Evangelical Lutheran Church when it came to matters of the teaching of the church. The paradox is that the Danish "No" to Porvoo largely depended on the theological understanding of the office of bishop, but the process helped to stress the importance of that same office in practice.

After Porvoo, the bishops said "No" to signing the Joint Declaration on the Doctrine of Justification formulated by the Lutheran World Federation and the Roman Catholic Church, but stated their intention to participate in the continuation of the Porvoo process. In May 2001 the bishops and the Council of Interchurch Relations decided together to sign the Leuenberg Concord. This was more than twenty-five years after the bishops in 1973 decided that the Evangelical Lutheran Church could not sign any theological document because nobody is allowed to speak on behalf of the Danish church. The signing of the Leuenberg Concord, and the change of attitude towards the principles involved, cannot be understood without reference to the Porvoo process.

For the present, the issue of signing the Porvoo Common Statement is not being discussed in the Evangelical Lutheran Church. The wounds after the debate are still too deep, and a change of mind has not taken place. Perhaps contacts between parishes in Denmark, Great

Britain, and Ireland will help to establish good relationships that one day will make it possible to reopen the debate and to enter naturally into a new process. It took more than twenty-five years to decide to sign Leuenberg. Patience is also a virtue when it comes to Porvoo.

II. Central Theological Concerns in the Porvoo Common Statement — Ecclesiology, Unity, Episcopacy, Apostolicity, and Mission

The Doctrine of the Church in the Porvoo Common Statement

STEPHEN W. SYKES

There is by definition a gap between on the one hand the theological content of a doctrine in an ecumenical document and the same doctrine developed and justified within a particular theological or ecclesial tradition. If there were not such a gap there would have been no need for an ecumenical statement in the first place. A hermeneutical issue, thus, always arises when an ecumenical statement is discussed by those who are members of one or another of the churches party to the agreement. The question is this: Is it satisfactory to assume the interpretative stance of one ecclesial tradition and use that pre-understanding to test the level of agreement achieved in the text? Do Lutheran or Anglican theologians resume their Lutheran or Anglican theological identities and consider the agreement simply from the point of view of the pre-existing norms of Lutheranism or Anglicanism? Or is something else demanded of them? On the one hand such a test is bound to have been applied by the participants to the agreement, because they cannot simply have presumed in advance of discussion that agreement was possible. On the other hand, if ecumenism is a feasible enterprise in any shape or form, it must consider at least the possibility of extending or enriching one ecclesial tradition; and the achievement of an ecumenical text requires of the interpreter a genuine effort of revision of his or her traditional standpoint.

Two events in contemporary ecumenism bear on the importance of this hermeneutical observation. The first is the question asked the churches in relation to the so-called Lima text from 1982, *Baptism, Eu-*

charist and Ministry — "Can your church recognize in this statement the faith of the Church throughout the ages?"[1] Most churches in their replies found it possible to acknowledge that there might indeed be a broader way of viewing that question than simply by means of their own traditions. The second event is the official reply of the Roman Catholic Church to the Final Report of ARCIC I (Anglican–Roman Catholic International Commission).[2] To the dismay of many ecumenists, both Anglicans and Roman Catholics, this reply plainly used traditional Roman Catholic ways of formulating doctrinal questions as the criteria for evaluating the ecumenical document. One participant, the distinguished Anglican Church historian Professor Henry Chadwick, went so far as to say that the tone of the reply implied that there had been a search to discover these discrepant vocabularies.[3]

The issue is not, of course, a simple one. An official reply is a different genre of document from a personal theological statement. And it is perfectly legitimate for non-participants to press questions that may have eluded participants. In the case of this essay, however, which is from a participant deeply involved in the development of the text, the hermeneutical stance presumes that Anglican ecclesiology is capable of development and enrichment. The questions addressed to the text are, therefore, not those deriving from consonance with Anglican sources; though, as I shall insist, Anglicans have traditionally held that Christian traditions other than their own have valid insights to offer.

The problem that the conversations leading up to the Porvoo Common Statement set themselves to resolve was plainly disagreement about the nature and role of the episcopate within the life of the church (see §34; "there is a long-standing problem about episcopal ministry and its relation to succession"). The consequence was that though six pages of the English text are devoted to ecclesiology, and six to further wide-ranging doctrinal agreements, eight pages are

1. See *Baptism, Eucharist and Ministry, 1982-1990,* Report on the Process and Responses, Faith and Order Paper 149 (WCC: Geneva, 1990).

2. "The Official Roman Catholic Response to the Final Report of ARCIC I" (1991) in Christopher Hill and E. J. Yarnold, S.J., eds., *Anglicans and Roman Catholics: The Search for Unity* (London: SPCK/CTS, 1994), pp. 156-66.

3. "There is a kind of search for unidentified submarines below the surface of apparently tranquil waters." In "Unfinished Business" (1992), in Hill and Yarnold, *Anglicans and Roman Catholics,* p. 214.

given over to episcopacy, supported by a further hundred pages of essays on "Episcopacy in Our Churches." Superficial commentators, and people looking for points of objection, were immediately able to criticize the alleged imbalance of the document's theological content. For them it merely confirmed the Anglican exaggeration of episcopacy. But since episcopacy was the major difficulty, and not least because the difficulty was of long standing, it was bound to be given disproportionate attention. The key issue for the Commission, however, was not so much episcopacy in itself, as the significance of the episcopate for the life of the church. There is complete agreement between Anglicans and traditional Lutherans that one cannot separate the doctrine of the ministry from the doctrine of the church. How, then, does the Porvoo Common Statement (PCS) set ministry *within* ecclesiology?

A strong feature of PCS is its mission orientation. "Above all, we face a common challenge to engage in God's mission to the people of our nations and continent at a time of unparalleled opportunity" (§6). Though the words are conventional, it is in fact the case that European churches have a major communicational difficulty with young people that at least some of them regard as a situation of primary evangelism. The task for the Porvoo churches can no longer be regarded as that of pastoring predominantly Christian nations.[4]

A section on "Our Common Mission Today" precedes the chapter on ecclesiology, which opens with the pregnant sentence, "Our times demand something new of us as churches." That new thing is defined as a *common* mission, requiring a degree of mutuality and interdependence not attained by churches engaged in parallel missions. Thus the first of the commitments listed in the Porvoo declaration reads: "We commit ourselves to share a common life in mission and service, to pray for and with one another, and to share resources" (§58b.i).

To see the church first in terms of its mission has profound implications for the way in which the apostolicity of the church is understood and valued, and thus, of course, the "apostolic ministry." This

4. That the young of people of Europe "have effectively lost touch with the institutional churches in terms of anything approaching regular practice" is a major conclusion of Grace Davie's study *Religion in Modern Europe: A Memory Mutates* (Oxford: Oxford University Press, 2000), p. 180.

doctrinal sequencing is visible also in the Niagara Report (the report of the Anglican-Lutheran Consultation on Episcope, 1987). This in turn coheres with the work of the Lutheran-Episcopal Dialogue in the United States, *Implications of the Gospel* (Cincinnati, 1988). §15 of the Niagara Report begins: "It is the whole Christian Church which has been sent on its mission and been given the necessary gifts."

PCS likewise addresses the issue of episcopacy from the standpoint of the apostolicity first of the whole church. What the church *is* arises out of the nature of the gospel, which the whole church and every member of it is *sent* to proclaim. The church is for mission by divine commission. In a crucial transitional sentence PCS claims:

> The Church and the gospel are thus necessarily related to each other. Faith in Jesus, the Christ, as the foundation of the reign of God arises out of the visible and audible proclamation of the gospel in word and sacraments. And there is no proclamation of the word and sacraments without a community and its ministry. (§17)

There is an obvious intention in this formulation that the unity of the church, which is a consequence of conformity to Christ's mission to draw all things into unity with himself (§14, citing Eph. 1:9f.), should be both visible and audible. Thus PCS adopts the formula that "the Church is sent into the world as a sign, instrument and foretaste of a reality which comes from beyond history — the Kingdom of God" (§18). This formulation is repeated in a later paragraph where the task of more fully embodying in structured form the unity of the church is accepted, "so that the Church may be seen to be the sign, instrument and foretaste of the Kingdom" (§22). One notes in this sentence the accent on visibility.

PCS is, of course, alert to the charge that what it has in mind is uniformity — the imagery of "one body" extensively used in a Church of England document on its internal processes of governance (the so-called "Turnbull Report," *Working as One Body* [1995]), ran into substantial, if misplaced criticism on this score. It is, of course, always a matter of judgment at what stage diversity, disagreement, and conflict cease to be a stimulus to serious mission and become a threat to it. It is rarely the case that simple distinctions such as those between essentials or inessentials, substance or form, fundamentals or non-fundamentals, can achieve the status of unchallengeable *arbiter in disputes.* But at the least, PCS shows itself alert to the diversity of gifts from the Holy Spirit (§19), to the fact of sin in the church (§20), and to the need to sustain a God-given diversity (§§23 and 24). The latter is carefully distinguished, one should note, from a "mere concession to theological pluralism" (§23).

At this point one must draw attention to a strategic and innovative aspect of PCS, namely the attempt at a scriptural "portrait" of the church. As already remarked, it occupies a position at which both diversity and sin are acknowledged as inevitable features of the life of the church, raising the question of the means whereby we recognize the presence in one another's church of the Church of Jesus Christ (§31, citing the resolution of the Lambeth Conference of 1988).[5] A traditional way of achieving this recognition is to define in advance what constitutes the essence of the church, and in the light of that to determine whether or not the partner to the dialogue is genuinely church. In both Lutheran and Anglican history the doctrine of "fundamentals" has functioned in this way.[6] A related but not identical attempt is embodied in the distinction between essentials and adiaphora. The "essence of Christianity," which has a long conceptual history and prehistory, belongs to the same problematic. It is, therefore, significant that PCS contains no mention of any of these traditional means for categorizing and ordering elements of Christian faith and life, preferring instead the idea of "portraiture." This approach is described and applied in §20:

> The Church is a divine reality, holy and transcending present finite reality; at the same time, as a human institution, it shares the brokenness of human community in its ambiguity and frailty. The Church is always called to repentance, reform and renewal, and has constantly to depend on God's mercy and forgiveness. The Scriptures offer a portrait of a Church living in the light of the Gospel:

5. *The Niagara Report* (London: Church House Publications, 1988), p. 15. See the section titled "The Nature of the Church and Its Mission."

6. S. W. Sykes, "The Fundamentals of Christianity," in Stephen Sykes, John Booty, Jonathan Knight, eds., *The Study of Anglicanism,* 2nd ed. (London: SPCK, 1998).

- it is a Church rooted and grounded in the love and grace of the Lord Christ;
- it is a Church always joyful, praying continually and giving thanks even in the midst of suffering;
- it is a pilgrim Church, a people of God with a new heavenly citizenship, a holy nation and a royal priesthood;
- it is a Church which makes common confession of the apostolic faith in word and in life, the faith common to the whole Church everywhere and at all times;
- it is a Church with a mission to all in every race and nation, preaching the gospel, proclaiming the forgiveness of sins, baptizing and celebrating the Eucharist;
- it is a Church which is served by an ordained apostolic ministry, sent by God to gather and nourish the people of God in each place, uniting and linking them with the Church universal within the whole communion of saints;
- it is a Church which manifests through its visible communion the healing and uniting power of God amidst the divisions of humankind;
- it is a Church in which the bonds of communion are strong enough to enable it to bear effective witness in the world, to guard and interpret the apostolic faith, to take decisions, to teach authoritatively, and to share its goods with those in need;
- it is a Church alive and responsive to the hope which God has set before it, to the wealth and glory of the share God has offered it in the heritage of his people, and to the vastness of the resources of God's power open to those who trust in him.

This portrait of the Church is by no means complete; nevertheless, it confronts our churches with challenges to the fidelity of our lives and with a constant need for repentance and renewal.

Before we look at this approach in more detail, we must notice the deployment of the concept of "bonds of communion" in §24, and the listing of beliefs and practices constituting "fundamental agreement in faith" or "substantial agreement in faith" in §32. Of course it is necessary to itemize those matters in which the unity that has become recognizable consists. But this is not the same procedure as the attempt to define "fundamentals," "the essentials," or "the essence" of Christianity. That procedure, one must bluntly say, was a failure.[7]

Portraiture, by contrast, suggests that no definitive checklist of features of Christian life and doctrine exists, but that, as with a drawing or a character portrayal, there is an interaction between perceiver and perceived; and that there can take place a disclosure of the one to the other which is never finally complete. It is no accident that PCS's portrait begins with the identification of a church "rooted and grounded in the love and grace of the Lord Christ" (§20). For love is both a gift of the Holy Spirit and a means of knowing. The lists of fundamentals were usually drawn up in the interests of excluding those who thought differently. Though love may be eventually obliged to say no to heresy or vice, its first instinct is to be inclusive and to "keep no score of wrongs" (1 Cor. 13:5). Similarly, a church that is joyful, prays continually, and gives thanks even in the midst of suffering carries the marks of an authentic church. PCS's portraiture does not claim to be complete; but its inclusion of features of the life of churches of the New Testament, which are often simply overlooked, is of considerable ecumenical importance. This attempt to portray the church of the Christian Scriptures makes possible the act of re-cognition of a partner as truly embodying those features, as in a family likeness.

Likewise belonging to the metaphor of portraiture is the language of "sign," which we have already noted, and which is repeated in the section of the following chapter devoted to "historic episcopal succession as sign" (D, §§50-54). Anglicans have frequently been impaled on the horns of a dilemma formulated in the following way: Is the historic episcopate part of the essence of the church or is it not? If they affirm that it is, they plainly fall foul of the *satis est* of the Augsburg Confession (CA 7); if they confirm that it is not, then their record of commending or requiring it in ecumenical dialogues stands condemned, and they apparently contradict the fourth item of the Chicago-Lambeth Quadrilateral.[8]

7. This was already clear in the eighteenth century. See Daniel Waterland, "A Discourse of Fundamentals" (1735), in *The Works of the Rev. Daniel Waterland* (Oxford: Clarendon Press, 1823).

8. This reads: "The Historic Episcopate, locally adapted in the methods of its administration to the varying needs of the nations and peoples called of God into the Unity

The method of portraiture suggests, however, that the initial question, framed in terms of the "essence of the church," needs itself to be subject to question. One must ask whether the church history knows any such thing as a final definition of the essence of the church. As has already been suggested, the quest for the fundamentals has never reached a satisfactory term. Indeed, from the start Roman Catholic theology has responded to Protestant attempts to define the fundamentals by asserting the prior need for an (unchallengeable) authoritative body, a definitively defining center of authority.[9] Though this challenge is supposed to lead to the requirement of papal authority, it is at least correct to say that all attempts to define the "essence of the church," not excluding those contained in Protestant confessional documents, unavoidably raise the question of authority. By what right and with what warrants are these confident assertions made?

The language of sign related to that of portraiture belongs to a different realm of discourse. Instead of belonging to the "essence of the church," historic episcopal succession is a feature of the life of a church intending that its ordained ministry should be what Christ himself meant it to be in a church engaged in the mission Christ himself gave it. Understood as a sign in a language system, it could be the case that the church conveys a similar message by other means. In PCS, Anglicans have in effect said that a church which has maintained the episcopal office without literally safeguarding the historic episcopate can still be confidently acknowledged (the terms used in §56; this is no hesitant or reluctant concession!) to belong to the "One, Holy Catholic and Apostolic Church of Jesus Christ and truly to participate in the apostolic mission of the whole people of God" (§58; the leading terms of the Porvoo declaration). How is this confidence possible? The answer is, by means of the recognition of the portrait in the other of a scriptural church.

The intention of PCS was to articulate the self-understanding of churches, all of which were episcopal, in such a way as to make possible a structurally visible unity to undergird their common mission.

---

of his Church" (Lambeth Conference, Resolution II [1888]). See J. Robert Wright, ed., *Quadrilateral at One Hundred* (Oxford: Mowbrays, 1988).

9. See Y. Congar, *Diversity and Communion* (London: SPCK, 1984), ch. 11. Pope Pius XI called the distinction between fundamentals and non-fundamentals "illegitimate" (p. 118).

The "normality" of the participation of one another's bishops in the laying on of hands at the ordination of bishops (§58b.vi) is one way of exhibiting that unity. Another way is constituted by "forms of collegial and conciliar consultation in matters of faith, life and witness" (§28). Formidable obstacles of language, custom, and national pride stand in the way of the realization of this goal, but confronting them is unavoidable if unity is to grow among the churches. To that extent whether PCS is a success has yet to be demonstrated. What is certain about the intention of the ecclesiology expressed in PCS is that unity of the church needs to be embodied in a sufficient collection of visible signs, the sufficiency being judged by the scriptural portraiture of a church living in the light of the gospel.

The Ecclesiology of the Porvoo Common Statement — A Lutheran Perspective

HEINRICH HOLZE

1. The Communion Ecclesiology of Porvoo

Since its publication in 1993, the Porvoo Common Statement (PCS) has provoked intense discussions. On the one hand, the statement has been celebrated as an important step forward and as a possible ecumenical breakthrough concerning church communion and the recognition of ministries.[1] On the other hand, it has caused anxiety and fears, especially in the Lutheran churches on the European continent.[2]

The discussion on PCS has focused on the doctrine of episcopacy and the historic succession. The matter in dispute was the episcopal ministry within the apostolicity of the whole church, particularly the interpretation of the historic episcopate as a prerequisite of full mutual recognition of the ministries. This topic is clearly of central importance in PCS. Nevertheless, it only makes up the fourth chapter of the text, "Episcopacy in the Service of the Apostolicity of the Church," and it is embedded in a broader ecclesiological and theological perspective including the nature of the church and an agreement in faith. In my con-

1. Cf. Ola Tjørhom, "The Porvoo-Statement — A Possible Ecumenical Breakthrough?" in *Pro Ecclesia* 3 (1994).

2. Cf. Ingolf Dalferth, "Ministry and the Office of Bishop according to Meissen and Porvoo: Protestant Remarks about Several Unclarified Questions," in *Visible Unity and the Ministry of Oversight: The Second Theological Conference Held under the Meissen Agreement between the Church of England and the Evangelical Church in Germany* (London, 1997), pp. 9-48.

tribution, I will go into the question of episcopacy and apostolicity only insofar as it is necessary with regard to the topic I have been asked to deal with: the ecclesiological perspective.

Generally, the contextual and historical framework is of particular importance here. Both the Anglican and the Nordic churches are national churches; the Nordic and the Baltic churches have enjoyed eucharistic communion for a long time; and together with the Anglican churches some of them have preserved the historic episcopate. The background of PCS is therefore characterized by "a growing closeness between European Anglicans and Lutherans, which convinces us that the time has come for us to review and revise the existing agreements" (§1). The statement takes up this "growing common understanding of the Church" (§4). Simultaneously, it refers to the Meissen Common Statement from 1988 and to the results of the longstanding dialogues between Orthodox, Roman Catholic, and Protestant churches and their "ecumenical convergence" regarding the doctrine of the church, especially to the Faith and Order statement *Baptism, Eucharist and Ministry* from 1982 (§5).

The ecclesiology of PCS can be recognized throughout the statement, from the very beginning to its end. Although the second chapter, "The Nature and the Unity of the Church" (§§14-28), deals explicitly with the ecclesiological aspects, ecclesiology is not a single topic set apart but the very basis of the whole document. The church is characterized by four aspects: the Trinitarian dimension, the sacramental dimension, the apostolic dimension, and the eschatological dimension. These aspects express the vertical and the horizontal level of the church, its eternal and temporal character, and they are connected in the concept of communion (koinonia).

The Trinitarian Communion

The point of departure of PCS's ecclesiology is God's work of salvation in Jesus Christ: "To bring us to unity with himself, the Father sent his Son Jesus Christ into the world. Through Christ's life, death and resurrection, God's love is revealed and we are saved from the powers of sin and death (John 3:16-18). By grace received through faith, we are put into a right relationship with God. We are brought from death to new life (Rom. 6:1-11), born again, made sons and daughters by adoption and set free for life in the Spirit (Gal. 4:5; Rom. 8:14-17)" (§15). The Triune God is the foundation for the doctrine of the church. The life of the church is not rooted in itself but is a fruit of God's work, it is a gift: "Communion between Christians and churches should not be regarded as a product of human achievement. It is already given in Christ as a gift to be received, and 'like every good gift, unity also comes from the Father through the Son in the Holy Spirit'" (§21). To speak about the church requires therefore a focus on the divine activity related to the world. It points to the fact that the church is dependent on divine activity: "We believe that the Church is constituted and sustained by the Triune God through God's saving action in word and sacraments" (§32f).

PCS emphasizes that the unity of the church is fundamentally linked both to Christ and to the unity of the Triune God. It is "rooted and grounded in the love and grace of the Lord Christ" (§20). And it exists within a strong relationship to the inner-Trinitarian life of God: "The unity of the Church is grounded in the mysterious relationship of the persons of the Trinity, this unity belongs by necessity to its nature" (§21). The relationship with God establishes the unity of the church. Simultaneously, it is the fundamental criterion for the identity of the church. According to the statement, the life of the church cannot be separated from its divine foundation. The church has been set in a constant relation to God and participates in his life: "By the gift of God's grace we have been drawn into the sphere of God's will to reconcile to himself all that he has made and sustains (2 Cor. 5:17-19)" (§14). These quotations make perfectly clear that the vertical dimension is the core of PCS's ecclesiological account — and that the Trinitarian understanding of the church has a strong basis.

The Sacramental Communion

"We believe that the Church is constituted and sustained by the Triune God through God's saving action in word and sacraments" (§32f). This directs the focus from the Trinitarian to the sacramental dimension of the church. The fundamental gifts that the church is entrusted with are word and sacraments. Word and sacrament are the unambiguous signs of God's presence in the world. The church can be recognized where the word is preached and the sacraments are administered. In word and sacrament God is giving himself. They are the guarantee that it is God and not human persons who constitutes and safeguards the church. Word and sacraments are therefore the fundamental signs of the church *(notae ecclesiae).*

Word and sacraments are received by faith as the fruit of the proclamation of the gospel: "Faith in Jesus, the Christ, as the foundation of the reign of God arises out of the visible and audible proclamation of the gospel in word and sacraments" (§17). Through faith the church cannot be separated from the life of the Trinitarian God: "Faith is the God-given recognition that the light has come into the world. . . . Faith, as life in communion with the triune God, brings us into, and sustains and nourishes us in, the common life of the Church, Christ's body" (§16). Through faith the communion of all believers takes shape: "There is no proclamation of the word and sacraments without a community and its ministry. Thus, the communion of the Church is constituted by the proclamation of the word and the celebration of the sacraments, served by the ordained ministry. Through these gifts God creates and maintains the Church and gives birth daily to faith, love and new life" (§17; cf. §§24; 27; 32g, h). Through faith the horizontal and the vertical dimension of the church are inseparably linked: "The Scriptures portray the unity of the Church as a joyful communion with the Father and with his Son Jesus Christ (cf. 1 John 1.1-10), as well as communion among its members" (§21).

The Trinitarian God relates to and works on the communion of the church in multiple ways: "The Holy Spirit bestows on the community diverse and complementary gifts. These are for the common good of the whole people and are manifested in acts of service within the community and to the world" (§19). The communion therefore does not exist for itself but in relation to and in responsibility for the world. It is an instrument of God's relation to the world: The church "manifests through its visible communion the healing and uniting power of God amidst the divisions of humankind" (§20). As a sacramental communion, the church is charged "with a mission to all in every race and nation, preaching the gospel, proclaiming the forgiveness of sins, baptizing and celebrating the eucharist" (§20).

The Apostolic Communion

The church exists in time and space and extends throughout history. It is a "visible communion" (§20). PCS emphasizes this aspect by pointing to the fact that the church — although in constant relation to the Triune God — is marked by the brokenness of the world: "The Church is a divine reality, holy and transcending present finite reality; at the same time, as a human institution, it shares the brokenness of human community in its ambiguity and frailty" (§20). This brokenness is part of the church from the beginning. It is recognizable in the divisions of the church and its splintering in numerous denominations. PCS points to tensions, conflicts, and clashes in Early Christianity: "Already in the New Testament there is the scandal of division among Christians (1 Cor. 1:11-13; 1 John 2:18-19)" (§27). Obviously, the history of Christianity has been a history of disunity more than of unity.

Nevertheless, PCS holds to the conviction that the criteria for the unity of the church can be recognized within history. The normative period is the Early Church. It is the time when Christ called the apostles to give witness of the gospel to the world: "The Church today is charged, as were the apostles, to proclaim the gospel to all nations. . . . The Church is called to faithfulness to the normative apostolic witness. . . . The Church receives its mission and the power to fulfill this mission as a gift of the risen Christ. The Church is thus apostolic as a whole" (§37). This points to the apostolic dimension that characterizes both the origin and the identity of the church. Moreover, the orientation towards the Early Church symbolizes the obligation to regain visible unity: "Churches not outwardly united, for reasons of history or through deliberate separations, are obliged by their faith to work and to pray for the recovery of their visible unity and the deepening of their spiritual fellowship" (§27).

However, the quest for unity in relation to the Early Church does not mean a quest for uniformity: "Visible unity . . . should not be confused with uniformity. 'Unity in Christ does not exist despite and in opposition to diversity, but is given with and in diversity.' Because this diversity corresponds with the many gifts of the Holy Spirit to the Church, it is a concept of fundamental ecclesial importance. . . . Both the unity and the diversity of the Church are ultimately grounded in the communion of God the Holy Trinity" (§23). Therefore, the goal is not a united structure and/or a standardization of liturgies and traditions but "the highest possible realization of communion between and within the churches" (§27). Communion includes the multiple expressions of faith and finds expression on various levels of church life: "It entails agreement in faith together with the common celebration of the sacraments, supported by a united ministry and forms of collegial and conciliar consultation in matters of faith, life and witness. These expressions of communion may need to be embodied in the law and regulations of the Church. For the fullness of communion all these visible aspects of the life of the Church require to be permeated by a profound spiritual communion, a growing together in a common mind, mutual concern and a care for unity (Phil. 2:2)" (§28). The church's task is to strengthen "the bonds of communion" on every level so that it is enabled "to bear effective witness in the world, to guard and interpret the apostolic faith, to take decisions, to teach authoritatively, and to share its goods with those in need" (§20).

Particular emphasis is given to the concept of continuity. The statement supports the idea that apostolicity has been preserved throughout history up to the present time: "The Church communicates its care for continuity in the whole of its life and mission, and reinforces its determination to manifest the permanent characteristics of the Church of the apostles" (§50). PCS also suggests that the church represents a continuous history and that this can be recognized in distinctive features that have not changed substantially throughout history: "The faith, worship and spirituality of all our churches are rooted in the tradition of the apostolic Church. We stand in continuity with the Church of the patristic and medieval period both directly and through the insights of the Reformation period" (§7). In quoting the Lima text, *Baptism, Eucharist and Ministry* (1982), PCS emphasizes: "In the Creed, the Church confesses itself to be apostolic. The Church lives in continuity with the apostles and their proclamation. The same Lord who sent the apostles continues to be present in the Church. . . . Apostolic tradition in the Church means continuity in the permanent characteristics of the Church of the apostles" (§36). Repeatedly, PCS refers to the concept that the church is characterized by an apostolic continuity that corresponds to its divine purpose: "The ultimate ground of the fidelity of the Church, in continuity with the apostles, is the promise of the Lord and the presence of the Holy Spirit at work in the whole Church" (§46).

Continuity with the apostles throughout time is preserved in several ways: "Faithfulness to the apostolic calling of the whole Church is carried by more than one means of continuity" (§52). The basic responsibility of the church is to take care of the proclamation of the gospel: "In every age from apostolic times it has been the purpose of the Church to proclaim this gospel in word and deed. . . ." (§15). This proclamation is the task of all believers: "The whole Church, and every member, participates in and contributes to the communication of the gospel, by their faithful expression and embodiment of the permanent characteristics of the Church of the apostles in a given time and place. . . ." (§38). Within the communion of believers the "ordained apostolic ministry" is of fundamental importance (§20). It is instrumental to the communion as a whole: "We are given a picture of how this ministry fosters the richness of diversity while also maintaining unity" (§25). It is the task of the ordained ministry to serve the communion of all believers: "We believe that within the community of the Church the ordained ministry exists to serve the ministry of the whole people of God. We hold the ordained ministry of word and sacrament to be an office of divine institution and as such a gift of God to his Church. Ordained ministers are related, as are all Christians, both to the priesthood of Christ and to the priesthood of the Church" (§32j).

PCS emphasizes that the ministry is no human invention but a divine institution that has been preserved throughout time: "God has given the apostolic ministry, instituted by our Lord and transmitted through the apostles" (§41). It is of central importance for the life of the church because it is, together with the proclamation of the gospel and the celebration of the sacraments, one of "the permanent characteristics of the Church of the apostles" (§51). The purpose of the ministry is to serve the faithfulness and the apostolicity of the church. Special attention is therefore given to safeguard the continuity of the ministry through succession: "Within the apostolicity of the whole Church is an apostolic succession of the ministry which serves and is a focus of the continuity of the Church in its life in Christ and its faithfulness to the words and acts of Jesus transmitted by the apostles. The ordained ministry has a particular responsibility for witnessing to this tradition and for proclaiming it afresh with authority in every generation" (§40; cf. §49). This particular importance is expressed in the act of ordination or "the setting aside of a person to a lifelong ordained office by prayer, invocation of the Holy Spirit and the laying on of hands" (§41).

The episcopal ministry is given particular tasks. First of all, it has an instrumental function and is related to the communion of all believers: "The diversity of God's gifts requires their coordination so that they enrich the whole Church and its unity. This diversity and the multiplicity of tasks involved in serving it calls for a ministry of coordination. . . . Episcope (oversight) is a requirement of the whole Church, and its faithful exercise in the light of the gospel is of fundamental importance to its life" (§42). In addition, the episcopal office carries a particular responsibility for the apostolic identity of the church: "We believe that a ministry of pastoral oversight (episcope), exercised in personal, collegial and communal ways, is necessary as witness to and safeguard of the unity and apostolicity of the Church. Further, we retain and employ the episcopal office as a sign of our intention, under God, to ensure the continuity of the Church in apostolic life and witness" (§32k). PCS argues for the need of "(securing) the apostolic continuity of the Church as a Church of the gospel served by an episcopal ministry" (§34). Moreover, "within the apostolicity of the whole Church is an apostolic succession of the ministry which serves and is a focus of the continuity of the Church in its life in Christ and its faithfulness to the words and acts of Jesus transmitted by the apostles" (§40; cf. §46). In this connection, Porvoo also refers to a continuity in episcopal sees. Generally, historic continuity is regarded as a fundamental sign of apostolicity. And the episcopal office has a distinctive role for the doctrine of the church. Therefore, PCS stresses that "the retention of the sign remains a permanent challenge to fidelity and to unity, a summons to witness to, and a commission to realize more fully, the permanent characteristics of the Church of the apostles" (§51).

The Eschatological Communion

The church as communion is not only taken up with a view to its temporal existence, but also points towards an eschatological future: "The Church is sent into the world as a sign, instrument and foretaste of a reality which comes from beyond history — the Kingdom of God" (§18; cf. §§32f.; 50). This is why the church is more than a communion in which the gospel is proclaimed and the sacraments are administered. Being in relation with the Triune God, the church is a preeminent instrument for the eschatological goal: "The Church, as communion, must be seen as instrumental to God's ultimate purpose. It exists for the glory of God to serve, in obedience to the mission of Christ, the reconciliation of humankind and of all creation (Eph. 1:10)" (§18).

The orientation towards the eschatological goal has consequences for the church in the present: ". . . the unity to which we are summoned has already begun to be manifested in the Church. It demands fuller visible embodiment in structured form, so that the Church may be seen to be, through the Holy Spirit, the one body of Christ and the sign, instrument and foretaste of the Kingdom. In this perspective, all existing denominational traditions are provisional" (§22). This means that the church existing in time and space has to become transparent for the eschatological goal. "Set before the Church is the vision of unity as the goal of all creation. . . . Communion is thus the fruit of redemption and necessarily an eschatological reality" (§27). Accordingly, the church is "a pilgrim Church, a people of God with a new heavenly citizenship, a holy nation and a royal priesthood" (§20). And as a human institution, the church is still in a process of renewal, change, and alteration that points towards the goal of visible unity. This is reflected when the statement calls for "a deeper realization of communion" (§29), "a deepening of fellowship" (§29), an overcoming of "remaining obstacles to still closer communion" (§33), and a "sharing of our life and ministries in closer visible unity" (§54). According to PCS, the task at hand consists in "making more visible the unity and continuity of the Church at all times and in all places" (§53). This process does not come to an end within time and space. Its fulfillment is a gift to be received: "God's ultimate purpose and mission in Christ is the restoration and renewal of all that he has made, the coming of the Kingdom in its fullness" (§14).

2. Apostolicity in the Lutheran Tradition

Although using a different language, the ecclesiology of PCS is in accordance with the Lutheran doctrine of the church. The classic starting point for Lutherans is the focus on word and sacrament as it is expressed in the Augsburg Confession Article VII: "The church is the assembly of saints in which the Gospel is taught purely and the sacraments are administered rightly." PCS refers to this doctrine by emphasizing the sacramental dimension of the church. This sacramental dimension implies that the church is not a mere human institution but created and nourished by God, dependent on God's word and his work of salvation.

PCS interprets this doctrine in the context of the ecclesiology of communion. This widens the perspective in a twofold manner. Seeing the church as a communion points both to the communion between the Triune God and the church and to the communion of all believers, which extends throughout time from the apostles to the consummation of the kingdom of God. Already Luther refers to the communion-ecclesiology of the Early Church.[3] In his early writings Luther makes use of communion-language to indicate the sharing of the gifts Jesus Christ is giving to the believers as well as the resources the members of the Christian community are giving one another. For Luther, the term "communion" had therefore both ecclesiological and ethical implications. The development of doctrine in the Lutheran churches, particularly the influence of Melanchthon's theology, led to a doctrinal emphasis: the Christian community was understood more as a group of scholars ("coetus scholasticus") than as a communion of believers.[4] On this background the criteria of Lutheran ecclesiology focusing on word and sacrament, and the "satis est"–clause of CA VII, led to a puristic understanding of the church excluding aspects that could be interpreted as human: "For the true unity of the church it is enough (satis est) to agree concerning the teaching of the Gospel and the administration of the sacraments. It is not necessary that human traditions or rites and ceremonies, instituted by men, should be alike everywhere."[5]

It was not until the late nineteenth century that new theological insights paved the way for interpreting the church in the context of a communion ecclesiology. At this time the concept of "Volkskirche," the

3. Alejandro Zorzin, "Luther's Understanding of the Church as Communion in His Early Pamphlets," in Heinrich Holze, ed., *The Church as Communion*, LWF Documentation 42 (Geneva, 1997), pp. 81-92.

4. Rolf Schäfer, "Communion in Lutheran Ecclesiology," in Holze, ed., *The Church as Communion*, pp. 133-62.

5. Augsburg Confession, Article 7.

church for and of the people, took the place of the former "Pastorenkirche," which focused on the pastors.[6] The ecumenical dialogues of the late twentieth century went further. The inner-Lutheran movement to strengthen world-Lutheranism increasingly employed communion terminology.[7] It was the controversial discussion on apartheid in the 1970s that accelerated this theological development by emphasizing the link between communion ecclesiology and ethical decisions.[8] The Seventh LWF Assembly in Budapest passed two resolutions employing the concept of communion to broaden the concept of unity. In "The Self-Understanding and Task of the LWF," it is stated that the Lutheran communion, "rooted in the unity of the apostolic faith . . . , finds its visible expression in pulpit and altar fellowship, in common witness and service, in the joint fulfilment of the missionary task, and in openness to ecumenical cooperation, dialog and community." This statement represents a turning point in the inner-Lutheran discussion: "The language of communion now becomes the central category for understanding the LWF."[9] In the second resolution, "The Unity We Seek," the LWF gives "a pregnant description of the goal of its ecumenical efforts" by making extensive use of communio/koinonia-terminology.[10] The Eighth Assembly in Curitiba, Brazil, finally draws the constitutional consequences by defining the LWF as "a communion of churches which confess the triune God, agree in the proclamation of the Word of God and are united in pulpit and altar fellowship" (Art. 3 of the Constitution). Moreover, the dialogue with the orthodox churches, which took place simultaneously, led to a rediscovery of the Trinitarian dimension of communion.[11] The

6. Ingun Montgomery, "The Understanding of the Church in the Sixteenth and Early Twentieth Centuries," in Holze, ed., *The Church as Communion,* pp. 163-84.

7. Harding Meyer, "'Koinonia/Communio' and the Notion of 'Kirchengemeinschaft/Church Fellowship' in Lutheranism, particularly in the LWF," in Holze, ed., *The Church as Communion,* pp. 339-56.

8. Günther Gassmann, "Confession and Communion: Ecclesiological Implications of the LWF's 1977 Status Confessionis Statement," in Holze, ed., *The Church as Communion,* pp. 185-203.

9. Michael Root, "Ecclesiological Reflection in the LWF," in *From Federation to Communion: The History of the Lutheran World Federation* (Minneapolis, 1997), pp. 237-38.

10. Harding Meyer, "Ecumenical Commitment in the LWF," in *From Federation to Communion,* p. 274.

11. Christoph Schwöbel, "The Quest for Communion: Reasons, Reflections and Recommendations," in Holze, ed., *The Church as Communion,* pp. 227-86.

Lutheran terminology of word and sacrament was not forgotten in these discussions, but played a minor role because of the broadening of the perspective through references to the Trinitarian, the apostolic, and the eschatological dimensions of communion.[12]

In summary, one can say that the basic assumptions of the Porvoo ecclesiology are convergent with Lutheran theology. The Trinitarian dimension corresponds with the insistence that the church is a creature of the gospel of the Triune God who creates, reconciles, and renews the world. The sacramental dimension stresses that word and sacrament are the distinctive features of church. The apostolic dimension expresses the existence of the church across time and space. Finally, the eschatological dimension emphasizes that the church — as a sign of God's purpose with the whole creation — points beyond itself.

As I see it, however, questions remain regarding PCS's interpretation of the apostolic dimension of the church, especially in view of the doctrine of the ministry, the episcopate, and the historic succession. For Luther, the witness of history is only important to the extent that it is in accordance with the gospel of Jesus Christ. He is the criterion for the biblical canon, but also for the persons and institutions of the Early Church. Luther therefore acknowledges the Apostolic Creed as a short summary of the Bible.[13] Moreover, he praises the Roman Emperor Constantine because the gospel could be preached during his reign without persecutions. And he respects Augustine highly because of his works on God's grace and the forgiveness of sins.[14] Luther bestows special esteem on the martyrs because they are regarded as examples that Christian faith has to be proven in afflictions.[15] In contrast, he criticizes Tertullian as a montanist, as a "real Carlstadt between the church fathers," and Jerome because of his ascetic ambitions.[16] For Luther, the church as church exists only in the cross because this highlights the relation to Christ. The true church, therefore, has to suffer and to be persecuted. God is working in contrast to appearance: Where Christ is,

12. Risto Saarinen, "The Concept of Communion in Ecumenical Dialogues," in Holze, ed., *The Church as Communion*, pp. 287-316.

13. WA TR 5, 581, 36ff.

14. WA 24, 551, 10.

15. WA 12, 77, 10ff.

16. WA TR 1, 330, 3; 399, 12ff.

17. WA 10 I 1, 403, 21ff.

there are afflictions; and where people are suffering, there Christ can be recognized.[17] The question of where the true church can be recognized is for him, therefore, no question of history but of exegesis, and the decision is taken according to the criterion "the Scripture alone."

Certainly, Luther also praises the Early Church: "The spring, the loveliest time of the year, this is the time of the Early Church, when the Holy Spirit produces flowers and fruits."[18] Nevertheless, Luther did not interpret the Reformation as a simple return to Early Christianity. He did not agree with the humanistic respect of antiquity. On the contrary, he appreciated the faith of the Early Church not for its venerability and its high age but only insofar as it gave expression to the gospel. For Luther, it is the gospel of Jesus Christ that is the basis and the goal of the interpretation of history. This goes also for the councils of the Early Church that have no separate authority besides the Holy Scripture. Luther writes: "If you have all the councils you are still no Christian because of them; they give you too little. If you also have all the Fathers, they too give you too little. You must still go to Holy Scripture, where you find everything in abundance."[19] Although Luther appreciated the confession of the Early Church, when he had to make a choice between Scripture or tradition, he decided without hesitation in favor of the Scripture. For him, the Scripture, meaning the gospel and Christ himself, is the only criterion both for the Early Church and for the church in his own time.

Using this criterion, Luther notices that the church during history, from its beginning to the present time, often has not been in accordance with the gospel, that Christ has been hidden under human tradition, and that the true church has not been present in the papal church but rather in small groups of believers. He therefore was not engaged in preserving the visible continuity of the church but in rediscovering the real church of the gospel. And he claimed that the church of the Reformation was in continuity with the true church of the apostles just because of its discontinuity with the papal church. The continuity Luther is talking about is not external, not visible continuity. It is not a continuity that can be shown in institutions, traditions, or minis-

18. WA 3, 25, 23ff.

19. Martin Luther, "On the Councils and the Church," in *Luther's Works,* vol. 41, ed. Eric W. Gritsch (Philadelphia, 1966), p. 136.

tries. It is a continuity that is defined as the continuity of the gospel, as the continuity of Christ present in the Holy Spirit. This spiritual continuity is essential for Luther's understanding of the church.

His emphasis of spiritual continuity is, however, not in contrast to the conclusion that the church exists in time and history. In his work "On the Councils and the Church" (1539) Luther mentions seven marks by which the church can be recognized:[20] the holy word of God, the holy sacrament of baptism, the holy sacrament of the altar, the office of keys exercised publicly, the fact that the church consecrates or calls ministers or has offices that it is to administer, the prayer, public praise and thanksgiving to God, and finally the holy possession of the sacred cross. In this context, Luther explains the role and the necessity of the ministries: "The church is recognized externally by the fact that it consecrates or calls ministers, or has offices that it is to administer. There must be bishops, pastors, or preachers. . . . The people as a whole cannot do these things, but must entrust or have them entrusted to one person. Otherwise, what would happen if everyone wanted to speak or administer, and no one wanted to give way to the other?"[21] As we can see, Luther gives a functional reason for the establishment of ministries. It is the task and the purpose that justify their existence in the church: "Now, if the apostles, evangelists, and prophets are no longer living, others must have replaced them and will replace them until the end of the world, for the church shall last until the end of the world. Apostles, evangelists, and prophets must therefore remain, no matter what their name, to promote God's word and work."[22]

For Luther, the focus is not on the ministry itself but on the persons the ministry is serving: "For all of us it is given, not to him who has the office, but to him who is to receive it through this office."[23] Christ uses the ministry for the proclamation of the word. In view of the priest that means: "What he says or does is not his, but Christ, your Lord, and the Holy Spirit say and do everything, in so far as he adheres to correct doctrine and practice."[24] Some pages later, Luther adds: "Besides these external signs and holy possessions the church

20. Martin Luther, "On the Councils," pp. 148-64.
21. Martin Luther, "On the Councils," p. 154.
22. Martin Luther, "On the Councils," p. 155.
23. Martin Luther, "On the Councils," p. 156.
24. Martin Luther, "On the Councils," p. 156.

has other externals that do not sanctify it either in body or soul, nor were they instituted or commanded by God. . . ."[25] According to Luther, this understanding of the ministries is consistent with the church of the apostles. In his work "Against Hanswurst" (1541), he concludes: "Thus we have proved that we are the true, ancient church, one body and one communion of saints with the holy, universal, Christian church."[26] With this strong sentence Luther emphasizes that the churches of the Reformation are in continuity with the Early Church: "We have remained faithful to the true ancient church," "we are the true ancient church," and he adds with regard to the Romans: "you have fallen away from us, that is, the ancient church, and have set up a new church against the ancient one."[27] Repeatedly, Luther uses the phrase "true ancient church,"[28] by which the emphasis shifts from the mere "antiquitas" of the church to the correspondence with the Holy Scripture. He could not accept the humanistic position because he was convinced that the true church, founded on the word of Christ, has always existed in spite of all distortions and aberrations. At the same time, it was not his intention to identify the churches of the Reformation with the Early Church but to see them in an analogy or continuity of faith: "The purpose of all this is to show that the church must teach God's word alone, and must be sure of it."[29]

For the sake of continuity, Luther stressed that the confession and the theology of the Reformation is in correlation with the confession and the theology of the Early Church. On the other hand, he refused to idealize and to restore the Early Church. He was convinced that the continuity of the church he was aiming at could not be guaranteed by traditions or institutions but by God alone. The continuity of the church exists in nothing else but the proclamation of the word and the

25. Martin Luther, "On the Councils," p. 173.

26. Martin Luther, "Against Hanswurst," *Luther's Works,* vol. 41, pp. 179-256, specifically p. 199. In this work ten marks are mentioned by which the church can be recognized: baptism; the sacrament of the altar; the keys to bind and loose sins; the preaching office; the Apostles' Creed; the Lord's Prayer; the teaching that one should honor the temporal powers; marriage as a divine ordinance of God's creation; the experience of suffering and persecution; prayer for others (pp. 194ff.).

27. Martin Luther, "Against Hanswurst," p. 194.

28. Martin Luther, "Against Hanswurst," pp. 194, 199, 205.

29. Martin Luther, "Against Hanswurst," p. 217.

administration of the sacraments. Further marks are only important insofar as they witness to or are instruments of word and sacrament.

In PCS we recognize a different approach. In accordance with Faith and Order's *Baptism, Eucharist and Ministry,* PCS characterizes the historic episcopate and the apostolic succession of the ministry as one of "the permanent characteristics of the Church of the apostles" (§51): "Apostolic succession in the episcopal office is a visible and personal way of focusing the apostolicity of the whole Church" (§46). It is "a sign" (§50) that underline the need to regain "that fullness which God desires for his people" (§54).

PCS does not, however, derive the continuity of the church exclusively from the historic episcopate: "The use of the sign of the historic episcopal succession does not by itself guarantee the fidelity of a church to every aspect of the apostolic faith, life and mission. . . . Nor does the sign guarantee the personal faithfulness of the bishop" (§51). On the contrary, PCS makes it clear that the church is built on Christ alone and his word: "The ultimate ground of the fidelity of the Church, in continuity with the apostles, is the promise of the Lord and the presence of the Holy Spirit at work in the whole Church" (§46).

This reservation is important. It expresses an awareness that the ministry and the historic episcopate have to be distinguished from word and sacrament. The ministry is necessary, even indispensable, for the proclamation of the gospel and the administration of the sacraments — however, it is only an instrument in the service of the church. This reservation is in accordance with Article 5 of the Augsburg Confession, which stresses the instrumental character of the ministry: "To obtain such faith God instituted the office of the ministry, that is, provided the Gospel and the sacraments. Through these, as through means, He gives the Holy Spirit, who works faith . . . in those who hear the Gospel."

Obviously, this indicates that the existing consensus on apostolicity and ministry is much broader than the dissent. Building on this consensus, the dialogue between Anglicans and Lutherans on the historic episcopate has to continue. The communion ecclesiology of PCS is a suitable basis for our efforts to solve the tasks of the church in a changing world.

The Concept of Unity in the Porvoo Common Statement: Visible Unity and Ecclesial Diversity

MARY TANNER

The Background

It helps to understand the concept of visible unity in the Porvoo Common Statement when something of the history of the participating churches, as well as the context of Europe in the beginning of the 1990s, is remembered. All of the participating churches in the conversations were churches of the western catholic tradition which, from the Reformation period, were conscious of continuity with the apostolic church and of being part of the One, Holy, and Catholic Church of Jesus Christ. As the Porvoo Common Statement (PCS)[1] itself puts it:

> The faith, worship and spirituality of all our churches are rooted in the tradition of the apostolic Church. We stand in continuity with the Church of the patristic and medieval periods both directly and through the insights of the Reformation period. We each understand our own church to be part of the One, Holy, Catholic Church of Jesus Christ and truly participating in the one apostolic mission of the whole people of God. (§7)

There was thus a commonality of experience and ecclesial understanding as well as the shared pre-Reformation history. Moreover, the participating churches had been actively engaged in the twentieth-

1. Published in *Together in Mission and Ministry* (Church House Publishing, 1993).

century search for the visible unity of the church, through participation in the multilateral work of the World Council of Churches, the international bilateral conversations, and regional and local councils of churches. Over the years close relations had been established between some of the Nordic and Baltic Lutheran churches and the Anglican churches of Britain and Ireland through agreements that had resulted in a greater visibility of communion. For example, from the 1920s eucharistic hospitality was practiced between the Church of England and the Church of Sweden; Swedish bishops took part in Anglican episcopal consecrations and vice versa. From the middle of the 1930s the same mutual relations became the accepted norm with the Church of Finland, and by the late 1930s were extended to Latvia and Estonia. In the 1950s communicants from Norway, Denmark, and Iceland were welcomed to receive Holy Communion in the Church of England, though not to take part in episcopal consecrations. Although these agreements were between the Nordic and Baltic Lutheran churches and the Church of England, they were generally accepted by the other Anglican churches of Britain and Ireland, as well as by other parts of the Anglican Communion.[2] The implementation of these piecemeal agreements, together with the participation of Lutheran representative bishops from these churches at Lambeth Conferences, already by the 1990s demonstrated visibly the degree of communion that these churches shared in faith, sacramental life, and ministry.

In addition to this experience of a degree of visibly shared life there were other things that contributed to the understanding of visible unity and ecclesial diversity that lies behind PCS. These Anglican and Lutheran national churches had, through membership in their own world communions, an experience and sense of what it means to be part of a worldwide communion and an understanding of how worldwide communion is made visible. Moreover, both the Anglican Communion and the Lutheran World Federation in the twentieth century had come to deepen their understanding of what it means to be a world communion and what is required to make that communion visible. For example, as Anglicans spread into the different regions of the world they had to discover what it is that holds them together in an

2. Christopher Hill, "Existing Agreements between our Churches," in *Together in Mission and Ministry*, pp. 53ff.

Anglican Communion. The Chicago-Lambeth Quadrilateral, with its reference to scriptures, creeds, the two dominical sacraments, and ministry in the historic episcopal succession, came to describe not only the elements that were constitutive of Anglican unity, but also provided the clue to the sort of unity Anglicans were called to live with other Christians. At the Lambeth Conference of 1988 Archbishop Robert Runcie, in his opening address on the nature of the unity we seek, emphasized that the unity of the church also requires the service of councils or synods and the ministry of primacy, a personal focus of unity and affection. He asked sharply, could not all Christians come to reconsider the kind of primacy exercised within the Early Church, "a presiding in love for the sake of the unity of the Churches"?[3] Archbishop Runcie's speech and the discussions at the 1988 Lambeth Conference show Anglicans seeking to understand and develop instruments of unity and communion to strengthen the interdependence of the provinces and make more visible and effective the unity of the communion. It was usual for Anglicans to refer to the visible unity of the church, held together with these constitutive elements, as "organic union."

In a similar way the Lutheran World Federation in the second half of the twentieth century was reflecting upon its own experience and understanding of being a worldwide communion. Since 1947 Lutheran member churches had come to see themselves as a communion of churches enjoying pulpit and altar fellowship. Later on, some were beginning to ask whether the name Lutheran Communion was not a more appropriate name than Federation to describe the nature of their unity. Lutheran commitment to the visible unity of a wider Christian fellowship came to be described in terms of a commitment to "unity in reconciled diversity." This was put forward, in part, as a corrective to the notion of organic union that was regarded by some Lutherans as an organizational straight jacket with no possibility of ever being attained. Harding Meyer and Gunther Gassmann wrote of reconciled diversity:

3. Robert Runcie, "Opening Address to the Lambeth Conference," in *The Truth Shall Set You Free: The Lambeth Conference, 1988* (Church House Publishing, 1988), pp. 21ff.

> The principle must be adhered to that at every level — local, regional, and universal — of the ecumenical quest for unity and its realisation room must be allowed, in principle at least, for confessionally determined convictions and structures of fellowship, including their indispensable, institutional and structural presuppositions.[4]

Commenting on this, Michael Root explains that what is foreseen is not simply the communion of highly diverse local churches or the ongoing institutional identifiability of confessional traditions, but parallel church structures. Here, he suggests, there seems to lie the specificity of unity in reconciled diversity.[5]

So, by the early 1990s both Anglicans and Lutherans, while committed to developing and deepening their own unity, were also thoroughly committed to seeking to manifest visibly the unity of all Christian people. For both communions, their own experience of unity and their understanding of what holds a world communion together provided clues about the sort of life they believed God was calling them to live together in a wider Christian fellowship.

There is little doubt that the developments taking place in both world communions were in their turn influenced by the reflections and statements of the international theological dialogues that blossomed after Vatican II. Both Anglicans and Lutherans were heavily involved in bilateral conversations. In the multilateral context, successive Assemblies of the World Council of Churches had produced statements on the goal of visible unity and gradually put content into the phrase "the visible unity of the Church." The New Delhi Assembly talked of unity made visible when "all in each place" are united to "the whole Christian fellowship in all places and all ages," when Christians were in one fully committed fellowship, "holding the one apostolic faith, preaching the one Gospel, breaking the one bread, joining in common prayer, and having a corporate life reaching out in

4. G. Gassmann and H. Meyer, "Requirements and Structures of Church Unity," in G. Gassmann and H. Meyer, eds., *The Unity of the Church: Requirements and Structure* (Lutheran World Federation Report, no. 15, 1983), p. 23.

5. Michael Root, "'Reconciled Diversity' and the Visible Unity of the Church," in *Community, Unity, Communion: Essays in Honour of Mary Tanner,* ed. C. Podmore (Church House Publishing, 1998).

witness and service to all." This fellowship would "act and speak together as occasion requires."[6] Eight years later the Uppsala Assembly developed the notion of the fellowship as a "conciliar fellowship" and described the unity as "a sign of the coming unity of humankind."[7] The Nairobi Assembly in 1975 clarified the notion of "conciliar fellowship" further as a fellowship of local churches that are themselves truly united. They are united by "the same apostolic faith . . . the same baptism . . . share in the same eucharist" and "recognise each other's members and ministries." "Relationships are sustained in conciliar gatherings called for the fulfilling of their common calling."[8] The Vancouver Assembly in 1982 offered a threefold description of visible unity, bringing together the constitutive elements of visible unity with unity in service and mission in a world in need of healing and reconciliation.

> First, the churches would share a common understanding of the apostolic faith, and be able to confess this Message together in ways understandable, reconciling and liberating to their contemporaries. Living this apostolic faith together, the churches help the world to realise God's design for creation.
>
> Second, confessing the apostolic faith together, the churches would share a full mutual recognition of baptism, the Eucharist and ministry, and be able through their visible communion to let the healing and uniting power of these gifts become more evident amidst the divisions of humankind.
>
> Third, the churches would agree on common ways of teaching authoritatively, and be able to demonstrate qualities of communion, participation and corporate responsibility that could shed light in a world of conflict.
>
> Such a unity — overcoming church division, building us together in the face of racism, sexism, injustice — would be a witnessing unity, a credible sign of the new creation.[9]

6. *The New Delhi Report* (SCM Press Ltd., 1962), p. 116.

7. *The Uppsala 68 Report*, ed. N. Goodall (World Council of Churches, 1968), pp. 17ff.

8. *The Report of the Nairobi Assembly* (World Council of Churches, 1976), pp. 60ff.

9. D. Gill, ed., *Gathered for Life: Official Report of the VI Assembly of the World Council of Churches* (World Council of Churches, 1983), p. 45.

These are important statements describing the goal of the ecumenical movement as visible unity. However, in all of these Assembly statements there is some ambiguity. It is possible to interpret the reference to "churches" as applying to local churches, in which case the vision of visible unity tends toward a communion of local churches joined by the faith, the sacraments, and conciliar structures. On the other hand, some would maintain that "churches" in these statements refers to denominations. This gives a rather different perspective to the concept of visible unity, making it more akin to that of reconciled diversity. It is likely that these Assembly statements are read differently by those coming from different traditions, who espouse different models of unity. An Anglican might interpret these statements as describing a communion of local churches. Lutherans might think more readily of continuing denominational structures living in reconciled diversity. But in either case the constitutive elements of visible unity are the same — the faith, the sacraments, the ministry, and structured conciliar communion supporting a common life of praise, service, and mission.

The reflections of the international bilateral conversations on visible unity also provided an important resource for the Porvoo conversations. As references in the Porvoo statement show, Anglican and Lutheran conversations with the Roman Catholic and Orthodox churches in particular helped to shape the understanding of the sort of visible unity God calls us to live together. Among the bilateral conversations the Anglican-Lutheran dialogue, understandably, was the one that had the most relevance for the Porvoo conversations. On the basis of substantial agreements reached in the international dialogue, including those on the church, sacraments, and apostolic ministry, the Anglican-Lutheran European regional conversations had gone on to explore whether it was now possible to move into closer visible fellowship.[10] The European report suggests that the aim of the conversations was "organic union" (§43) or "full communion" (§62). What was not clear was whether the two terms were being used synonymously. Nor is it clear what the report sees as constituting either "organic unity" or

10. *Anglican-Lutheran International Conversations: The Pullach Report* (London: SPCK, 1973). *Anglican-Lutheran Dialogue: The Report of the European Commission* (London: SPCK, 1983).

"full communion." It was the task of the Anglican-Lutheran Joint Working Group, meeting in 1983, to focus on the notion of "full communion."[11] In the Cold Ash Report, full communion is taken to imply a life in which members may receive the sacraments of the other; bishops of one church may take part in the consecration of bishops of the other; a bishop, pastor/priest, or deacon may exercise liturgical functions in a congregation of the other body if so invited; and there would be recognized organs of regular consultation and communion.

> By full communion we here understand a relationship between two distinct churches or communions. Each maintains its own autonomy and recognizes the catholicity and apostolicity of the other, and each believes the other to hold the essentials of the Christian faith.[12]

To this is added that to be in full communion means that churches become "interdependent while remaining autonomous."[13] When the Church of England came to debate these various Anglican-Lutheran international and regional reports, the background paper for the General Synod asked, "Is the description of full communion in the Report of the Joint Working Group consonant with the present understanding of full communion within the Anglican Communion?" The Cold Ash Report, in spite of its emphasis on organs of consultation and communion, seems to support the view that each Communion should retain its own autonomy and thus not to envisage the creation of a single church in one locality under a single ministry.

It is clear that when the Porvoo conversations began, Lutherans and Anglicans shared a commitment to the gospel imperative for unity to be made visible, holding that unity in faith and sacraments belongs to a life of visible unity. It is also clear that both were world communions that in the second part of the twentieth century were developing an understanding of what it means to be a world communion. The understanding of their own identity in turn had an effect upon the

11. *Anglican-Lutheran Relations: Report of the Anglican-Lutheran European Commission* (London: SPCK, 1983).

12. *Anglican-Lutheran Relations,* paragraph 25.

13. *Anglican-Lutheran Relations,* paragraph 27.

sort of visible unity they were committed to seek with other Christians. This was not simply a matter of blind acceptance that the future must be "themselves writ large," for both were clear that the pilgrimage to unity entails conversion and re-formation. At the same time, there were, not surprisingly, differences of emphases in the way they understood themselves and what constituted their own unity, and this tended to influence their thinking about the sort of visible unity they believed God was calling them to manifest. There was also a lack of clarity in the ecumenical dialogues about the kind of visible unity that the churches were committed to seek. Churches, moreover, including Anglicans and Lutherans, tended to use different models to describe unity — reconciled diversity, united not absorbed, organic unity, full communion.

All of this formed the background to the Porvoo conversations. What was new and decisive in the early 1990s was a heightened sense of the necessity for a united Christian witness in the context of the sudden, dramatic changes taking place in Europe. Anglicans and Lutherans in Northern Europe recognized a moment, a *kairos* — a time of "unparalleled opportunity" (§6). The Porvoo conversations were driven by the conviction that visible unity is utterly required for credible and effective mission and more than ever urgent now for authentic mission in a Europe looking for its own unity and identity.

Visible Unity in the Porvoo Common Statement

In the Porvoo statement unity is not something humans can ever create by their own clever ecumenical endeavors. Unity is divine gift, the gift of being drawn into, and living in, the fellowship *(koinonia)* of the Triune God, Father, Son, and Holy Spirit.

> Unity is given in Christ as a gift to be received, and like every good gift, unity also comes from the Father, through the Son, in the Holy Spirit. (§21)

Here the Porvoo statement is quoting the report *Ways to Community* (1980/81) of the Roman Catholic-Lutheran Joint Commission. In its view of what constitutes the unity of the church, the Porvoo statement is in line with an ecclesiology of *koinonia* so central in the understanding of Vatican II and foundational in so many bilateral dialogues since Vatican II. But while unity is divine gift, it is also human task. The church as communion has two dimensions that belong together, a vertical one, and a horizontal one. There is communion with the Father through participation in Christ through the power of the Holy Spirit. And there is communion with one another, a communion between members of the body of Christ. It is the vocation of the church to be seen in the world as the one body of Christ, a sign of the reconciliation and unity God desires for all, an effective instrument to help in bringing about God's purpose, and a foretaste of God's kingdom here and now. Christian disunity is anomalous and contradicts the gospel message. Denominational traditions are provisional and even the degree of visible unity already enjoyed by Anglicans and Lutherans in Northern Europe at the beginning of the 1990s was not enough. What was required was a "fuller visible embodiment in structured form" (§22).

What then has Porvoo to offer in terms of its understanding of visible unity? One of the most striking things is the way the statement eschews the use of any particular model to describe visible unity. It uses neither the one-time preferred Anglican term of "organic union," nor the preferred Lutheran term "reconciled diversity." The document is also cautious about using the term "full communion." The phrase only occurs once in the Porvoo statement, in a quotation from the Lutheran World Federation Assembly in Curitiba (§31). By avoiding the use of "full communion" the statement might perhaps be thought to be distancing itself from the description set out in the Cold Ash Report. Whether this was the conscious intention of the drafters or not is not stated. What is more important is that the report does not identify itself with any one particular model of visible unity. Instead it offers what in two places it calls a "portrait" of the sort of life together Christians in Northern Europe believe they are called to live (§20).

The notion of portraiture is crucial for the Porvoo statement. For its portrait of visible unity it goes back to the Scriptures. It underlines nine aspects of the church living visibly in the light of the gospel. A church living in unity will be seen to be grounded in the love and grace of Christ; always joyful; a pilgrim people. It will confess the apostolic faith; celebrate baptism and Eucharist; be served by an apostolic ministry that unites the local with the church universal. It will manifest visible communion in a divided humanity; and have bonds of communion that enable it to make effective witness by taking decisions, teaching authoritatively, and sharing goods with those in need (§20).

This "thumbnail" portrait is attractive in summing up something of both the qualitativeness of a life of visible unity, as well as pointing to the elements that constitute unity — the faith, the sacraments, the ministry, and the bonds of structural communion, all working together in the witness to the love of Christ and empowering the church for mission. The portrait, as the statement admits, is by no means complete. It nevertheless contains within itself a challenge to Anglicans and Lutherans, reminding them of their need to repent and be renewed and re-formed together for unity in mission and service.

The biblical sketch of visible unity is repeated in several places in the statement. In paragraph 28, for example, it is stressed that the different elements, or aspects, of visible communion — the faith, the sacraments, the ministry, and the forms of collegial and conciliar consultation — are interrelated aspects. The Porvoo statement sees all these elements as part of an interlocking package of those things that properly belong to visible unity. They are not isolated elements but belong together, constituting and supporting a unity of life and mission (§28). These elements are not arid structure. They need to be permeated by a profound spiritual communion — "a growing together in a common mind, mutual concern and a care for unity (Phil. 2:2)" (§28).

The portrait of visible unity espoused in the Porvoo statement is then biblically based and also consonant with much Anglican and Lutheran ecclesiological reflection. By preferring the way of portraiture rather than the use of any model of unity like organic union, or reconciled diversity, or even full communion, the Porvoo statement opens the way for a more creative and imaginative description of visible unity that avoids past polemics. It thus avoids the accusation that organic union overemphasizes the structural, or that reconciled diversity seems to justify continuing separation. It also avoids the accusation that Anglicans seem in the past to have defined full communion in a number of different ways.

The portrait of visible unity in chapter II, with its skeletal frame of faith, sacraments, ministry, and conciliar structure, ought not to be separated from what follows in the rest of the Porvoo statement. Both the statements of agreement in faith and the commitments of the declaration that the churches were invited to make on the basis of those agreements serve to fill out what Porvoo understands as pertaining to a life of visible unity. So visible unity is demonstrated in confessing together the faith grounded in Scriptures and set forth in the Nicene-Constantinopolitan and Apostles' Creeds with the basic Trinitarian and Christological dogmas to which those creeds testify, and upholding together a belief in God's justifying grace. The common faith is celebrated in forms of common worship, spirituality, liturgy, and sacramental life with common texts, hymns, canticles, and prayers. The common life of faith issues in good works, in love of God, and in love of neighbor (§32).

Visible unity is manifested in a common sacramental life. Unity in a common baptism (followed by the reaffirmation of baptismal faith in confirmation) is seen in the way baptized members of all the participating churches are regarded as members one of another. Eucharistic communion with a shared faith that the body and blood of Christ are truly present, distributed and received under the form of bread and wine, is demonstrated in the welcome of each other's members to eucharistic celebrations in all the churches. Such eucharistic unity goes beyond the practice of eucharistic hospitality to individuals, which was hitherto the practice (§32).

Visible unity is demonstrated in a single ministry, ordered in the threefold pattern of bishop, priest, and deacon with a shared understanding of the relation of the priesthood of the ordained to the priesthood of Christ and to the priesthood of the church (§32). Most significantly, unity is manifested in the ministry of bishops in the historic succession in communion with one another. The breakthrough on apostolicity and succession and the role of the historic episcopate made this episcopal unity possible.[14] The participation of a group of bishops sharing together in the laying on of hands at the consecration of a new bishop signifies the unity of the ministry as well as the unity of the communities represented by the participating bishops (§48). The consecration of bishops in the historic succession is another sign of unity and continuity (§50). Unity in ministry is made visible in the life of the churches by welcoming those episcopally ordained to the office of bishop, priest, or deacon to serve, by invitation, in any of the participating churches without reordination (§58).

14. See the essays by Ola Tjørhom and Kirsten Busch Nielsen in this volume.

Unity is further visibly demonstrated in gatherings of bishops and conciliar consultations on significant matters of faith and order, life and work. Such oversight, *episkope,* is necessary as a witness to, and safeguard of, the unity and apostolicity of the church. Unity is visible above all in a common life of mission and service, prayer for and with one another, in sharing of resources, and exchange of ideas on theological and practical matters (§58).

One of the most obvious signs of unity is precisely in places where in the past congregations of two traditions have lived side by side. Unity is visible in the welcoming of diaspora congregations into the life of indigenous churches, to their mutual enrichment (§58).

It is possible to fill out the portrait of visible unity in chapter II with what comes in the agreements in faith and the commitments in the declaration. All of this enables us to get some clearer picture of what is implied in the Porvoo understanding of a life in visible unity. Anglicans might well reflect that this picture is hardly different from the sort of unity enjoyed by Anglicans in the Anglican Communion. It is little surprise that the first meeting of the Contact Group, set up to monitor the new life in visible unity, agreed to call the new relationship "the Porvoo communion." There has been some criticism of this title but many would say that it precisely describes the communion they now enjoy in the new relationship.

Ecclesial Diversity

Living out the unity of the church visibly brings with it inevitably questions of diversity in relation to unity. Right from the outset the Porvoo statement is insistent that visible unity is not to be confused with uniformity. Quoting again from the report of the Lutheran-Roman Catholic Joint Commission, *Ways to Community,* it stresses that "unity in Christ does not exist despite and in opposition to diversity, but is given with and in diversity." Diversity is seen not as negative but like unity itself as gift:

> Because this diversity corresponds with the many gifts of the Holy Spirit to the Church, it is a concept of fundamental ecclesial importance, with relevance to all aspects of the life of the Church, and is

> not a mere concession to theological pluralism. Both the unity and diversity of the Church are ultimately grounded in the communion of God the Holy Trinity. (§23)

The stress on unity with diversity is made again in a quotation from another report of the Roman Catholic-Lutheran Joint Commission, *Facing Unity: Models, Forms and Phases of Catholic-Lutheran Church Fellowship* (1985):

> Unity needs a visible outward form which is able to encompass the element of inner differentiation and spiritual diversity as well as the element of historical change and development. This is the unity of a fellowship which covers all times and places and is summoned to witness and serve the world. (§26)

As with unity so with diversity. Diversity is upheld in chapter II as integral to a life of visible unity, and it is in the agreements and the commitments of the declaration that we get hints of what some of that diversity might be in practice. The section on agreements in faith ends with the statement that there is already a "high degree of unity in faith and doctrine" (§33). At the same time this unity in faith and doctrine "does not require each tradition to accept every doctrinal characteristic of our distinctive traditions." The common faith will have a variety of expressions in different cultural contexts. In initiation the practice of infant and adult baptism is practiced; confirmation, while common to all, may be administered by bishops or in some cases by the local priest. The diversity of gifts of ministries expresses a common priesthood of the whole people of God. While there is a basic oneness of the ordained ministry, that ministry is expressed in three orders. Oversight is exercised in a variety of different ways — personal, collegial, and communal. The ministry of oversight has a particular task of coordinating the diversity of gifts and the multiplicity of tasks: it is "a ministry of coordination" (§42). As Bishop John Hind put it, "We are quite used to speaking of bishops as ministers of unity. Porvoo helps us understand that bishops are also ministers of diversity."[15]

15. John Hind, "Diversity in the Porvoo Communion," delivered at the First Theological Conference, Durham, 2000.

There is one further matter relating to diversity that is interesting to note. A single, fully interchangeable ministry is an important characteristic of visible unity. At the same time it is made clear that such interchangeability is subject to the canonical regulations in existence in the churches (§58). The co-chairmen in their Preface refer to one specific limitation to ministerial interchangeability that was there at the outset. The different positions in relation to women's ordination, both in the churches themselves and between the churches, especially the different positions in respect to the consecration of women as bishops, restricts the interchangeability. For example, the Church of England's official position remains that no woman bishop, or those ordained by her, whether male or female, may exercise their ministry in the Church of England. The same situation applies to those ordained by a Dean in the Church of Norway and who have, therefore, not been episcopally ordained. However, while the Porvoo communion is living with these differences, and thus with restricted interchangeability, it ought not to be implied that such differences are permanently acceptable, authentic diversity. How could they be when both place restrictions on visible unity?

The Porvoo statement nowhere says that diversity extends to the continuation of recognizably Lutheran and Anglican identities as part of a life in visible unity, though some of the language of the statement must be interpreted in that way. For example, the report refers in the commitments to welcoming "one another's members," "inviting one another's bishops" to participate in the laying on of hands, encouraging consultations of "representatives of our churches," etc. While such language may suggest the continuation of separate and recognizable Anglican and Lutheran regional churches, yet at the same time the report is clear that all denominational traditions are provisional. The assumption here is surely that the future demands such radical transformation of us all that there will be a unity and communion beyond what we presently know as Anglicanism, beyond what we presently know as Lutheranism. This is a familiar thought for Anglicans who have lived with the notion of the radical provisionality of the Anglican Communion. It may well be that we ought not to press for more definition, for it is only as Anglicans and Lutherans live into the Porvoo agreement that it will become clear whether Anglican and Lutheran identities will constitute legitimate diversity in the future. This is likely to be affected by the relationship that develops between the two traditions in other regions of the world and developments at the level of the two world communions. Already there are those who are suggesting that the next step is for an agreement at the world level that would bring together the different Anglican-Lutheran regional agreements that presently exist in North America, Australia, and Northern Europe.

So in Porvoo both unity and diversity are values to be cherished and promoted. The "bonds of communion" — common confession of the apostolic faith, one baptism, a united celebration of the Eucharist, a single ministry, and collegial and conciliar consultation — constitute the unity and also support the diversity of the Porvoo communion. But the report is equally aware that diversity has its limits. There is a diversity that serves unity, but there is also a diversity that contains destructive elements and goes beyond what is tolerable (§25). Thus criteria for maintaining the unity of the church are necessary to set the limits for legitimate diversity. "What is constructive in the Church for its *communio* is, at the same time, the foundation and the limit for its unity."[16] The statement is clear that there will be times when diversity is intolerable and threatens division. This was always so from the beginning of the church. The controversy over the radical decision to admit Gentiles without circumcision to baptism was ratified by the calling of the Jerusalem Council, recorded in Acts 15 (§25). So conciliar gatherings remain important today for guarding unity and sustaining legitimate diversity. The Porvoo statement suggests that oversight is to be exercised with personal, collegial, and communal aspects at the local, regional, and universal levels (§45).

The portrait of visible unity with rich diversity which the Porvoo statement sets as the goal of Anglican-Lutheran relations in Europe is not exclusive to these partners. Porvoo is not about establishing an exclusive Anglican-Lutheran bloc in Northern Europe. It was conceived of as one step towards the visible unity that needs to be expressed by all Christian people. Indeed the report ends with a strong encouragement for each participating church to pursue the same goal of visible unity at local, national, and international levels. (§§60, 61) It has to be

16. John Vikstrom, "Setting the Scene: The Porvoo Agreement and Its Vision," unpublished paper delivered at the First Theological Conference, Durham, 2000.

pursued by the Anglican Communion and the Lutheran World Federation, and also with other world communions.

Living into Visible Unity and Ecclesial Diversity

Lesslie Newbigin was surely right in his insistence that we cannot simply be committed to unity in some vague unspecified sense. We have to be able to put some content into that commitment. The same point is made by Harding Meyer when he writes that a goal-oriented movement must articulate as clearly as possible the aims commonly agreed on by its adherents. Michael Root makes the same point about the need to make statements that can serve as "criteria and orientation points as we structure and implement the steps now possible." One of the strengths of the Porvoo Common Statement is that it does precisely this. It describes a portrait of visible unity with diversity that can act as "criteria and orientation points." The portrait shares many characteristics of the Anglican view of organic union with its unity in faith, sacraments, ministry in the historic succession, and structured communion. At the same time its emphasis on diversity shares something of the Lutheran insistence on reconciled diversity. But to identify Porvoo with either model, or with the model of full communion, would not do justice either to its own description or to its openness to discover more about visible unity as the churches live into the new relationship. The Porvoo statement is clear that as the churches share together more and more of their faith, life, and mission they will get hold at a deeper level of what visible unity and ecclesial diversity entail. That will surely explode all existing models of visible unity.

In the six years since the signing of the Porvoo agreement, as other essays in this volume show, the churches have been learning to make their unity more visible.[17] The sheer affection and sense of commonality between the Porvoo churches has been experienced and expressed on many, many occasions. Twinnings at the levels of parishes and dioceses, the serving of ordained ministers from one Porvoo church in another, the participation in each other's consecrations, the

17. See, inter alia, the contributions of Charles Hill, John Neill, Juhani Forsberg, Tiit Pädam, and Jan Schumacher in this volume.

presence of Nordic and Baltic bishops at the Lambeth Conference in 1998, the exchange of information, the gatherings of Primates and Presiding Bishops, the meeting of the first theological conference, new joint work on the diaconate, pastoral conferences, the ongoing work of the Porvoo Contact Group to oversee the growth of the relationship, and above all the communion in prayer maintained through the Porvoo prayer cycle *An Invitation to Prayer,* are all visible signs of a shared unity.

It is significant that the first Theological Conference of the new Porvoo communion, in Durham, England, in September 2000 had as its title, "Diversity in Communion." It recognized that in the early years of the life of the Porvoo communion issues had already arisen that raise the question of the limits of tolerable diversity. The conference named in particular those of the ordination of women and homosexuality. It recognized that there are "profound differences of conviction between and within the member churches." It was noted that differences comprised not merely diverging judgments but also varieties of approach, method, and understanding in theological issues. The report of the conference was clear that communion such as that now enjoyed in the Porvoo communion demands interaction and points of exchange. It requires sharing a common life and then reaching a common mind. Among its recommendations the conference included the need to provide an account of *communio* that supports diversity but is also aware of the need to identify limits. An important insight comes in the recognition of the need to develop stronger means of "mutual accountability" between the churches. The conference noted sharply that "where a signatory church of the Porvoo communion intends to take an action which is likely to affect the boundaries of diversity within the Communion that some structure of sharing information and concerns should be established." Put like this, this sounds like a mild requirement. But in a communion that aspires to maintain visible unity and legitimate diversity, surely some structures that can call for restraint, encourage continuing joint exploration, discern, make a common decision and then monitor the response to that decision, are what is needed to live out mutual accountability. Any communion of churches needs ways to protect and strengthen its own unity and sustain its proper diversity.

If the Porvoo communion is to live in visible unity with an ever richer, more authentic, and more confident diversity true to the portrait of its founding document, then attention will have to be paid to discovering the right persons, structures, and processes that will enable mutual accountability to take place. These are needed to discern what makes for unity and what is enriching tolerable diversity, and to call for restraint or decision when appropriate. The Porvoo statement was clear that visible unity requires oversight exercised in personal, collegial, and communal ways. Whether the Porvoo communion deepens its unity in a convincing way in the future will have much to do with whether, and how, it develops those personal, collegial, and communal ways of common decision making and teaching with authority that are integral to the Porvoo portrait of visible unity, and whether the members are willing to heed the advice and decisions of those structures. Without this it is hard to see how issues of diversity that threaten unity can be responded to in the communion, how mutual accountability can be the way of the communion.

We would not do justice to the vision of visible unity and ecclesial diversity in the Porvoo statement if we did not stress the relation of the church to eschatology. For the vision of visible unity with diversity is contained within one grand, overarching eschatological vision — a restored and renewed creation and a reunited humanity (§27). "God's ultimate purpose and mission in Christ is the restoration and renewal of all that he has made, the coming of the Kingdom in its fullness" (§14). To that kingdom, with its unity and diversity, the visible unity and diversity of the church here on earth is to point. The prize of the Porvoo communion is the way of fidelity to this calling.

Some Observations Concerning the Unity Concept of the Porvoo Common Statement

HARDING MEYER

The Issue of Unity Concepts in Historical Retrospective[1]

The great and occasionally passionate debate at the end of the 1960s and in particular the 1970s about concepts or models of unity is already long ago. At that time, in a considerably changed environment of the ecumenical movement at large, this debate was unavoidable. With the entry of the Roman Catholic Church into the ecumenical movement and, almost simultaneously, the intensified ecumenical engagement of the Confessional Families, now called Christian World Communions, new and rather forceful agents had appeared on the ecumenical scene. The former shape of the ecumenical movement could not remain unaffected by these changes.

The crucial issue was whether these Christian World Communions in their ecumenical endeavor could embrace the concepts of church unity as they had developed over the preceding decades of the ecumenical movement, represented mainly by the World Council of Churches (WCC) and its Commission on Faith and Order.

It must be emphasized that the problem was not the *understanding of the unity of the church.* What the WCC Assembly in New Delhi (1961) in its famous "unity declaration" had affirmed concerning the

1. Here and sometimes also in what follows I must refer to my book *That All May Be One: Perceptions and Models of Ecumenicity* (Grand Rapids/Cambridge, UK: Eerdmans, 1999) in which the issue of and the debate on concepts of unity are described and documented extensively.

nature and the constitutive elements of unity was substantially shared by all Christian World Communions as well as by the Roman Catholic Church in its conciliar "Decree on Ecumenism." Rather, the real problem was, what *shape or model* the unity of the church should adopt when it came to concrete realizations of unity. This distinction between, on the one hand, the *"understanding of unity"* on which one agreed and, on the other, the *"model"* or *"concept of unification,"* which remained problematic, was and still is important. And the debate of the '60s and '70s clearly focused on the latter, i.e., on the question of "models" or "concepts of unification." But in the midst of all debate it was never controversial that the *criterion* for the legitimacy and authenticity of a certain "model" or "concept of unification" was, in the last analysis, the common "understanding of unity," i.e., the question whether a "model" or "concept of unification" met the "basic requirements for unity" implied in the "understanding of unity."

Almost inevitably, this issue incited conflict. The reason was that within the ecumenical movement as represented particularly by the WCC, the opinion prevailed that, ultimately, only one concept of unity could be regarded as legitimate and authentic: the *"corporate"* or *"organic union"* in which the unifying churches within a determinate territory give up — "surrender," it was said — their confessional or denominational identity and autonomy, forming from now on one single church with a new name and with a new and common identity. And this opinion drew its strength from the widespread conviction that the very existence of different confessional or denominational church bodies was the ecumenical problem *par excellence* that had to be overcome for the sake of unity.[2]

The Christian World Communions did not share this conviction of a fundamental opposition between confessional diversity and church unity. Rather, they considered "the variety of denominational heritages legitimate insofar as the truth of the one faith explicates in history in a variety of expressions." They felt, therefore, unable to wholeheartedly engage in an ecumenical movement, which had as its only and primary goal — as its "ideal"[3] — the *anti-* or *trans*-confes-

2. More details in my book *That All May Be One,* pp. 103-7.

3. This was said repeatedly, e.g., in the report of the World Conference on Faith and Order in Edinburgh, 1937.

sional concept of "organic unity." Even if they did not simply reject this concept as such, they pleaded, alongside this concept, for another and equally legitimate concept of unity that "encompasses a plurality or diversity of convictions and traditions" on the condition that the "existing differences between churches lose their divisive character." They called this concept, which was in some aspects very close to the earlier concept of "unity of mutual recognition,"[4] *"unity in reconciled diversity."*[5]

The debate, finally, led to the insight that there are *various but equally legitimate concepts or models of unity,* provided that they conform with the commonly agreed upon *understanding of unity.* The concrete choice of which one of these *concepts* should be pursued in a specific interchurch dialogue depends on "the ecumenical necessities and possibilities of different situations and of different church traditions,"[6] i.e., of the churches involved, their specific self-understanding and historical context.

Since then, an irenic spirit reigns in all deliberations about "concepts of unity," and it is pointless to bring the discussion back to its former edge — be it by declaring one or the other concept as obsolete or by claiming one concept for a successful realization of unity, thus considering it as superior or victorious over the other.

This should be kept in mind also in dealing with the topic of this paper, "the unity concept of the Porvoo Common Statement."

4. The preparatory document for the Edinburgh Conference, entitled "The Meanings of Unity," described this concept. However, the report of the Edinburgh Conference itself reduced it to mere "intercommunion." See my book *That All May Be One,* pp. 89-93.

5. The quotations in this paragraph are taken from a "discussion paper" on "The Ecumenical Role of the World Confessional Families in the One Ecumenical Movement," which summarizes the results of two consultations among representatives of the World Confessional Families in Geneva, 1974. See my book *That All May be One,* pp. 118-26. Concerning, in particular, the idea and concept of "unity in reconciled diversity" see also my article "'Einheit in versöhnter Verschiedenheit'. Hintergrund, Entstehung und Bedeutung des Gedankens" in Harding Meyer, *Einheit in versöhnter Verschiedenheit. Aufsätze zur ökumenischen Theologie,* vol. 1 (Frankfurt/Paderborn, 1998), pp. 101-19.

6. This is what the Commission on Faith and Order said at its meeting in Bangalore, 1978. See again my book *That All May Be One,* pp. 123-25.

I. The Affirmations of the Porvoo Common Statement on the Unity of the Church

In its part II ("The nature and unity of the church") the Porvoo Common Statement speaks about "The nature of communion and the goal of unity" (§§21-28), summarizing in §26, with a quotation from the Lutheran/Roman Catholic dialogue document "Facing Unity: Models, Forms and Phases of Catholic-Lutheran Church Fellowship" (1985). This affirmation indicates right at the beginning that the two partners share a "substantially common understanding of the nature of unity" and that the "models of unity" with which "Facing Unity" deals later on are "realizable forms of the fundamental understanding of unity."[7] This shows that in this document, too — as in the debate of the '60s and '70s — there is a clear differentiation between "understanding of unity" in which one agrees and the question of "models" or "concepts of unity," which requires further pursuit.

By using this quotation from "Facing Unity," the Porvoo statement affirms that the understanding of unity in which Lutherans and Catholics concur and which expressly refers to the "unity declaration" of New Delhi,[8] is common also to the Anglican and Lutheran churches of the Porvoo statement.

The Porvoo statement does not continue by explicitly developing its own "unity concept." The question, therefore, is whether the Porvoo statement implicitly conveys something with regard to that issue.

If one puts the question in this way it is striking to see how emphatically the Porvoo statement, in its section on "The nature of communion and the goal of unity," affirms that the unity of the church is essentially a unity in diversity and must never be confused with "uniformity." "The maintenance of unity and the sustaining of diversity" belong together (§§24 and 25). Theologically, this is undergirded by referring to "the many gifts of the Holy Spirit to the church" and to the unity and diversity within the Trinity (§23). In the same sense the decisions of the so-called "Council of the Apostles" (Acts 15) are being referenced.

In light of the debate on concepts of unity, a question immedi-

7. "Facing Unity," §§1 and 2.

8. "Facing Unity," §4.

ately arises as to whether the diversity, which has to be "sustained" within the unity of the church, also includes the diversity of existing confessional or denominational traditions. This is neither affirmed nor denied explicitly. As for diversity, it is self-evident and true that in the light of the kingdom of God, of which the church is the "sign, instrument and foretaste," "all existing denominational traditions are provisional" and stand under an eschatological proviso. The Porvoo statement, however, implicitly affirms that during the earthly pilgrimage of the church, the diversity of denominational or confessional traditions belongs to the sought-for unity. In any case it never speaks of "leaving behind" or of "surrendering" these traditions for the sake of unity.

Thus, the Porvoo Common Statement, in principle, has to be understood as integrating a central concern of the concept of "unity in reconciled diversity."

This is confirmed by the fact that, in this setting, the Porvoo statement again quotes a Lutheran/Roman Catholic dialogue document, "Ways to Community" (1981): "Unity in Christ does not exist despite and in opposition to diversity, but is given with and in diversity" (§23). This affirmation could be used against its original meaning if one overlooked its context, which expressly speaks of the unity of the church as "reconciled diversity."[9] Or, as the Decree on Ecumenism puts it,[10] "a proper freedom (is preserved) in the various forms of spiritual life and discipline . . . the variety of liturgical rites and even . . . the theological elaborations of revealed truth."

On the other hand, the Porvoo statement clearly integrates the concept of "organic" or "corporate union," although this concept as such does not apply to the relationship between *national churches* as the Porvoo statement does, but rather to the unity of churches "within the same territory."[11]

Despite this basic difficulty in applying the concept of "organic union" to the Porvoo statement, one can say that this document's emphasis on the *"structured form"* required for visible unity (§22) incorporates a concern that is characteristic for the concept of "corporate" or

9. "Ways to Community," §36.

10. "Ways to Community," §37; cf. Decree on Ecumenism, §4.

11. Cf., e.g., the description of "corporate union" in the report of the World Conference on Faith and Order in Edinburgh (see my book *That All May Be One*, pp. 94-100, in particular p. 95), confirmed by the actual church unions in various countries and regions.

"organic union."[12] It is a concern that is certainly not absent from the concept of "unity in reconciled diversity," although there it is less pronounced.

In the last paragraph of this section (§28), the same concern becomes even more palpable. It is said that the "agreement in faith together with the common celebration of the sacraments" necessary for communion is "supported by a *united ministry,*" and not just by a mutually recognized ministry. Here one can clearly discern what is, for the concept of "organic union," the "governmental unity" without which, according to the Edinburgh World Conference,[13] a corporate union "can hardly be imagined." This is why in the ecumenical endeavors of Anglicans, to which the concept of "organic union" goes back historically, the fellowship or communion in the episcopal office always was and still is essential for an authentic realization of church unity.

Thus, one can say: The affirmations of the Porvoo statement on the unity of the church do show that there is a common *understanding of church unity* and its nature which is nearly identical to the view maintained in the ecumenical movement at large. However, with regard to the *shape or form* this unity should assume, the Porvoo statement does not commit itself to one particular idea among the models or concepts of unity advocated in the ecumenical movement, but does integrate some of their basic concerns. Thus it reflects the procedure of the Lutheran/Roman Catholic dialogue document "Facing Unity," which also does not commit itself to one particular concept of unity, but describes, although much more extensively, the shape or form of unity by incorporating the concerns of several concepts.[14]

However, the question of the "unity concept of the Porvoo Common Statement" poses itself once again, and in a particular manner, in dealing with the *episcopal office* (part IV, §§34-57).

12. In dealing with "corporate union" the Edinburgh World Conference spoke of "some measure of organizational unity."

13. Harding Meyer, *That All May Be One*, pp. 94-100.

14. "Facing Unity," §§46-47 and all the preceding paragraphs.

II. The Episcopal Office and the Agreement Reached in the Porvoo Common Statement

Before reviewing the details, I want to state that I consider the Porvoo statement, with its agreement on the episcopal office, the basis on which the British and Irish Anglican churches and the Nordic and Baltic Lutheran churches could establish communion with one another, as a major ecumenical achievement that should be welcomed and celebrated without reserve. The Apology of the Augsburg Confession emphatically says that it is "our deep desire to maintain the church polity and various ranks of the ecclesiastical hierarchy, although they were created by human authority."[15] This desire, including the preconditions there mentioned, is fulfilled for the Lutheran churches that signed the Porvoo statement.

If in what follows I shall address certain questions to the Porvoo statement, this by no means contradicts my preceding evaluation of its final result. These questions, rather, concern the overall argumentation — one could also say: the "concept" that supported and led to this result. They reflect some problems of potential misunderstanding and will, finally, lead me to the question whether and how far this argumentation or "concept" could be applied also to the dialogue of the other Lutheran churches with Anglican churches or with episcopally structured churches in general.

My focus is on the fourth and last chapter of the Porvoo statement. It deals, as the title runs, with "episcopacy" understood as "service of the apostolicity of the church" and sets out with the affirmation that this episcopal service cannot be dealt with in isolation but has to be seen in a broader setting. What is being said here has already been stated, in a more concise manner, in part III as common basic convictions (§32i-k):

"The primary manifestation of apostolic succession is to be found in the apostolic tradition of the *Church as a whole*" (§39), since it is the Holy Spirit who "keeps the Church in the apostolic tradition" and maintains the "continuity in the permanent characteristics of the Church of the apostles" (§36). The *ordained ministry* is being seen on this

15. Apology, Article 14 (The Book of Concord, 214). Instead of "various ranks of the ecclesiastical hierarchy" the German version speaks of "der Bischöfe Regiment."

background: "Within the apostolicity of the whole Church is an apostolic succession of the ministry" (§40). This ministry has a "particular responsibility for witnessing to this tradition and for proclaiming it afresh with authority in every generation" (§40). It fulfills this responsibility by "different tasks" (§41) and with a view to diverse "gifts" granted by God. Such "diversity of God's gifts" and "diversity and multiplicity of tasks . . . call for a ministry of co-ordination": "the ministry of oversight, *episcope*" (§42), and this "oversight of the Church . . . is the particular responsibility of the *bishop*." Bishops are "representative pastoral ministers of oversight, continuity and unity in the Church" (§43), although their ministry is exercised not only "personally" but, at the same time, "collegially and communally" (§§44 and 45).

From this point forward, the text (§§46-57) focuses entirely on the episcopal office, more precisely: on the question of "*continuity* of the ministry of oversight," the "*apostolic succession* in the episcopal office" (§46), a question that still has to be settled between the churches of the Porvoo Common Statement (cf. §34).

The argumentation that follows is not always easy to understand and, by implication, is easily misunderstood. This difficulty in understanding refers mainly to the relation between the "*reality*" of the episcopal office in apostolic succession and its "*sign*," i.e., the "historical episcopal succession" (§§51; 52) in the form of "ordination or consecration of a bishop" through the "laying on of hands" by other bishops themselves standing in apostolic succession, as "the apostles did, and the Church through the ages" (§47).

With regard to the *reality* of the episcopal office the Porvoo statement clearly and repeatedly affirms: This "reality of the episcopal office" (§57) has been maintained and is given in the Nordic and Baltic Lutheran churches, not just the reality of *some kind* of episcopal office, but the reality of an episcopal office standing in "*orderly succession*" (§56) and therefore the reality of an "*authentic* episcopal ministry" (§52).

One would think that with this affirmation the problem had been settled and that, henceforth, fellowship in the episcopal office and full communion between the Anglican and Lutheran churches could be declared and practiced. Thus, the result of the dialogue would be that both parties today *recognize and acknowledge* that they *do have* one and the same "authentic episcopal office" in "orderly succession." The declaration of the Lambeth Conference of 1920 with regard to the Church of Sweden would have been, as it were, "extended" and applied also to the other Nordic and Baltic Lutheran churches. At that time, Resolution 24 of the Lambeth Conference had officially adopted the report and the conclusions of a Commission, appointed by the preceding Lambeth Conference, on "The Church of England and the Church of Sweden." The report said: "That the succession of the bishops has been maintained by the Church of Sweden, and that it has a true conception of the episcopal office. . . ."

In this perspective the unity concept of the Porvoo statement would have been the *"concept of mutual recognition,"* a concept closely related to the unity model of "unity in reconciled diversity" as I mentioned earlier. And, indeed, the terms "to recognize" and "to acknowledge" do play important roles in crucial places of the Porvoo statement (§§52-57).

However, the Porvoo Common Statement is not so straightforward because, here, the *"theory of sign,"* if I may say so, interferes.

The notion of *"sign"* occurs also in other places of the Porvoo statement. The Church, e.g., is a "sign . . . of the Kingdom of God" (§§32f; 50) and ordination to the ministry is a "sign of God's faithfulness to his Church" (§50). Particularly frequent, however, is the use of the term "sign" where the episcopal office is concerned. In this setting "sign" is "the sign of the historic episcopal succession" (§§50-54) and it means that, at the ordination or consecration of a bishop, other bishops who themselves are standing in "historic episcopal succession" perform the *"laying on of hands"* on the newly ordained bishop, as "the apostles did, and the Church through the ages" (§47). Therefore, the heading of this entire section is "The Historic Episcopal Succession as Sign."

It is true that the term "sign" can also be applied to the episcopal office *as such* in the sense that it is "a sign of our intention . . . to ensure the continuity of the Church in apostolic life and witness" (§32k; similarly §58a.vi). The term and its use, therefore, have a certain ambiguity in the Porvoo statement. Nevertheless, it is clear what the Porvoo statement properly means when, in connection with the episcopal office, it speaks of "sign": it is the "historic episcopal succession" realized in the ordination or consecration of a bishop through the act of laying on of hands by other bishops themselves standing in this succession (§47).

In contrast to the episcopal office in the Anglican churches, the episcopal office in some of the Nordic and Baltic Lutheran churches, because of an "interruption of the episcopal succession" (§34), has *not preserved this "sign."* Although, with regard to its *"reality,"* the episcopal office in these Lutheran churches is an "authentic episcopal ministry" (§52) standing in "orderly succession" (§56) and being *"acknowledged"* by Anglicans (§52), such "acknowledgment" or "recognition" *alone* does not suffice. What, on the Lutheran side, is still needed is the *appropriation of the "sign."* With the words of the crucial §52: the Lutheran churches with their authentic episcopal office are "free to enter a relation of mutual participation in episcopal ordinations with a church which has retained the historical episcopal succession, and to *embrace this sign. . . ."*

Anglican "recognition" of the *"reality"* of an authentic episcopal office in the Lutheran churches, and *Lutheran appropriation* of the *"sign"* of the historic episcopal succession, together lead to *"a reconciled and mutually recognized episcopal ministry"* (§54), and the "recognition" of the "reality," it is emphasized, *precedes* the appropriation of the "sign" (§53).

One can see in the words "reconciled" and "mutually recognized" an implicit, although unintended hint to the question of "unity concepts." Indeed, for the concept of "unity in reconciled diversity" *both* elements, "reconciliation" and "recognition," are fundamental. Sometimes, this concept has been understood as a "static" concept dominated by the idea of mere recognition of what already is. This is a blatant misunderstanding since "reconciliation of diversity" can never happen by "mutual recognition" alone but necessarily includes modification and change.[16]

16. The declaration on "Models of Unity" of the Assembly of the Lutheran World Federation in Dar es Salaam (1977) is unambiguous at this point. It says that the concept of "unity in reconciled diversity" is pointing towards a "way to unity" that is "a way of living encounter, spiritual experience together, theological dialogue and *mutual correction,* a way in which the distinctiveness of each partner is not lost sight of but *rings out, is transformed and renewed,* and in this way becomes visible and palpable to the other partners as a legitimate form of Christian existence and of the one Christian faith. There is no glossing over the differences. *Nor are the differences simply preserved and maintained unaltered.* On the contrary, they lose their divisive character and are reconciled to each other."

III. Some Comments on the "Theory of Sign" in the Porvoo Common Statement

If now, in concluding my observations and reflections, I shall put some questions to the Porvoo statement this does not mean that I want to criticize the result of the Porvoo conversations. Quite the contrary! The *questions I still have* are essentially no more than questions of understanding, and they mainly concern the "theory of sign."

In particular I wonder what the *significance of the "sign"* is or is supposed to be *for the "reality" of the episcopal office.* The Porvoo statement emphasizes that "the sign is *effective*" and it describes the effect in four affirmations (§48). However, the first three affirmations remain, in my understanding, on the merely "significative" level and, in the strict sense, i.e., with regard to the "reality" of the episcopal office, do not "effect" anything. If it is said that the "sign" "bears witness" to something, that it "expresses" and "signifies" something, this does not lead beyond the merely significative level since all three verbs have a definitely "significative" and not an "effective" meaning. Only the fourth and last affirmation points to something clearly "effective." It is said: "It (*sc.* the sign) *transmits* ministerial office and its authority in accordance with God's will and institution." But if this is so then one cannot avoid asking whether the *absence of the "sign" fundamentally questions the "reality" of an "authentic episcopal office"* in the Lutheran churches, which, after all, had been expressly "acknowledged" by the Anglican partner.

Here resides (for me and for others) the basic problem in understanding the crucial §52. The first of its two decisive affirmations reads: ". . . a church which has preserved the sign of historic succession (*sc.* as the Anglican Church) is free to acknowledge an authentic episcopal office in a church (*sc.* as some of the Nordic and Baltic Lutheran churches) which has preserved continuity in the episcopal office by an occasional priestly/presbyteral ordination at the time of the Reformation." The difficulty in understanding this is: How can an "authentic episcopal office" and the "continuity in the episcopal office" be "preserved . . . *by an occasional priestly/presbyteral ordination,*" i.e., by an ordination that *exactly failed to preserve* the "sign of historic succession" and, thus, had "*interrupted* the episcopal succession" (§34)? I would understand and, indeed, endorse an affirmation saying that an "authentic episcopal office" that maintained the "continuity in the episcopal office" can be preserved *"in spite of* an occasional priestly/presbyteral ordination," i.e., *in spite of* the missing "sign." But I cannot understand that such an episcopal office can be preserved *"by* an occasional priestly/presbyteral ordination," i.e., by an ordination that has lost the sign, especially if it is true that this "sign" *"transmits"* the "ministerial office [of the bishop] and its authority" (§48). Let me here add that I recently saw a Spanish translation of the Porvoo statement that translated the "by" as "a pesar de" (in spite of) and I, myself, in a German paper thought I should translate it as "vorbei an," which means "by-passing" priestly/presbyteral ordination.[17]

It may well be that I have failed to really grasp the "theory of sign" that underlies the Porvoo statement's affirmations. If this should be the case, the reason for my failure could well be that the Porvoo statement itself does not sufficiently elucidate the *significance* of the "sign of historic episcopal succession" for the "reality" of the episcopal office.

Concluding my observations, I would like to focus briefly on the question whether and how far the Porvoo statement and its "concept" could be applied to the dialogue of the other Lutheran churches with Anglican or with episcopally structured churches in general. I dare to phrase this important question in a somewhat casual fashion:

IV. Porvoo Beyond Porvoo?

The fact that, on the basis of the Porvoo Common Statement and the signing of the declaration, the Nordic and Baltic Lutheran churches and the British and Irish Anglican churches will now have a common episcopal office and thus could establish full communion with each other is of significance for the whole of Lutheranism. Since this does not reduce the communion of these Lutheran churches with the other Lutheran churches in the world, the Porvoo statement can be welcomed by all Lutheran churches as a legitimate fulfillment of the de-

17. I, maybe wrongly, thought I could do so after consulting the Oxford Advanced Learner's Dictionary of Current English, edition of 1980.

sire expressed in the Book of Concorde to "maintain" the ancient episcopal church polity.[18]

However, it seems to me very unlikely that the Porvoo statement will appear to the other Lutheran churches as a model or concept as they try to come to grips with the issue of episcopacy in their dialogue with Anglican churches. In my mind, the reason for this is that the *particular and basic presupposition* of the Porvoo statement, i.e., the fact that, also according to Anglican judgment, the Lutheran churches involved have preserved the "reality" of an "authentic episcopal office" and the "continuity of the episcopal office," does not apply to most of the other Lutheran churches. As a matter of fact, Anglicans have not — either in the German and North American or in the international Anglican/Lutheran dialogues — pronounced a "recognition" of such an "authentic episcopal office" in other than the Nordic and Baltic Lutheran churches.

If, therefore, the dialogue between these other Lutheran churches and Anglicans ultimately aims at reaching *the same goal,* it has to take another path than the Porvoo dialogue and follow a *different concept.*[19] Such a path would be more demanding for Lutherans than the way the Nordic and Baltic churches were able to take. It would not only demand *embracing the "sign"* of historic episcopal succession but rather *sharing in the "reality"* of an authentic episcopal office standing in historic continuity.

That is why the dialogue between the Evangelical Lutheran Church in America and the Episcopal Church in the USA as well as the international Lutheran/Roman Catholic dialogue has developed another concept. It has been proposed and described, with certain variations, both in the North American proposal "Concordat of Agreement,"[20] which in the meantime and in a revised version[21] has been adopted by the Lutheran and the Episcopal churches, and in the Lu-

18. Apology of the Augsburg Confession (see above and footnote 15).

19. Only while writing this paper I learned about the Waterloo Declaration between the Evangelical Lutheran Church in Canada and the Anglican Church of Canada. The declaration was adopted by both churches in July 2001 and is said to come close to the Porvoo Common Statement. However, since I do not yet know the wording of this declaration I must, for the time being, refrain from any judgment.

20. "Toward Full Communion" and "Concordat of Agreement," 1991.

21. "Called to Common Mission."

theran/Roman Catholic dialogue document "Facing Unity."[22] Due to the inherent difficulty of the matter the proposal itself is quite complicated. Since it cannot be the task of this paper to describe the proposal in detail I only want to highlight its *main idea:* It presupposes that the Lutheran churches do have an authentic *ordained ministry,* but that they did not preserve the "continuity in the episcopal office."[23] Therefore, a way or, better, a "process," extended over a longer period of time, is being proposed in the course of which the Lutheran churches, as it were, "grow into" the historic episcopacy and, at the end, share it with their Anglican or Roman Catholic partner church in such a way that the theological and ecclesiological convictions of the Reformation are not being surrendered or curtailed.

This clearly is a concept different from that of the Porvoo Common Statement. However, with these different "concepts" for regaining fellowship in the episcopal office it is the same as with the different "concepts of unity" in general: The *goal* is identical, but "the concrete choice of which one of these *concepts* should be pursued in a specific dialogue depends on 'the ecumenical necessities and possibilities of different situations and of different church traditions.'" With these words I have, at the beginning of this paper, summarized an important insight of the earlier debate on concepts and models of unity. It appears to be true also for the dialogue on episcopacy.

22. The proposal of "Facing Unity" is being explained extensively in §§86-119 and summarized in its main points in §§117-119 ("Approach to a jointly exercised ministry of fellowship") of that document.

23. In "Called to Common Mission" it is expressly said: "At present the Episcopal Church has bishops in historic succession, as do all the churches of the Anglican Communion, and the Evangelical Lutheran Church in America at present does not . . ." (§11).

Sign but Not Guarantee: Reflections on the Place of the Historic Succession of Bishops Within the Apostolic Continuity of the Church in Some Current Ecumenical Texts

JOHN HIND

The perpetuity of the Church was an article of faith; but its diminutions and corruptions, and its jeopardy by the follies of its members were part of the canon of history. There was plenty of ground for cynicism. . . . The faithful put it down to the indwelling of the Holy Ghost. Either way there was an uncomfortable mystery: how the chaos of history could issue in so consistent a hold on dogma or why an omniscient God chose such a messy method of preserving His foothold in the minds of His creatures.[1]

Introduction

This essay seeks to understand a phrase that is frequently used in modern ecumenical discussions about the so-called "historic episcopate." A typical formulation of the phrase occurs in the Porvoo Common Statement: "The use of the sign of the historic episcopal succession does not by itself guarantee the fidelity of a church to every aspect of the apostolic faith, life and mission" (§51).[2]

That the church as a whole should be thus faithful may be taken for granted. Whether she/it[3] has any divine assurance of such fidelity

1. Morris West, *The Shoes of the Fisherman* (Fontana, 1976), p. 15.

2. *Together in Mission and Ministry* (Church House Publishing, 1993). Hereafter Porvoo.

3. Catholics tend to prefer the feminine pronoun, Protestants the neuter, to de-

either as a whole or in any particular part is one of the points at issue, although all Christians will want to take seriously the Lord's own promise that the "other" Paraclete, the Holy Spirit, would guide Jesus' chosen disciples into all truth (cf. John 16:13).

This is not an abstract question. Christian believers need to be confident that what they learn in the church is authentic and has the authority of Christ himself. This is just as true of those who consider the Bible to be the *ipsissima verba* of God as it is of those who acknowledge the Spirit's guidance in the living tradition of the church (and of course of those many who hold to both).

In this connection it is becoming increasingly common ecumenically for the historical continuity of the church to be regarded as a significant factor in its authority. The Anglican-Reformed dialogue, for example, refers, with no apparent disapproval, to the fact that the "succession of public episcopal ministry could be appealed to [in the Early Church] as a ground of assurance that what was being taught was the authentic message of Jesus and the apostles."[4]

The Porvoo phrase quoted is an echo, although not a direct quotation, of a well-known passage in Faith and Order's *Baptism, Eucharist and Ministry*,[5] where, in the course of a discussion of the apostolicity of the church and the role of the orderly transmission of ministerial authority, it is said that some recent reconsiderations of the relationship between the historic episcopal succession and the apostolicity of the church as a whole "enable churches which have not retained the episcopate to appreciate the episcopal succession as a sign, though not a guarantee, of the continuity and unity of the Church" (BEM/Ministry §38).

This way of speaking was itself distilled from earlier stages of the production of the Lima text, for example from the memorandum concerning "Episkopé and Episcopate in Ecumenical Perspective" drawn up by a Faith and Order consultation held in 1979, which concluded that "although apostolic succession does not offer any guarantee for

scribe the church. In this essay I shall normally use the latter out of deference to the most frequent English usage, although biblical and theological principle would generally favor the former.

4. *God's Reign and Our Unity* (1984) §99.

5. *Baptism, Eucharist and Ministry*, WCC, Faith and Order 1982. Hereafter BEM.

maintaining the truth, non-episcopal churches may gain a new dimension in their life by introducing the sign."[6]

BEM adapted the idea but used the expression in a purely descriptive way. It drew attention to the way in which growing mutual theological understanding in a changed ecumenical atmosphere was making it possible for some non- or even anti-episcopal churches to accept the possibility that some form of the episcopal succession might have something to commend it so long as too much is not claimed for it.

In other words it was not, in BEM, a prescriptive assertion by the Faith and Order Commission either approving or recommending this limitation on the role of the episcopal succession in the apostolic continuity of the church. Rather, it simply described the way in which dialogue was helping to create the possibility of overcoming one of the apparently most intractable of ecumenical problems, namely, how to reconcile episcopal and non-episcopal churches, saving all essential principles and yet without requiring faithful believers to doubt the authenticity of the gospel or the sacraments they had received.[7]

The use of the expression in Porvoo did, therefore, go further than BEM in returning to the earlier, more evaluative position of the 1979 consultation, implying not only that there was a changed situation but also that the particular slant on this suggested by the expression in question was in some sense desirable.

The Church of England's response to BEM commented, with apparent approval, "it is . . . clear that episcopal succession does not of itself guarantee continuity."[8]

By contrast, the Roman Catholic Church, in its response to BEM, claimed that "episcopal succession can rightly be called a *guarantee* of the continuity and unity of the church, if one recognizes in it the ex-

6. Faith and Order paper 102, p. 12. Apostolic succession in this sense is defined as "through continuity in the succession of the ministry through personal episcopal ordination."

7. The importance of such confidence is well expressed in the Thirty-Nine Articles of the Church of England. Article XXV describes the sacraments as "certain sure witnesses, and effectual signs of grace," while Article XXVI reassures the faithful that "the effect of Christ's ordinance" in word and sacrament is not "taken away" by the unworthiness of the ministers.

8. *Towards a Church of England Response to BEM and ARCIC* GS661 (CIO Publishing) §99.

pression of Christ's faithfulness to the church until the end of time. At the same time it lays upon each individual office-bearer the responsibility to be a faithful and diligent pastor." This claim arises from an understanding of the bishop's ministry as "a sacramental sign of integration and a focus of communion. Through the episcopal succession, the bishop embodies and actualises both catholicity in time, i.e., the continuity of the church across the generations, as well as the communion lived in each generation. The actual community is thus linked up with the apostolic origins, its teaching and way of living."[9]

Despite the apparent contradiction, the Church of England House of Bishops in their response to the Encyclical *Ut unum sint* of Pope John Paul II claimed that, "While the Church of England hesitates, as BEM does, to use the language of 'guarantee' of historic episcopal succession, the House of Bishops is nevertheless clear that its understanding is not different from the one expressed by the Roman Catholic Church, as that is set out in its official response to BEM. When the Roman Catholic response makes use of the term 'guarantee,' it clearly does not claim that the indefectibility, infallibility and apostolicity of the Church are unquestionably assured merely by an historically demonstrable laying on of hands from the time of the apostles."[10]

This claim receives support from the description of episcopacy and apostolicity in the Methodist–Roman Catholic report *Authoritative Teaching in the Methodist and Roman Catholic Churches,* where we read, "The teaching of any individual bishop in itself is not guaranteed to be preserved from error by the Holy Spirit, and there have been and can be bishops whose teaching and way of life are contrary to the Gospel entrusted to them."[11]

As it is self-evident that there have been bishops and even whole provinces of bishops with impeccable "pedigrees" who have fallen into heresy or have become schismatic, no one considers continuity in

9. Published in *Churches Respond to BEM,* vol. 6, ed. M. Thurian. Faith & Order Paper 144 (WCC, 1988), p. 33.

10. *May They All Be One,* House of Bishops Occasional Paper (Church House Publishing, 1997) §43. This attempt at rapprochement had already been made in the earlier House of Bishops Occasional Paper, *Apostolicity and Succession* (1994), §63.

11. *Speaking the Truth in Love.* Report of the Joint Commission for Dialogue between the Roman Catholic Church and the World Methodist Council 1997-2000, paragraph 106.

itself to give absolute assurance that the teaching of a particular bishop (or group of bishops) is truly apostolic. Indeed, as the Munich statement of the Roman Catholic–Orthodox international dialogue puts the matter, "Apostolic succession . . . means something more than a mere transmission of powers. It is succession in a church which witnesses to the apostolic faith, in communion with the other churches which witness to the same apostolic faith."[12]

Part of the problem may be that neither the word "guarantee" nor the expression "apostolic succession" is being used in exactly the same sense by all parties to the discussion!

The 1973 Groupe des Dombes statement *Towards a Reconciliation of Ministries* helpfully distinguished between "the fulness of the apostolic succession of the whole Church" (implying continuity in the essential features of the church of the apostles), and "the fulness of the apostolic succession in the ministry" (implying continuity in the transmission of the ministerial function, fidelity in preaching to the teaching of the apostles, and a life in keeping with the gospel and the demands of mission). The statement rather delicately comments that "these three features are usually inseparable," clearly indicating that mere ministerial continuity does not always secure apostolic fidelity, while the "succession . . . as a ministerial sign, bears witness to the apostolic character of the Church and prepares the community for the coming and the action of our Lord himself."[13]

What Is the Question?

Christians need to know that they can have confidence in the teaching authority of the Church. Jesus' promise to be with his disciples to the end of the age and the gift of the Spirit to lead them into the whole truth are fundamental to this confidence, and from the earliest times the Christian community took care to develop instruments for safeguarding it. These include above all the canonical scriptures, the "rule of faith (or truth)" (later the creeds), and the orderly transmission of

12. "The Mystery of the Church and of the Eucharist in the Light of the Mystery of the Holy Trinity II.4," in P. McPartlan, *One in 2000* (St. Paul's, 1993), p. 47.

13. ET in *Modern Ecumenical Documents on the Ministry* (SPCK, 1975), pp. 95, 96.

apostolic ministry. All these means are intended to reassure believers that their faith is the authentic gospel and that God will honor the promise of Christ — that the gates of hell will not prevail against the church.

In the complex world of signs that constitute the sacramental symbolism of the church, what is meant by a sign that is not a guarantee? Is this intended, for example, to suggest a sign in the sense of a mere signpost, an indication of the way we should go if we want to reach a particular destination, rather than an active aid to progress, that is to say an efficacious sign, to use more traditional categories? More particularly, is the statement directed at (i.e., against) the position held by, or presumed to be held by, some other church or group of churches? Who, in short, is thought to believe that "the use of the sign of the historic episcopal succession" by itself guarantees "the fidelity of a church to every aspect of the apostolic faith, life and mission"?

One might then go on to ask whether if the historic episcopal succession does not *by itself* afford a guarantee of the fidelity of "a church" to every aspect of the apostolic faith, life, and mission, is there anything else that does afford such a guarantee? What is meant by "a church" and a "guarantee," not to mention the somewhat difficult expression "the use of the sign of" (cf. §51)?

The Use of the Phrase in the Porvoo Statement

Porvoo is rather stating the obvious with its declaration, "There have been schisms in the history of churches using the sign of historic succession. Nor does the sign guarantee the personal faithfulness of the bishop."

"Nonetheless," continues the agreed statement, "the retention of the sign remains a permanent challenge to fidelity and to unity, a summons to witness to, and a commission to realise more fully, the permanent characteristics of the Church of the apostles" (§51).

In this way, we are introduced both to what the authors and signatories of the Porvoo Common Statement do and do not want to claim for the historic episcopal succession and to some of the neuralgic points of church history that underlie the reservations they wish to express. In putting things in this way they hope to enable Northern European Anglicans and Lutherans to overcome their historic difficulties in this area.[14]

It is to be noted that what is at issue here is the historic episcopal succession and not more general questions of episcopal ministry or an episcopal ordering of the church. The issue sits somewhat awkwardly on the boundary between theology and history, given that for some Christians what is popularly called the apostolic succession is a theological question touching the very identity and authority of the church, while for others it is at the most a matter indifferent. For both groups of course the matter may involve issues concerning the theological interpretation of history and how we may be confident in the teaching of the church. In other words, it is not really (or merely) a question of whether an episcopal form of church government is desirable or acceptable, but, more narrowly, whether what part the succession of bishops in supposed continuity from the apostles plays in the preservation of the identity of the church throughout the ages and her fidelity to gospel truth.

Quite a lot is at stake here. It affects not just the confidence of those for whom the historic episcopal apostolic succession is an essential part of their ecclesial landscape, but also that of others who may feel that stressing the succession in this form calls the authenticity of their own church tradition into question. Clearly if two church traditions, historically deeply divided over episcopal ministry, could overcome the legacy of history without inappropriate compromise on either side, that could be a major contribution to wider reconciliation.

To put the matter more simply than it deserves, Anglicans have for many years insisted in practice on the historic episcopal (apostolic) succession as an indispensable element in the full visible unity of the church. Despite their own internal disagreements over the theological significance of this, they have in effect made it an essential condition of any unity scheme. Lutherans, on the other hand, even episcopal Lutherans whose churches preserved the succession, cannot accept the necessity for unity of anything that goes beyond the pure preaching of the gospel and the due administration of the sacraments.[15]

14. How significant this difficulty has been may be inferred from the frequency with which Porvoo refers to it.

15. *Confessio Augustana,* Article VII — including the well-known reference to the "satis est" or to what is seen as sufficient for church unity.

The task therefore was to revisit the churches' understanding of the succession of bishops in the apostolic ministry, to discover how much load different understandings bear in different churches and try to find a way of describing matters that managed to safeguard both positions. On the surface this appeared an unachievable task. In recent years, however, a new ecumenical method has been developing, which involves going behind what are currently perceived to be the points of disagreement and trying to discover whether they may in some cases be contradictory ways of expressing a common truth.

A good description of this approach is to be found in the report that commended BEM and the *Final Report of ARCICI*[16] to the General Synod of the Church of England in 1985.[17]

> **A Developing Ecumenical Method**
>
> 11. The dialogues, bilateral and multilateral, are based upon the principle of "growing together" (the *Final Report*), a process of "convergence" (the Lima text) on the way to establishing sufficient agreement in the faith to maintain the full visible unity of the one holy, catholic and apostolic Church. The notion of convergence implies that theology is understood as having a direction, as going somewhere, rather than involving a mere repetition by each partner of long cherished dogmatic formulae. While not denying that serious issues have indeed divided the churches, commitment to the possibility of convergence entails acknowledging that emotive and polarised language has played a large part in continuing the separation of the churches. The process of convergence involves a willingness to leave behind the language of past polemic in the search for a common understanding.
>
> 12. All the dialogues look for ways of reconciling antithetical positions, avoiding the terms in which the antithesis was originally put forward. This method suggests that whatever may have

16. *ARCIC* is the Anglican–Roman Catholic International Commission which has produced an impressive series of agreed statements since its inception in 1968. *Final Report* is the name given to the report published in 1982 when the Commission had completed the first set of questions identified as historical areas of disagreement.

17. *Towards a Church of England Response to BEM and ARCIC* GS661 (CIO Publishing). The report was prepared by the Faith and Order Advisory Group of the Church of England.

been the case in the past is now no longer necessarily so. While there can be no justification in theological dialogue for glossing over differences, it is accepted that the pursuit of restatement is possible. That is, not more irenic restatements of where we once were, nor even restatements of where we are now in our separation, but restatements of our common Christian heritage. The dialogues, therefore, avoid controversial language and attempt to re-examine and re-appropriate our common heritage offered to us in the Scriptures and Tradition.

13. Several factors have combined in the last fifty years to create a new and promising climate in which convergence can be furthered. Not least among them is the sharing of the insights of biblical scholarship and knowledge of the history which led to the divisions between the churches. This, combined with genuine friendliness to each other's traditions, a sharing in worship, life and mission, has supported the theological search for agreement in faith.

14. More explicit agreement in faith is necessary for the uniting of divided churches than needs to be expressed between different groups within a single communion. Only explicit agreement in faith can provide that confidence needed to heal the wounds of division, jealousies and irrational fears. But agreement in faith is not to be solely as an assent to propositional formulations of doctrine, nor to rigid liturgical and devotional practice. Agreements reached in words in the convergence process must be carried by, and be expressive of, the life of communities which are themselves growing together and proclaiming the Gospel together. Convergence has to be in word and in life.

It was against the background of a long relationship between Anglican and Nordic and Baltic Lutheran churches as well as the bi- and multi-lateral dialogues in which those churches had been involved, that the discussions which led to the Porvoo Common Statement were undertaken. The "developing ecumenical method" and the approach of BEM referred to above helped create an atmosphere in which the historically sensitive issue of the apostolic succession of bishops could be handled in a fresh way.

It was important for both sides to try to understand the religious and emotional significance of the matter for the other. Anglicans (particularly Anglo-Catholics) needed to understand why it was important for Danish and other Lutherans that their ecclesial integrity was not impugned despite their churches' having been forced by historical experience and theological conviction to abandon a particular concept of the apostolic succession. On the other hand, Lutherans needed to appreciate why the issue was for some (although not all) Anglicans a matter of no less significance for their sense of being a church. The differences on this matter were particularly painful because both sides thought of themselves as "orthodox."[18]

We shall have to consider what is meant by the historic episcopal succession, and also examine what is signified by saying both that it is a sign and that it is not a guarantee of the continuity and unity of the church.

Apostolic Succession

The nineteenth-century wit and Anglican clergyman Sidney Smith is said once to have observed that of course he believed in the apostolic succession; how else could one explain the descent of the then bishop of London from Judas Iscariot?

As an expression, "apostolic succession" is commonly used to signify an unbroken line of episcopal ordinations from the apostles to the bishops of our own day.

This is usually understood to imply at the least, and to some minds only, that the persons ordained to the episcopate today received their ordination by the laying on of hands by normally not less than three bishops who themselves had been thus ordained, and so on back to the time when the apostles transmitted the communicable parts of

18. The term "orthodox" is at this point no kind of evaluative epithet. It refers merely to the position of those churches that claim a historic episcopal inheritance and who regard this as one of the marks of their own church. The post-Reformation Church of England has always regarded this as one of its own characteristics, although opinions have varied as to the significance or normative nature of this stance. As is well known, the Roman Catholic Church (and since the ordination of women to the priesthood many Eastern Orthodox churches as well) does not consider the episcopate of the Church of England to stand within this succession.

their ministry to those who, whether as missionaries or ministers of settled communities, would continue to plant and pastor the church.

Closely associated with this understanding is a sense that the historical continuity of the church from the apostles is theologically significant and that somehow "bishops" as such constitute the one indispensable ingredient in this.

Concern for the good ordering of the ministry and its transmission may be traced to the first century, to the New Testament (especially the Pastoral Epistles) and to the Letter of Clement of Rome to the Corinthians. The "apostolic succession" as popularly understood, however, emerged as a significant theme in the late second and early third centuries, when, in the face of heresy, such writers as Hegesippus, Irenaeus, and Tertullian were at pains to establish clearly how the authentic apostolic teaching was to be recognized and where and by whom it was found to be authoritatively preached.

It was, in other words, precisely in this context, along with a growing desire to identify those New Testament scriptures which should be regarded as canonical and to define the church's "rule of faith," that the historic continuity of the episcopate first came to be stressed. A central idea was that of the traceability of the teaching in the contemporary church back to the apostles. The point at issue is of course that it should be the same faith the apostles taught, and that the faith is the same in whatsoever church it is taught today. Because it is *apostolic* the succession witnesses to catholicity in space as well as time (what are sometimes called the "synchronic" and the "diachronic" aspects of catholicity).

There is thus a rich interplay between the historicity and the unity of the church; between Scripture, Creeds, and Tradition; between the faith that is handed on and those through whom it is handed on.

Succession in Apostolic Faith and Life

Underlying the debate about the historic episcopal succession are differences of conviction or emphasis about the nature of the church and its participation in the mystery of God's work in Christ. For example, is the church primarily an instrument for proclaiming the gospel and serving the world in Christ's name, or is it, rather, in the first place a mystery revealed by faith, manifesting the end to which all things are called? The same question already surrounds the ministry of the Twelve, who may be seen either as those called and sent by Jesus to further his mission, or as symbolic signs of the ingathering of Israel.

Of course, these are not necessarily incompatible alternatives, although stressing one extreme to the exclusion of the other can make them appear so. As a result, some Christians wish to stress the functional ministerial aspects of episcopacy, while others emphasize the symbolic, representational dimensions of this ministry, seen especially when the bishop acts as president of the eucharistic assembly.

What both sides in this debate should be able to agree on is that anything said about the succession of bishops is an element in the succession and continuity of the church as a whole, living throughout the ages as a witness (both sign and instrument) to what God has done and to the end to which that points.

Christ promised to be with his disciples until the end of the age and the Spirit is given to lead them into all the truth. Similarly, in the Eucharist, the church shows forth the Lord's death (a historic event in the past) until he comes (eschatological fulfillment). In the proclamation of the gospel, in liturgical celebration, in service to the world, and in mutual support and solidarity, Christians claim Christ's promise and find their confidence therein. Any talk of the inerrancy of Scripture, or of the church's indefectibility or infallibility (including papal infallibility) is based on this. This is also the context in which to understand the place of the historic episcopal succession within the apostolicity of the church as a whole.

Unfortunately, during the centuries, various pressures and particularly the schisms that split East from West, and, more recently, fractured the unity of the Western church, led to a breakdown of this balanced integrity of Christian truth and its authoritative proclamation. A consequence has been that separated churches have sought "guarantees" of the authenticity of their faith in different places or aspects of the Christian tradition or applied different hermeneutical tools.

It seems to me that it is within the context of this phenomenon that we should seek to evaluate the phrase "sign but not guarantee."

The expression has been widely used and quoted since BEM. In particular, as already observed, its use enabled the Anglican and Lutheran Porvoo churches to find a common formula for episcopacy, thus overcoming one of the apparently insurmountable obstacles in the way of ecumenical rapprochement. It enabled Anglicans, whose practical commitment to the historic-episcopal-apostolic-succession has been unwavering in practice since the Restoration, to maintain their pragmatic principles, even if they have never been able or willing to express that commitment in terms of dogma. It enabled Lutherans, for whom it was dogmatically necessary *not* to express any willingness to commit themselves doctrinally to any such necessity, to do so pragmatically.

Was this the supreme ecumenical fudge, or a useful and commendable ecumenical instrument? Some critics, to be sure, have suggested that this has been at the price of evacuating the concept of the succession per se of any serious instrumental value. This is because they understand it as implying that episcopacy in its commonly understood historical form is an optional, albeit desirable, form of church government but lacking any particular theological mandate or charism.

A lot depends on how we understand the significative-symbolic character of sacramental practice and language. This raises huge questions, whose treatment lies far beyond the scope of this brief essay or the competence of its author. They are, however, vital for the proper consideration of these matters. For example, among some who are most suspicious of sacramental language there is however a strong commitment to understanding the Bible as "the word of God" and who make correspondingly high claims for the place of Holy Scripture as the supreme authority in the church.

What is at stake is the way bishops exercise oversight over the continuity, fidelity, and unity of the whole church. Episcopé involves guardianship of the Christian tradition as a whole. Central to this is the celebration of the liturgy, preaching, teaching, and pastoral care, including the right direction of the church. No less important is guardianship of all that makes for *koinonia:* fellowship, unity, sharing in spiritual and material goods, solidarity in suffering — and all this not merely within that particular (part of the) church directly committed to their care, but in their "care of all the churches." All this is implied in apostolicity.

It should go without saying, that in every aspect of this guardianship bishops should never be seen as individual actors, but as fellow disciples alongside their baptized brothers and sisters, for whom they have been called to exercise this particular ministry.[19]

This is well expressed in the *Valamo Statement* of the Catholic-Orthodox international commission.

> (44) The one and only ministry of Christ and his apostles remains active in history. This action is, through the Spirit, a breakthrough of "the world to come," in fidelity to what the apostles transmitted of what Jesus did and taught. (45) The importance of this succession comes also from the fact that apostolic tradition concerns the community and not only an isolated individual, ordained bishop. Apostolic succession is transmitted through local churches ("in each city," according to the expression of Eusebius; "by reason of their consanguinity of doctrine," according to Tertullian in the *De Praescriptione*, 32, 6). It is a question of a succession of persons in a community, because the *Una Sancta* is a communion of local churches and not of isolated individuals. It is within this mystery of *koinonia* that the episcopate appears as the focal point of apostolic succession.[20]

Conclusion

The Church of England House of Bishops paper *Apostolicity and Succession* answers in a sentence the fundamental question explored in this essay: "The various elements of apostolicity, working together, maintain and nurture the local churches and bind the local churches together in continuity with the Church of the apostles."[21]

The issue is how the elements work together, and whether some are more load bearing than others. No church claims that the apostolic succession of bishops is a guarantee of fidelity apart from wider considerations of faithfulness to the apostles' teaching and fellowship. It is

19. Cf. St. Augustine: "With you I am a Christian; for you I am a bishop."

20. "The Sacrament of Order in the Sacramental Structure of the Church with particular reference to the importance of Apostolic Succession for the Sanctification and Unity of the People of God," *Valamo 1988* paragraphs 44, 45.

21. *Apostolicity and Succession* §41.

however apparent that for some it is a possibly useful element in the apostolic succession of the church, while for others it is one of the indispensable marks and instruments of it.

The churches have thus some way to go before we would be able to speak of ecumenical consensus or convergence even among the historically episcopal churches themselves.[22]

I find myself left intrigued by certain differences in the language used by different churches and dialogues about the extent to which the historic episcopal succession is a guarantee or sign of the apostolicity of the church.

The Porvoo Common Statement says that it "first . . . bears witness to the Church's trust in God's faithfulness to his people and in the promised presence of Christ with his Church, through the power of the Holy Spirit, to the end of time; secondly, it expresses the Church's intention to be faithful to God's initiative and gift, by living in the continuity of the apostolic faith and tradition; thirdly, the participation of a group of bishops in the laying on of hands signifies their and their churches' acceptance of the new bishop and so of the catholicity of the churches; fourthly, it transmits ministerial office and its authority in accordance with God's will and institution" (§48).

The Vatican response to BEM said, "episcopal succession can rightly be called a *guarantee* of the continuity and unity of the church, if one recognizes in it the expression of Christ's faithfulness to the church until the end of time."

The Porvoo expression of the matter is concerned with the way in which "the use of the sign" of episcopal succession witnesses to the earthly church's response to God's faithfulness ("it bears witness to the Church's trust in God's faithfulness to his people"). The Roman Catholic statement refers to its conviction that the episcopal succession is "the expression of Christ's faithfulness to the church."

It is of course all too easy to read more into words than is intended, but it seems reasonable to press the question of this divergence of language. Are those who talk about "the use of the sign" of episcopal succession referring to the same reality as those who talk about the episcopal succession? Is the episcopal succession a gift of God to the

22. This does not of course begin to take account of those Christian communities and groups who see no place at all for a historically transmitted ministry.

church or part of the way in which the church may structure itself for a faithful response?

This essay may raise more questions than it answers. I conclude however that the expression "sign but not guarantee" may be ecumenically useful provided the word "sign" is understood strongly ("efficacious sign") and "not guarantee" is taken as an indication that none of the several "signs" of the church's apostolicity can stand alone and apart from the others.

Apostolicity and Apostolic Succession in the Porvoo Common Statement — Necessary or a Mere "Optional Extra" in the Church's Life?

OLA TJØRHOM

Within some of the Nordic Lutheran churches — and even more within the larger Lutheran constituency, it has been argued that the Porvoo Common Statement (PCS) pays too much attention to questions related to ministry, episcopacy, and apostolicity. For some, this emphasis points towards a largely hierarchical perception of the church. Moreover, it has been indicated that the Porvoo approach may be somewhat counterproductive in view of the essential contemporary challenges that are at the core of the church's mission.

There are several reasons why the Porvoo commission felt it necessary to emphasize episcopacy and apostolicity. One is the simple fact that these questions always have been central in the official dialogues and the theological discussions between Anglicans and Lutherans. Another reason is a growing awareness among the commission members that apostolicity and the need of apostolic leadership is crucial precisely in relation to the mission of the church. Additionally, such leadership was seen as a bond of continuity in the church's life — and, thus, as a fundamental requirement in manifesting the church as a *communio* across time as well as space.

This means that we were firmly set on depicting apostolicity and apostolic continuity *not* as a retrospective, predominantly "nostalgic" concern, but as a reality that contributes fruitfully to the life and mission of the church today. More concretely, we were determined to picture episcopal leadership in apostolic succession as something that effectively serves the unity of the church — or rather the church's witness to unity in a divided world. We also saw such leadership as a feasible answer to the leadership vacuum — or even crisis — which increasingly comes through as an obstacle to the church's mission.

For me personally, the Porvoo process led to a partly new understanding of apostolicity, apostolic succession, and apostolic leadership: These factors cannot be seen solely as links — or as a kind of "pipeline" — to the past. What is at stake here is rather the following: (a) A living bond with the apostolic witness to Christ — and, thus, to Christ as the cornerstone of the church; (b) a similarly living bond to and manifestation of the church as a communion across time and space; and (c) an effort to respond to the most vital — and ever more burning — issue or requirement of securing a functioning spiritual leadership in our churches.

Clearly, questions relating to episcopacy, apostolicity, and succession were not easy to handle among the Porvoo partners. Not the least at this point, the participating churches reflected widely diverging theological positions as well as structural or ministerial practices. However, as far as I am concerned, we largely succeeded in locating an approach that had the capacity of reconciling differing views and providing the basis of communion between the involved churches. In the following, I shall try to explain this approach further — using a model which, in my opinion, possesses an ecumenical potential that may prove to be of relevance significantly beyond the Porvoo partners.

I. What Is Apostolicity? Some General Theological Observations

Let me begin with some terminological and conceptual remarks. The three central terms in this connection are "apostolicity," "apostolic succession" or *successio apostolica,* and "the historic episcopate" in apostolic succession.[1] On the one hand, these terms cannot be seen as identical. "Apostolicity" is a fundamental mark of the *Una sancta* — i.e., something that is absolutely indispensable in the church's life. Even if

1. Admittedly, the expression "historic episcopate" has its limitations. And as far as I can see, it has been used regularly only within an Anglican context. However, since it is difficult to find appropriate alternatives, I have decided to stick to this expression. What is meant here is obviously "episcopacy in historic apostolic succession."

"apostolic succession" often is associated primarily with the episcopal office, it can also be applied as a description of the wide process by which the apostolic nature of the church is kept up and manifested today. And then "the historic episcopate" becomes one sign among many of the *successio apostolica*. This *inter alia* indicates that we have to avoid identifying or confusing "apostolicity" with "the historic episcopate." On the other hand, there is, in my opinion, a vital interconnection among these three concepts which can be described along the following lines: "Apostolicity" is continued and becomes manifest in the lives of the churches through "apostolic succession." And this succession is expressed through a number of signs, among which "the historic episcopate" plays a crucial role. Accordingly, "apostolicity" and "the historic episcopate" can also not be torn completely apart from each other. In the wake of this brief account, a number of vital theological observations can be deduced. I shall here have to settle with mentioning five essential points — points that I see as being basically in keeping with the Porvoo statement:[2]

First, apostolicity is not simply a "pipeline" to the past, but must primarily be perceived as an expression of living continuity with Jesus Christ through the ministry of his apostles. Now, this continuity is anchored in the apostolic witness to Christ — or more precisely, in the historic reality of what the apostles saw and heard in their fellowship with Jesus on earth. And it is being transmitted to us within the framework of a historic form or pattern that is by no means random — a pattern that should not be exposed to our desperate desire to reinvent the wheel every now and then. At this point, John Henry Cardinal Newman is clearly correct in criticizing Protestantism for having lost the sense of history. However, our vital continuity with the Early Church must always be understood as a continuity in Christ and not

2. Seen in the light of the evident ecclesiological and ecumenical significance of the question of apostolicity and its implications, it is somewhat surprising to note that the systematic-theological literature on this question is relatively modest. And while a significant amount of the existing contributions deal with apostolicity and "something," comparatively few of them can be seen as attempts to account for the apostolicity of the church and of Christian life in a broader perspective. On the Roman Catholic side, Otto Karrer and Yves Congar must be mentioned here. Among Anglicans, *inter alia* Oliver Tomkins and Richard Norris should be registered. And on the Lutheran side, Carl Braaten and Hans Asmussen in my opinion call for particular attention.

as mere nostalgia — indicating that Christology is more important than history here. Furthermore, while the apostles are essentially instrumental to apostolicity, Christ is its main content. Seen in this perspective, apostolicity comes through as a pointer to the church's Christological foundation as the body of Christ. And it is only in this sense that apostolicity can be described as absolutely indispensable to the church — or as a constitutive *nota* or mark of the *Una sancta.* Subsequently, one may even argue that among the four ecclesiological marks or attributes that are listed in the Nicene Creed, apostolicity emerges as the key factor — just as Jesus Christ is the church's cornerstone.

Second, being a fundamentally Christologically-anchored *nota ecclesiae,* apostolicity cannot be confined to certain sectors, but must be manifested in the church in its totality. Accordingly, the apostolic *nota* cannot be restricted to the ordained ministries of the church, but must be attached to and reflected through the life and mission of the whole people of God. This becomes particularly visible when the people together or individually affirm the apostles' witness to Christ by confessing the apostolic faith in accordance with Holy Scriptures as contained in the symbols of the Ancient Church. Seen on this background, there can be no true apostolicity without a confession of the one apostolic faith as being handed over from the apostles. However, this does not mean that apostolicity can be reduced to a doctrinal concern in a narrow sense. What is at stake here is rather an expression of Christian and ecclesial life in its fullness. And it definitely includes the church's apostolic mission in the world.

Third, within this broader approach to apostolicity, there is a need for specific expressions and signs that will help us to avoid a vague and abstract perception of the apostolic nature of the church. Such signs are essential in manifesting and visualizing apostolicity — at the same time serving as specific markers of its fundamental significance. Generally, the rather "docetic" approach to apostolicity that has become pre-eminent within Pietism as well as Liberal Neo-Protestantism has proved to be clearly insufficient and must be avoided. Trying to concretize the relevance of the sign in this connection, I would like to underline the following points: (a) On the one hand, *signum* and *res* — the sign and the "thing" itself must not be flatly identified. There is always the possibility that the *res* can survive even if several of its *signa* have been lost. (b) On the other hand, *signum* and *res* should also not be torn completely apart. At this point, there may be a certain relevance to the Lutheran Reformers' insistence that the sacramental promise or grace will only be fulfilled in connection with the sacramental element or sign. (c) This implies that the churches should not apply a reductionist or juridical approach at this point — asking which signs of apostolic continuity can be seen as absolute requirements in terms of validity. Here we should rather open up for as many appropriate apostolic signs as ever possible as an expression of how crucial this aspect is — without confusing *signum* and *res*. This, furthermore, implies that signs of apostolicity should never be seen as entities that belong to the "private property" of individual or parochial churches. Apostolicity is best and most fully expressed in fellowship — i.e., when we share each other's apostolic signs within the framework of a living communion.

Fourth, within the rich multitude of feasible apostolic signs, the church's ordained ministries in general and the episcopal office in particular are of fundamental significance. This does not mean that these signs are more important than others, but that ordained servants of the church have a special responsibility to witness to, safeguard, and express apostolicity. And they have been equipped with a distinct authority in order to be able to execute this task. These apostolic leaders are not supposed to repeat what the first apostles did — since this neither can nor needs to be repeated. However, their vocation is to represent an appropriate continuation of an apostolically based leadership under new circumstances — simply because the church can neither fulfill its mission nor safeguard its identity without a functioning spiritual leadership. Subsequently, the apostolicity of the ordained ministries is expressed most directly through ordination — being understood as an integration in a college of fellow bishops and priests across time as well as space.[3] The fact that the practice of continuous episcopal ordinations occasionally has been broken, and still may be broken,

3. A most helpful account of ordination in this perspective can be found in a brief appendix to the Roman Catholic–Lutheran dialogue statement "Facing Unity: Models, Forms and Phases of Catholic-Lutheran Church Fellowship" from 1985. Cf. H. Legrand, *The Practice of Ordination in the Early Church*, pp. 68ff. It should be remembered that ordination can be described as a sacrament within Lutheran theology, too. See Melanchthon's account in his Apology of the Augsburg Confession (art. XIII, BSLK 293, 10f.).

does not negate its potential as an essential sign of apostolicity. And it certainly does not mean that we are today at liberty to dispense with this practice at any given moment. Seen in this perspective, Jerome's defense of a "presbyteral succession" emerges as an exception that should not be made the rule.

Fifth, to be an apostle means to be sent by Christ. Accordingly, the apostolic church is the church that has been sent *(apostellein)* by its Lord to serve humanity, the world, and God's creation as a whole — making it perfectly clear that mission forms an essential part of its apostolic nature. Furthermore, the aim and purpose of this church is not only that a number of souls shall be saved, but that God's creation shall be liberated from its slavery to corruption. Hence, the apostolic church should be perceived as the priest of creation and as the sign and anticipation of a reunited humankind. Seen in this perspective, an evident link between catholicity and apostolicity also emerges: The apostolic mission of the church is the project that aims at the full realization of its catholicity — i.e., at the time when God will "bring everything together under Christ, as head, everything in the heavens, and everything on earth" (Eph. 1:10).[4]

This brings my very brief presentation of the church's apostolicity to an end. The goal here has certainly not been to give a full theological account of apostolicity, but rather to emphasize certain features that are crucial when it comes to understanding Porvoo's approach at this point. However, before I move on to the background and contents of PCS, I would like to add an even shorter observation on the ecumenical dialogue on the present topic. As far as I can see, this dialogue has for a long time been seriously hampered by two positions that both come through as obvious dead ends: On the one hand, we have those who, at least in practice, falsely identify apostolicity with only one of its signs — most often with the sign of the historic episcopal succession. On the other hand, there are those who are prepared to settle with a purely abstract approach to apostolicity — bluntly disregarding all feasible signs. Both positions come through as clearly lacking — *inter alia* in the sense that neither of them manages to realize that

4. With regard to the vital interrelation and dialectics between apostolicity and mission, cf. C. Braaten, *The Apostolic Imperative: Nature and Aim of the Church's Mission and Ministry* (Minneapolis, 1985).

apostolicity must be seen as a comprehensive ecclesiological category anchored in the life of the church as a whole. In my opinion, one of the most important achievements of the Porvoo Common Statement is its constructive efforts to identify an intermediate position between the two mentioned extremes. And in developing such an intermediate position, a broad and dynamic ecclesiological approach is applied — an approach which makes it clear that apostolicity must be grounded in the reality of the church in its totality.

II. The Larger Framework of Porvoo's Deliberations on Apostolicity

In many respects, the Anglican communion and the Lutheran churches can be seen as converging entities. This depends on the historical fact that both traditions are somehow anchored in the Reformation, as well as on a significant amount of theological consensus. However, the understanding of apostolicity and the *successio apostolica* has for a long time been a significant problem in this connection. This mainly stems from the following discrepancy: While apostolic succession in the historic episcopate plays a key role within the Anglican churches, only a limited number of Lutheran churches have kept up this particular sign of apostolicity.[5] And in several of the European Lutheran churches — such as Denmark, Iceland, and Norway — there was a break in this form of succession. This occurred when Luther's collaborator, Johannes Bugenhagen — who was never consecrated as a bishop — ordained so-called "superintendents" in Copenhagen in 1536. In my opinion, however, this act should primarily be seen as a kind of contextually governed emergency solution. The point was simply that there was an evident need for episcopal oversight in the

5. I am unable to produce a complete list of which Lutheran churches have kept the episcopate in apostolic succession. In this connection the Church of Sweden plays a key role — already from the time of the Reformation keeping and safeguarding this sign of apostolicity. This was also the case with the Evangelical-Lutheran Church of Finland, partly due to the fact that Finland at that time was ruled by the Swedish king Gustav Vasa. From these churches the Lutheran "version" of the historic episcopate spread — first to the Lutheran churches in Estonia and Latvia, and later to a number of Lutheran churches and dioceses in Africa.

emerging evangelical congregations and churches. And since such oversight could not come from the Roman Catholic Church, the most plausible solution seemed to be to perform their own ordinations. But these acts were not conceived as theologically motivated breaks with the traditional order of the church. They should, thus, neither be theologized and canonized nor perpetuated. Totally misplaced is any impression that the whole identity and integrity of the Reformation movement depends on Bugenhagen's non-episcopal ordinations. Let me add in this connection that even the "superintendents" were basically ordained to a distinct service of oversight in the life of the church. Accordingly, this incident does not represent a total break with the church's episcopal ordering.

Against this background, one might expect that it would be possible for Anglicans and Lutherans to find ways of handling the problem of apostolicity and succession between them. But for a long time, this was clearly not the case. On the contrary, more or less extreme positions were developed within both traditions — extremes that occasionally even became predominant. On the Anglican side, there are examples that the sign of historic continuity in the episcopal office has been overemphasized in a rather isolated manner — pointing in the direction of a mechanical so-called "pipeline" theory in which the key concern was "hands on heads and bottoms on seats." And among Lutherans, this special sign of apostolicity has often, at best, played a marginal role — at worst, no role whatsoever. This has, in some cases, even led to a disregard of all signs or visible manifestations of apostolicity and apostolic continuity — turning this crucial mark of the church into a largely abstract theory. A fresh example of this can be found in the heated U.S. debates on the Episcopal-Lutheran agreement "Called to Common Mission" (CCM) from 1999. Here the militant Lutheran opposition to CCM has insisted on "word alone" as the sole principle — also describing the historic episcopate as "Episcopal DNA," which in the rhetoric of the critics almost sounds like a mortal disease.[6] Generally, there is much in evidence that apostolicity comes through as a more vital concern in churches that have kept the episcopal sign than among those that have lost it.

6. Cf. Meg Madson, "On Adopting Episcopal DNA," *Dialogue* 39, no. 1 (2000): 68ff.

In the 1970s and '80s, official theological dialogues were conducted between Anglicans and Lutherans on international and regional levels.[7] These conversations documented a significant theological convergence, but led to almost no forms of concrete fellowship between the involved churches. And as far as I can see, this simply resulted from the fact that the dialogue commissions were unable to propose feasible and practicable solutions to the problems related to apostolicity and succession — the very problem that was blocking the transformation of achieved theological consensus into real communion. In this way, it was clearly demonstrated that the *successio apostolica* was the main dividing question between the two traditions. In 1982, the publication of Faith and Order's Lima report represented a notable step forward in this area. This was especially the case with regard to its affirmation that episcopal succession can be seen as "a sign, though not a guarantee" of the unity and continuity of the church.[8] However, this statement did not make clear, in more positive terms, what the historic episcopate had to offer in the churches' life. And even if *Baptism, Eucharist and Ministry* (BEM) identified a formula that enabled non-episcopal churches to relate to episcopal succession, this formula did not say much — or anything — about how concrete communion in the episcopal office of unity could be achieved. Accordingly, it soon became clear that the Lima text also needed further elaboration at this point.

Turning to the Porvoo process, it is important to note that all the Lutheran dialogue partners can be described as episcopally ordered. This is demonstrated by the fact that they have kept a personally exercised episcopal office, that this office, at least in practice, functions as a particular "order" distinct from the office of the local pastor, and that persons are being installed in this office for life terms by an act that content-wise and structurally must be seen as an ordination — even if this expression in some cases is not applied explicitly to the consecration of bishops. Admittedly, only the Church of Sweden has officially endorsed a threefold ministerial pattern, while the others adhere more

7. Cf. respectively the international Pullach Report (1972) and the regional European Helsinki Report (1982).

8. Cf. BEM/Ministry §38 — i.e., *Baptism, Eucharist and Ministry*, Faith and Order Paper 111 (Geneva, 1982).

or less explicitly to the traditional Lutheran insistence on the basic "oneness" of the ordained ministry. In my view, however, this "oneness" should mainly be understood as a theological concern — implying that all ministries are one in the sense that they must be anchored in what constitutes the church, namely the service with word and sacrament. But this definitely does not exclude a differentiation of tasks within the "one" ministry that at least in practice comes very close to the threefold ministerial pattern that was developed within the Ancient Church. Personally, I know of few if any Lutheran churches that have fully realized the oneness principle in terms of their ministerial structures. Most of them seem to operate with a certain distinction between the local pastor and some kind of episcopal oversight — often also having an ordained diaconate.

When it comes to apostolicity and the *successio apostolica,* however, the situation is somewhat different. Here the Porvoo process started out with three differing positions — or even three varying ecclesial types: First, churches that have kept up episcopal succession and cherish it as essential in their lives — which with some practical variations was the case with all the Anglican participants. Second, churches that have preserved this kind of succession without necessarily seeing it as theologically essential — i.e., Sweden and Finland, Estonia and Latvia. And third, churches that have lost this sign of apostolicity and traditionally have not been particularly committed to regaining it — i.e., Denmark, Iceland, Norway, and Lithuania.[9] Obviously, these significantly differing approaches were taken into account as a serious challenge at the beginning of the dialogue process. But in spite of this, the goal of the conversations was to produce a solution that would reconcile these three differing positions — at the same time providing the basis for concrete unity between the participating churches in the episcopal office. Seen against this background, the following can be identified as the more specific aim of the Porvoo process: (a) A commitment to contribute to the conversion of achieved doctrinal agreement into concrete communion; (b) an awareness that this would require some kind of solution to the problems connected

9. See on this the essays on the different Porvoo churches in *Together in Mission and Ministry: The Porvoo Common Statement with Essays on Church and Ministry in Northern Europe* (London, 1993).

with episcopal succession; and (c) an attempt to locate an approach that could be applied to the Lutheran churches that have kept the historic episcopate as well as the partners that have lost this particular sign of apostolicity.[10]

III. "The Porvoo Model" — Porvoo's Approach to Apostolicity and Succession

Before looking more closely at the account of apostolicity and apostolic succession in the Porvoo Common Statement, three fundamental concerns should be registered: First, in its deliberations on apostolicity, PCS does not delve directly into the problem of how the historic episcopate should be perceived and how it can be restored in the churches that have lost it. On the contrary, the statement is careful to place this problem in a wider ecclesiological context or — more precisely — to anchor it in the life and mission of the whole people of God. Second, Porvoo aims at locating an intermediate position between two extremes at this point: On the one hand, those who identify apostolicity with only one of its signs, namely the historic episcopate — and on the other hand, those who tend to disregard all concrete signs of apostolic continuity and, thus, often end up with a rather abstract comprehension of this essential *nota ecclesiae.* And third, PCS is less concerned with questions relating to the formal validity of previous ministerial structures. Here the text is more focused on the future — that is, on finding solutions that will be acceptable to all partners, without forcing anyone to renounce their own past. These concerns are essential in understanding what Porvoo tries to achieve — theologically as well as ecumenically.[11]

10. Here it should be noted that agreements between the Church of England and most of the Lutheran Porvoo churches already existed — with the Church of Sweden from 1911, with the Evangelical Lutheran Church of Finland from the 1930s, with the churches in Estonia and Latvia from the later part of the 1930s, and with Denmark, Iceland, and Norway from the 1950s. However, there were significant differences between the agreements with churches that had kept the episcopal succession and those that had lost this apostolic sign.

11. Many commentators have already written on Porvoo and apostolicity — cf. i.a., several of the contributions in J. Puglisi and D. Billy, eds., *Apostolic Continuity of the*

Since the Porvoo Common Statement is readily accessible, there is no need to recapitulate its deliberations on apostolicity and the *successio apostolica* in great detail. I will, therefore, settle with underlining some points and concerns that in my view are particularly important in this connection:

First, PCS pays due attention to the mission and service of the church in the world. This is expressed in the text's initial chapter, where the tasks and challenges that face the Porvoo partners on the contemporary European scene are emphasized. The text further stresses that in light of our common hope, "we are called to . . . work for the furtherance of justice, to seek peace and to care for the created world" (§32l). Moreover, "the church today is charged . . . to proclaim the gospel to all nations, because the good news about Jesus Christ is the disclosure of God's eternal plan for the reconciliation of all things in his Son" (§37). Thus, it becomes clear that the church's apostolicity includes historic continuity as well as an apostolic mission in and for the world. On the one hand, this vital dimension could — and probably *should* — have been stressed more strongly in the statement. On the other hand, the present concern is underlined more explicitly in PCS than in most other bilateral dialogue texts.

Second, PCS affirms that "all members of the church are called to participate in its apostolic mission" — also including a reference to "the corporate priesthood of the whole people of God" (§32i). Furthermore, "the Church is . . . apostolic as a whole" (§37). And this crucial concern is expressed even more strongly when it is stated that "the primary manifestation of apostolic succession is to be found in the apostolic tradition of the Church as a whole" (§39). Accordingly, PCS does not, in any sense, relate apostolicity solely to the ordained ministries, but anchors this essential *nota ecclesiae* in the life and reality of the church and God's people in its totality. This approach is further affirmed by the fact

---

Church and Apostolic Succession, Louvain Studies 21, no. 2 (1996); and H. Roelvink, "Apostolic Succession in the Porvoo Statement," *One in Christ* 30 (1994): 344ff. (Fr. Roelvink was a Roman Catholic observer in the dialogue process.) Moreover, *Internationale Kirchliche Zeitschrift* 90, no. 1 (2000) is dedicated to the discussions on Porvoo at the 35th International Old Catholic Theological Conference in Wislikofen, Switzerland, in September 1999. See further O. Tjørhom, "The Church and Its Apostolicity: The Porvoo Common Statement as a Challenge to Lutheran Ecclesiology and the Nordic Lutheran Churches," *Ecumenical Review* 52, no. 2 (2000): 261ff.

that Porvoo includes a comprehensive section on "The Nature and Unity of the Church" (cf. chapter II). Seen in this perspective, it seems to be difficult to characterize PCS as particularly "hierarchical."

Third, "within the apostolicity of the whole Church is an apostolic succession of the ministry which serves and is a focus of the continuity of the Church in its life in Christ" (§40). The main responsibility of the ordained ministry is "to assemble and build up the body of Christ by proclaiming and teaching the Word of God, by celebrating the sacraments and by guiding the life of the community in its worship, its mission and its caring ministry" (§41) — thus making it clear that the ordained ministry should be seen as a service to the church and the faithful. Subsequently, ordination is described as follows: "The setting aside of a person to a lifelong ordained office by prayer, invocation of the Holy Spirit and the laying on of hands reminds the Church that it receives its mission from Christ himself and expresses the Church's firm intention to live in fidelity to and gratitude for that commission and gift" (§41).

Fourth, according to Porvoo, there is a special "continuity of the ministry of oversight (which) is to be understood within the continuity of the apostolic life and mission of the whole Church" (§46). This "apostolic succession in the episcopal office is a visible and personal way of focusing the apostolicity of the whole Church" (ibid.). The continuity in apostolic succession is in a special manner "signified in the ordination or consecration of a bishop" (§47). Here the particular sign of the laying on of hands is effective in four ways: "First it bears witness to the Church's trust in God's faithfulness to his people and in the promised presence of Christ with his Church, through the power of the Holy Spirit, to the end of time; secondly, it expresses the Church's intention to be faithful to God's initiative and gift, by living in the continuity of the apostolic faith and tradition; thirdly, the participation of a group of bishops in the laying on of hands signifies their and their churches' acceptance of the new bishop and so of the catholicity of the churches; fourthly, it transmits ministerial office and its authority in accordance with God's will and institution" (§48).

Fifth, the practice of "(ordaining) a bishop in historic succession" — or "the historic episcopal succession" — is seen as "a sign" (§50). This sign must be placed "in its full context of the continuity of proclamation of the gospel of Christ and the mission of his Church" (§50).

The use of the sign of episcopal succession "does not by itself guarantee the fidelity of a church to every aspect of the apostolic faith, life and mission" (§51). And "faithfulness to the apostolic calling of the whole Church is carried by more than one means of continuity" (§52). Yet, "the retention of (this) sign remains a permanent challenge to fidelity and to unity, a summons to witness to, and a commission to realize more fully, the permanent characteristics of the Church of the apostles" (§51). Thus, episcopacy should be perceived as "a sign of our intention, under God, to ensure the continuity of the Church in apostolic life and witness" (§32k).

Having given an account of what Porvoo actually says about apostolicity and succession, I would like to offer my interpretation of what this means in terms of our aim to provide a basis for communion between the involved churches in the episcopal office in historic succession. Obviously, the ensuing interpretation is personal and colored by my own theological position. Yet, it is my view that the ten following — rather brief — theses are basically in keeping with PCS's intention:

1. At the outset, it should be emphasized that apostolicity has the church's continuity with the apostolic witness to Christ as its core. This continuity is a living reality and cannot be perceived as a mere "pipeline" to the past or as pure nostalgia. Accordingly, it must be accentuated that the mark of apostolicity does not only point to the apostles as such or in an isolated manner, but directs us to their witness to Christ — thus, actualizing the Christological basis of ecclesiology and Christ as the church's cornerstone.
2. It is in this sense that apostolicity must be seen as indispensable and essential in the life of God's people across time and space. Together with unity, catholicity, and holiness, apostolicity is a crucial *nota ecclesiae* that by necessity belongs to the church's nature. This simply means that without living continuity with our apostolic foundation as a pointer to Christ, no true church can exist.
3. As a fundamental mark of the body of Christ, apostolicity cannot be confined to certain "ecclesiological sectors." Rather, this mark must be seen as something that pertains to the church's existence in its totality — being anchored in and carried by the whole people of God. Thus, apostolic continuity can only be understood

properly within the framework of a broad ecclesiological approach. And in this connection, the continuity that is expressed in our common confession as well as in the doctrine and teaching of the church plays a crucial role, too.

4. However, the requirement of such a broad ecclesiological approach must not be allowed to lead to the reduction of apostolicity to a predominantly abstract or "internal" concern. Being essential to the church, it must be kept in our "living memory." And this indicates that apostolic continuity calls for concrete, visible expressions or signs that can serve as constant reminders of this fundamental ecclesial mark.
5. In the life of the church, there is a wide variety of apostolic signs — and it does not make much sense to try to present them within the framework of a theological ranking. But even if the ordained ministry in its different forms is only one among several signs of apostolicity, these ministries have been entrusted with a special responsibility for interpreting and safeguarding the church's apostolic nature and continuity.
6. This responsibility applies in a particular way to the office of the bishop and the exercise of *episkopé* — being a special sign of unity and continuity in the life of the church. Normally, episcopal continuity is manifested through prayer and the laying on of hands in the ordination of bishops by fellow bishops. But this concern can also be reflected in other ways, such as through a continuity in ancient episcopal sees.
7. On the one hand, apostolicity should not be exclusively identified with its signs — and especially not with only one of these signs. This indicates that a basic apostolicity can be kept up also in periods when some of its signs have been lost. On the other hand, *signum* and *res* — the sign and the "thing" itself — should never be torn completely apart. And it seems clear that no church can afford to neglect a single potential sign of the apostolic continuity that is essential to Christian life.
8. In view of the historic episcopate, Porvoo neither says that this sign is an absolute juridical requirement nor that it can be reduced to a mere "optional extra" in the church's life. At this crucial point, PCS argues that while churches that possess this special sign are enabled to affirm the apostolic continuity of others,

churches that have lost it are freed to regain their unity with the episcopal office in historic continuity (cf. §52).

9. Porvoo actually invites the participating churches to share their different signs of apostolicity with each other within the framework of a living communion. Accordingly, it is incorrect to claim that the Lutheran partners at this point are only passive recipients and not active contributors. On the contrary, all the concerned churches have vital gifts to bring here.
10. In general terms, the Porvoo Common Statement presupposes that apostolicity is expressed better and more fully in communion — advocating a "catholic" approach to the apostolic nature of the *Una sancta.* And in this way, PCS corrects the counterproductive attitude, ecumenically speaking, that signs of apostolicity can be seen as factors that belong to the "private property" of parochial churches.

The approach to the church's apostolicity presented in PCS can be described as "the Porvoo model." This is the core and main asset of the present text. On this basis, and together with the other parts of the statement, a foundation for communion in faith and confession, in sacramental life and ministry, in mission and service to the world is provided — also including full interchangeability of episcopally ordained bishops, priests or pastors, and deacons. I cannot here go into the discussion whether PCS should be understood as an expression of "full communion" in detail. But allow me the following brief remark: On the one hand, it is correct that Porvoo never speaks explicitly about "full communion." And in this way, what could be seen as an inappropriate "grading" of communion as well as an unjustifiable anticipation of the ultimate eschatological goal of our ecumenical efforts is avoided. On the other hand, it is definitely not possible to downgrade the outcome of PCS to a mere step towards unity. On the contrary, all the key marks of communion are being dealt with and explored here. This is confirmed by the fact that Porvoo succeeds in uniting the three differing "ecclesial types" listed earlier in this paper. This must be seen as a significant ecumenical achievement.[12]

12. Looking at the recent Anglican-Lutheran dialogue in this perspective, it seems clear that only "Called to Common Mission" from the USA, the Canadian Waterloo

One point must be emphasized in the wake of my presentation of the PCS approach to apostolicity. In its efforts to realize "a united ministry" (§28) and a similarly united episcopal ministry in historic apostolic succession, Porvoo deviates markedly from the Leuenberg Concord of 1973 between Reformed, United, and Lutheran churches on the European continent. To start with, episcopal succession is for obvious reasons a neglected concern in the Leuenberg text. Additionally, the Concord settles with a "mutual recognition" of ministries — while remaining silent on how these ministries are to be understood theologically and exercised practically in the lives of the churches. Thus, one is left with an unclear impression of what is supposed to be "recognized" — at the same time at least implicitly conceding to the static temptation of parochial churches to "remain as they are." At the risk of repeating myself, I must confess that it continues to astonish me that the Church of Norway has found it possible to sign Porvoo as well as Leuenberg. An echo of the enigma of the 1973 Concord can be identified in the Reuilly Common Statement from the talks between the British and Irish Anglican Churches and the Lutheran and Reformed Churches in France (1997). Here the Protestant dialogue partner — somewhat awkwardly — insists that "mutual recognition" includes "full communion" and interchangeability of ministries (cf. Reuilly, §27). This also represents a totally different approach than the one advocated in PCS. Generally, it is important to note that Porvoo transcends the traditional "models" of unity. This has made it difficult for some proponents of these models — be it of "organic union" or "reconciled diversity" — to fully grasp what PCS is aiming at. In my opinion, however, our efforts to find new ways forward have benefited much from our readiness to leave old models behind — models that more and more have come to function as ecumenical straitjackets.[13]

Agreement (2001), and Porvoo aim at realizing actual communion. The other texts — i.e., the German-English Meissen Statement (1991), the French-British Reuilly Statement (2001), and the Australian report "Covenanting for Mutual Recognition and Reconciliation" (not yet formally received by the churches) — primarily represent significant steps towards unity.

13. A critical assessment of the present tendency — especially among Protestants — to settle with static diversity can be found in O. Tjørhom, "The Goal of Visible Unity: Reaffirming Our Commitment," *Ecumenical Review* 54, no. 1 (2002): 162ff. Here I also deal more extensively with a Leuenberg type of ecumenism.

As indicated above, Porvoo does not maintain that the sign of historic succession in the episcopal office must be understood as "necessary" in the sense that churches that have lost this sign of continuity are seen as invalid or substantially deficient. Similarly, the text makes it clear that apostolicity is attached to and expressed by a multitude of signs. Yet, this definitely does not mean that the historic episcopate in apostolic succession can be considered as a mere "optional extra" in the church's life or something we are at liberty to pick and choose as it suits us. Here I would like to quote PCS §52, a key paragraph: On the one hand, "a church which has preserved the sign of historic episcopal succession is free to acknowledge an authentic episcopal ministry in a church which has preserved continuity in the episcopal office by an occasional priestly/presbyteral ordination at the time of the Reformation." On the other hand, "a church which has preserved continuity through such a succession is free to enter a relationship of mutual participation in episcopal ordinations with a church which has retained the historical episcopal succession, and to embrace this sign, without denying its past apostolic continuity." This effort to identify an intermediate position may not make total sense logically, but in my opinion it makes much sense theologically. And its key point is the conviction that *signs of apostolicity should not be perceived as juridical requirements or commands, but rather as God's rich gifts to his church in Christ through the Holy Spirit — gifts that none of us can afford to reject and that we share with each other in communion.*[14] Thus, Porvoo receives BEM's position — at the same time moving beyond its "negative" affirmation that succession is "not a guarantee."

Along these lines, it becomes clear that even if Porvoo does not contain judgments on previous validity, it still presents concrete challenges to all the involved churches: Anglicans are challenged to acknowledge and integrate the signs of apostolicity that have been central to the Lutheran tradition such as the underlining of the authority of Holy Scripture, the focus on continuity in the service with word and sacrament, and the emphasis on mission. Obviously, none of these fac-

14. It should be noted that the focus on juridical requirements of unity can be presented within a maximalist as well as a minimalist framework. While the first approach lists all the factors that are necessary for unity or validity, the latter is more concerned with all the factors that must *not* be seen as necessary. On the Lutheran side, the last position is often associated with a minimalist interpretation of *Confessio Augustana* Art. VII.

tors are in any sense new to Anglicans. But to honor them as apostolic signs may represent a certain widening of a traditional Anglican perception of apostolicity. On the Lutheran side, the concern that continuity should be expressed in liturgy and worship, the broad sacramental approach to the church as well as to Christian life in general, and — for those churches who have lost it — the desire to regain the sign of episcopal succession are vital challenges. Generally, PCS does not settle with a static affirmation of the churches as they are, but invites them into a dynamic change or growth in unity. Thus, the text is in keeping with René Beaupère's important insistence that the reunited church lies beyond all existing ecclesial realities.[15] At stake here is our commitment to making our unity visible in and for the world.

In light of an in some cases less than convincing reception process,[16] there is much evidence that the element of change and growth in unity should have been stressed more strongly in the Porvoo text. This *inter alia* applies to the statement that mutual participation in episcopal ordinations should only occur "normally" (cf. §58b.iv). If such participation had been made an absolute rule, the three Icelandic Lutheran bishops would have had time for little else than traveling to episcopal consecrations in their Anglican and Lutheran sister churches. Still, it becomes a problem if this statement is taken as a sign that such mutual participation actually does not contribute significantly to our communion, and thus, that individual bishops can abstain from it. In the wake of this, I would like to underline that the main challenge for the Porvoo fellowship in the time ahead is to develop and sustain the achieved unity on the structural level. Such structures would promote dynamic growth in fellowship between the Porvoo churches and emphasize the binding character of our communion. But they would contribute first and foremost to making our unity visible as a witness in a divided world — a concern that is strongly endorsed in PCS's initial chapters.

15. Cf. R. Beaupère, "What Sort of Unity?" in *What Kind of Unity?* Faith and Order Paper 69 (1974): 38.

16. Here I shall settle with mentioning evident setbacks in the Porvoo process within the Church of Norway. This is *inter alia* reflected in the — totally unnecessary — decision of the Bishops' Conference that deans shall still be allowed to ordain. And more recently, an official report on the ministry has been issued (*Embetet i Den norske kirke* [February 2001]) containing viewpoints and suggestions that are by and large incompatible with PCS.

Regardless of this lack, however, I will argue that the Porvoo Statement should be seen as a considerable ecumenical achievement. And this particularly applies to the "Porvoo model" with its approach to apostolicity and succession. The point here is not that all aspects of the PCS model can be transferred directly to other partners. The present statement is contextual in the sense that it deals with concrete churches with specific features. Yet, in spite of its contextual nature, the approach that is set forth in Porvoo may contribute a solution to the ecumenically-speaking most vital, but still clearly controversial topic of apostolic continuity that will be relevant and applicable in a wider perspective, too. Surely, PCS does not say all there is to say about apostolicity. But there seems to be ample reason to hope that the present text will be helpful in finding new paths forward — when it comes to the theological understanding of apostolic continuity as well as the required ecclesial practice at this point. In this sense, the Porvoo Common Statement can be seen as a feasible "model" or even as a possible ecumenical breakthrough in our continued efforts to achieve visible unity in the episcopal office and to enter into a mutual sharing of our signs of apostolicity.

Apostolicity and Succession in the Porvoo Common Statement: Without Confusion, Without Separation

KIRSTEN BUSCH NIELSEN

The issue of apostolicity and succession takes us to the very heart of the Porvoo Common Statement (PCS). But it also leads directly into a hornet's nest of theological problems, both historical and systematic in character. These problems constitute the complex context within which PCS is to be read. By way of introduction to my account of PCS's conception of apostolicity and succession I shall offer an outline of some of the features of this context. As we shall see, however, the issue of apostolicity and succession as addressed in PCS points beyond the text itself. For in fact, PCS raises a range of questions left unanswered by the text but needing to be addressed in any further elaboration of the interpretation of the document. In my concluding remarks I shall venture a stab at this in respect to one of the outstanding questions, namely the relation between apostolicity and succession. But I begin elsewhere: with the straightforward question as to what apostolicity and succession are really about.

Apostolicity

The term "apostolicity" designates the particular quality attaching to the church's appeal to the gospel in preaching and sacraments, that it be congruent with the biblical witness to Christ's life, death, and resurrection — a witness that is apostolic in virtue of its resting, in a specific sense, on the apostles' witness to Christ. Apostolicity turns on the notions of authenticity and authority in the way in which the church conducts itself in its engagement with the word of God. In the early centuries of church history this normative sense of the term "apostolic" figured in the catholic confession as one of the predicates or marks of the church, which later, in the Lutheran context, were construed as determinations of the church in its true essence, the church of faith, i.e., the church in its hidden aspect. This should not be taken to mean that the church in its manifest aspect, its historical existence, is not constrained by such predicates.[1] Since no one individual Nicene ecclesial predicate can be insulated from the others, inasmuch as they must be viewed as forming an integrated whole, apostolicity applies to the church as one, holy, and catholic, and so to the church as such. That does not mean that apostolicity, both qua theological determination and qua commitment, cannot be distinctively bound up with certain sectors of the church; but that it does not make apostolicity a partial matter. That the meaning of the root *apost-* has to do with "mission" entails that apostolicity involves not only backward-looking credentials but also a forward-looking commitment to mission. The notion of "mission" confers an eschatological perspective on apostolicity. Thus does apostolicity become a prism for the church's relation to time, its existence between eternity and history.[2]

. . . and Succession

In theological vocabulary apostolicity has been coupled with the idea of succession. Implicit in the combination of the two terms in the concept "apostolic succession" is a premise to the effect that the notion of succession is integral to that of apostolicity. This assumption is one to which I shall return, not to contest it but to explore it further. For now, we can limit ourselves to the contention that the coupling of apostolicity and succession receives *prima facie* support from the fact that intrinsic to Christianity and church is the transmission from one genera-

1. See Gerhard Ebeling's dual interpretation of apostolicity (and the other Nicene ecclesial predicates): as the existential basis for the church of faith and qua problem or task for the church in its actual historical existence (1993: 375-78). Cf. the Augsburg Confession 7, and the Thirty-Nine Articles 19.

2. Cf. Pannenberg 1993: 443f. and Nørgaard-Højen 1995: 256-61.

tion to the next of the Christian faith, and that this ongoing reception and transmission (cf. 1 Cor. 15:3) is perforce bound up with continuity and progression.

Apostolicity points both backward and forward and is seen, in its normativity, as something which, in a certain sense, is "redeemed" in a kairos when its retrospective connectedness and its prospective mission are conjoined in the witness to Christ in the here and now in which, in his Spirit, he is present as the contemporary of faith. The notion of succession, by contrast, focuses in a more neutral fashion on the thread "linking" the apostolic origins of preaching with its eschatological perspective. The noun "succession" indicates that one thing follows upon another and that these things which so succeed each other constitute an order, series, or sequence as in the instance mentioned above, namely the transmission of the Christian faith from one generation to the next.

The notion of apostolic succession would seem to indicate that there is a particular form taken by the continuous transmission of the Christian faith, on which rests a special responsibility in respect to apostolicity and through which it finds distinctive expression. In virtue of the way in which the church was constituted in the first centuries, apostolic commitment was linked with succession in the episcopate in particular. This founding of apostolicity in episcopal succession and thus, in dogmatic terms, in ecclesiology, has been retained in Anglican theology. In contradiction to this, the Lutheran standpoint has it that apostolic succession attaches primarily to the proclamation of the gospel, a so-called *successio doctrinalis.* To make the point acutely, apostolic succession is, in a Lutheran understanding, fundamentally a hermeneutical project. It only becomes an issue for ecclesiology and the theology of ministry insofar as, in the words of Martin Luther, the church is engendered by the gospel, qua *creatura verbi.*[3]

3. I do not contravene this when — in drawing on the Christian tradition that forms my background — I echo the Danish pastor, theologian, and popular educationalist N. F. S. Grundtvig, by adding that the locus of succession is the worshiping community of believers when assembled around the word in creed, baptism, and Eucharist. On that understanding succession reposes on "[the] foundation . . . that the Apostles have laid in the name of Christ, and [that they] have laid not in a book, but in the Church itself" (Grundtvig 1984: 129). The quotation is from "Elementary Christian Teachings" (1855-61).

Features of PCS's Theological Context

This brings us to the complex of theological problems that constitute the systematic and historical context of the understanding of apostolicity and succession in the Porvoo Common Statement. I shall sketch some of the features of this context, five in all.

1. The credibility of the ministry of the word in modern times has seemed to the authors of PCS to be a crucial concern. This is attested by the structure of the text. PCS begins with an account of the political and religious realities of today. The political and religious situation is seen as "a new opportunity" for the church's mission and ministry (PCS §§1-2, 10-13). That PCS dedicates itself to this concern testifies to a conception of Christianity that gives priority to the ministry of the word in the world here and now, and by so doing suggests the need for an ongoing interpretation of the scriptures in fresh settings and contexts of understanding. An important feature of PCS's context is the actual *political and religious configurations* in which the text is situated. But more than that: PCS explicitly *contextualizes* itself and conceives of its own task as a task in a specific context. Precisely this contextualization is bound up with PCS's understanding of apostolicity and its accentuation of it as a pivotal theological concept. The connections might have been more clearly elaborated but they are certainly there: from the introduction of "witness and service in God's mission to the world" through "the common challenge to engage in God's mission to the people of our nations and continent" and on to the vision of the church as "participating in the one apostolic mission of the whole people of God" (PCS §§5-7).

2. PCS builds on a strong conception of church. Its second section lays out its ecclesiology while its account of the theological standpoints on which the Anglican and Lutheran churches behind PCS agree — and so which have never given grounds for mutual condemnation — follows only in the third section. In both Anglican and Lutheran eyes, it is untraditional to focus primarily on the issue of church. But PCS does so. It is understood that there is a (new) shared preoccupation with ecclesiology, including the issue of church unity, which has led to contemporary challenges being interpreted in terms of a call to missionary witness and ministry. *The conception of church* is an important strand in PCS's context.

This focused ecclesiological awareness is just what elicited PCS. The unity of the church qua gift and task is the starting point in the endeavor to formulate the conditions for a communion of churches (i.e., PCS §§11 and 21f.) And to this unity belongs apostolicity qua gift and task — or so it might be surmised. But the connection between unity and apostolicity, developed in PCS, remains surprisingly weak. The text merely describes the churches' "common ground" as founded in the shared apostolic tradition (cf. PCS §7) while "[the c]ommunion with God and with fellow believers" is seen as "manifested in . . . the common confession of the apostolic faith" (PCS §24). Instead of going on to unfold the relation between unity and apostolicity, the text immediately moves towards the much-debated issue of ministry (cf. PCS §25).

3. PCS does not primarily seek to resolve historical issues, where the theology of ministry figures as one of the most intractable of Anglican-Lutheran differences. Nor does PCS wish to neglect such issues. The relation between Anglican and Lutheran theology is at its most vexed in what concerns the question of *the understanding of ministry, particularly that of the episcopacy,* and this issue, in its historico-confessional form, is yet another important strand of the context within which PCS raises the question of apostolicity and succession.

4. Against the backdrop of church history it is not surprising that ecumenical studies and dialogue in the twentieth century were especially preoccupied with the understanding of episcopacy qua criterion for interconfessional communion and schism, respectively. What is striking in that relation is the endeavor to dilute the link between apostolicity and episcopal succession. This is related to the formulation of what might be called a *broad approach to the question of apostolicity.* And here we encounter yet another feature of PCS's context.

The endeavor to formulate such a view of apostolicity came to expression under the multilateral ecumenical auspices of the general assembly of the World Council of Churches in 1968. As the report puts it, "[t]he Church is faced by the twin demands, of continuity in the one Holy Spirit, and of renewal in response to the call of the Spirit amid the changes of human history. The Church is apostolic in the sense that all that makes the Church is derived from Christ through the apostles. Apostolicity also means the continuous transmission of the Gospel to all men and nations through acts of worship, witness and human service in the world. The Church is therefore apostolic because she remains true to the faith and mission of the apostles" (Uppsala Report, pp. 15f.). In Faith and Order's document *Baptism, Eucharist and Ministry* (BEM) from 1982, the idea that apostolicity attaches to the church as such is further elaborated and sharpened: "The Church lives in continuity with the apostles and their proclamation. The same Lord who sent the apostles continues to be present in the Church. The Spirit keeps the Church in the apostolic tradition until the fulfilment of history in the Kingdom of God" (BEM Ministry §34). These texts suggest that apostolicity is not merely a predicate of the church as such but also that apostolicity as task and commitment rests on the church as a whole. A distinction is made between "the apostolic tradition of the whole Church and the succession of the apostolic ministry" (BEM Ministry §34 commentary). So the ordained ministry has indeed "a particular task of preserving and actualising the apostolic faith" (BEM Ministry §35). With this commitment to apostolicity the document attempts — with the conception of "the episcopal succession as a sign, though not a guarantee" (BEM Ministry §38) — to forge a "loose" connection to succession in the episcopal ministry. It is also claimed that the church, qua apostolic, is not simply committed to a legacy that lies behind it, but also to a mission that lies before it.

5. That the conception of apostolicity in these texts compels our interest derives from the fact that it constitutes a key presupposition of the conception of apostolicity that took shape in the Anglican-Lutheran ecumenical conversations up to the 1990s and that forms, accordingly, part of PCS's wider context. At an international level this became manifest in 1987 in the Niagara Report. Reiterated in the latter is the emphatic intertwining of apostolicity and church as an accentuation of the idea that apostolicity and mission belong together. The Trinitarian foundation of apostolicity is stressed: "Mission indeed comes to special expression in the church's apostolicity. For apostolicity means that the church is sent by Jesus to be for the world, to participate in his mission and therefore in the mission of the One who sent Jesus, to participate in the mission of the Father and the Son through the dynamic of the Holy Spirit. . . . We believe that all members of the church are called to participate in its apostolic mission" (Niagara Report, §§21 and 68). The stress on the connectedness of apostolicity and church might, as already noted, be regarded as leading to a dilution of the link between apostoli-

city and episcopal succession. However, according to the Niagara Report, this dilution would not entail that the ministry of oversight, episcope — which is the proper concern of the report but which, in an Anglican-Lutheran conversation, cannot in practice be disengaged from the question of episcopacy and episcopal succession — would be nullified as a condition of the church's apostolicity. The text expressly states that "[w]e believe that a ministry of pastoral oversight (episcope), exercised in personal, collegial and communal ways, is necessary to witness to and safeguard the unity and apostolicity of the church" (Niagara Report §69). But the link between apostolicity and the episcopal ministry finds tentative expression, be it only negatively and indirectly. The dispute about episcope is characterized as the Anglican and Lutheran churches' "discharge of the ministry of episcope" and in respect of this "discharge" both churches now confess "[to] have fallen short of the unity and continuity of the apostolic commission" (Niagara Report §76). Since the point that has triggered this "discharge of episcope" is the very understanding of the notion of episcope in the episcopal ministry, including the understanding of the historical episcopacy and ministerial succession, it is precisely these that are in play when the text combines episcope and apostolicity.

The Context Summarized: A Broader and a Narrower Concept of Apostolicity

The conception of apostolicity indicated above has come to inform both the local and the regional Anglican-Lutheran (as well as Anglican-Evangelical) conversations and agreements, including PCS. What distinguishes this understanding of apostolicity also distinguishes PCS.

This applies in particular to the duality we have noted. On the one hand, there is the broad approach to apostolicity in which it is emphasized that apostolicity is something that characterizes the church as a whole — both as a statement about the true church of faith and as an expression of the church's commitment to apostolicity in its historical existence. On the other hand, there is a narrower approach that insists on a special tie linking apostolicity and the episcopal ministry, including episcopal succession, and builds on the premise that apostolicity implies succession and that succession is episcopal succession.

That this duality harbors potential tensions and obscurities is obvious. This is the case with regard to both systematic and confessional concerns. Viewed in a confessional light, the duality of approach disguises the fact that Anglican theologians have engaged in a broader interpretation of apostolic succession than that marking Anglican tradition since the *Act of Uniformity* of 1662 while, conversely, Lutheran theologians in dialogue have focused more sharply on the episcopal succession as the bearer of apostolicity than is implicit in Lutheran theology, whatever the view of episcopal ordination and succession actually presupposed by those theologians.

Having outlined the duality informing the understanding of apostolicity as the pivot of PCS's context we now turn to the text itself.

PCS on Apostolicity and Succession

With regard to apostolicity as a differentia of the church as such, PCS says in the section about the "principal beliefs and practices that (the churches behind the text) have in common," that "all members of the Church are called to participate in its apostolic mission" (PCS §32i). This standpoint is reiterated a little later but without repeating the theologically central emphasis on the common ministry of all the baptized which hallmarks PCS when, in the fourth section devoted to episcopacy and apostolicity, it says that "[t]he Church is called to faithfulness to the normative apostolic witness to the life, death, resurrection and exaltation of its Lord. The Church receives its mission and the power to fulfil this mission as a gift of the risen Christ. The Church is thus apostolic as a whole" (PCS §37).[4] Apostolicity, which as a predicate of the church in its true nature governs the entire church, is associated further by PCS qua task and commitment with the church as a whole. This perspective is one PCS is at pains to articulate.

But what is the relation between apostolicity and succession? Uncovering what PCS maintains on this head is no easy task. As we shall see by examining the subsequent paragraphs in the fourth section, other themes intrude themselves and dominate the picture: the cou-

4. These lines are both prefaced and followed by quotations from the sections of *Baptism, Eucharist and Ministry* as well as the Niagara Report, quoted from above.

pling of apostolicity to the church as well as episcopacy and episcopal succession.

To begin with, PCS conjoins the church's apostolicity with apostolic succession. But it is worth noting that this occurs without the latter being more nearly determined: "[T]he primary manifestation of apostolic succession is to be found in the apostolic tradition of the Church as a whole" (PCS §39, citing BEM Ministry §35). What does this mean? On the one hand, it cannot mean that the apostolic succession should "manifest itself" anywhere other than in the church's apostolic tradition. Were it to do so, then either the apostolic succession or the apostolic tradition would have to be non-apostolic. For what is apostolic succession? And what is apostolic succession in relation to apostolic tradition? These questions are left hanging in the air. On the other hand, the sentence is equally without meaning if it is read as a mere pleonasm. I read the sentence, then, as yet another statement — this time of an almost invocatory strain — to the effect that the apostolicity of the church is fundamentally an attribute of the church as a whole. This is the point that comes through via the questions the sentence leaves open.

With this emphasis in place the text has positioned itself to take the next — decisive — step, which reaches to the delicate question of episcopal succession: "Within the apostolicity of the whole Church is an apostolic succession of the ministry which serves and is a focus of the Church [and this] ordained ministry has a particular responsibility" with respect to witness and the ministry of the word (PCS §40). But the vagueness of the preceding paragraph is carried over. For it remains unclear how "apostolic succession" in the first sentence relates to "apostolic succession of the ministry" in the second. Is there a "primary manifestation of apostolic succession . . . in the apostolic tradition of the Church as a whole," without "[the] apostolic succession of the ministry" being involved? In what, then, does this "primary manifestation of apostolic succession" consist, and how does it relate to episcopal succession?

To enable us to trace the answer delivered by the text we need to get a grip on its understanding of the apostolic ministry as set out in the passages that follow upon those already mentioned. The apostolic ministry, instituted by God, PCS inclines to see as a threefold ministry. With good reason special attention is given to the ministry of oversight and the episcopal ministry. It is nonetheless striking how the apostolic ministry as such seems quietly to evaporate in the section dealing with "Apostolic Ministry" so that towards its close only the episcopal ministry is discussed (PCS §§41-45). Of the bishops it is said, inter alia, that "[t]hey serve the apostolicity, catholicity and unity of the Church's teaching, worship and sacramental life" (PCS §43).[5]

Concerning the service of the episcopal ministry in relation to the apostolicity of the church, the text makes it clear, once more, that this function, in line with the bishop's other ministerial functions, "should [not] be carried out in isolation from the whole Church," and that "[t]he continuity of the ministry of oversight is to be understood within the continuity of the apostolic life and mission of the whole Church" (PCS §§43 and 46). Here too we have to ask what is intended. What is it to *understand* the one (narrow, specific) continuity *within* the other (broad, general) continuity? This question is left open. It is clear, however, that the apostolicity of the church as a whole is, with the words "the apostolic life and mission of the whole Church," once more affirmed. Nor is there any hesitation with respect to the link between the apostolicity of the church and the episcopal ministry. In continuity with the earlier quotation it is stressed that "[a]postolic succession in the episcopal office is a visible and personal way of focusing the apostolicity of the whole Church" (PCS §46). While it was said earlier of the apostolic succession of the ministry that it served and was the focus of the life of the church (cf. PCS §40), in the later context it is the episcopal ministry that in virtue of succession has this commission. That the latter is the conclusion of the text in this area emerges from the following paragraphs that discuss the consecration of bishops. As stated, such consecration signifies apostolic succession (PCS §47). This paves the way for the closing paragraphs, which focus on the historical episcopate as a sign. This is held not only to *signify* but also to *communicate* something. With the consecration of bishops in historical succession "the Church communicates its care for continuity in the whole of its life and mission" (PCS §50, cf. §§50-54). With this sentence, the aposto-

5. Here it is not stated explicitly that the ordained ministry and deacons do not serve apostolicity, but nor is it stated that they do. So there remains an obscurity in respect of the interrelations obtaining between types of ministry and their respective functions as they structure the ordained ministry.

licity, of which the episcopal ministry is the bearer, is reconnected with the dominant theme, the apostolicity of the church. The discussion is brought full circle.[6]

Open Questions Regarding Apostolicity and Succession

However, the circle has been drawn only in respect to this one topic, the so-called broad approach to apostolicity as something that, as both predicate and the expression of a commitment, concerns the church as a whole (cf. PCS §§32i, 37, 39, 43, 46, and 50). On this PCS speaks unequivocally.

In other areas, however, questions remain open. They collect around the topics that lie within what I have termed the "narrow" approach to apostolicity according to which that concept leads to succession, and then leads on to episcopal succession, so that apostolicity and the episcopal ministry including ministerial succession are in effect conjoined (cf. PCS §46 and the ensuing paragraphs on the episcopal ministry and succession qua sign). If there is obscurity here it will shed a blurring light on the broad approach to apostolicity as something that concerns the church as such.

As we have seen, it is unclear whether PCS conceives of a "manifestation of apostolic succession," which — whatever it may be — is not anchored in "[the] apostolic succession of the ministry" (cf. PCS §40). What it means to say in arguing that "[t]he continuity of the ministry of oversight" is to be seen "within the continuity of the apostolic life and mission of the whole Church," also remains open (cf. PCS §46, cf. §43). So PCS leaves open what relation is *fundamentally* presupposed between apostolic succession as such and apostolic succession as bound up with the succession of bishops, just as it leaves open what is meant by "apostolic tradition" in relation to apostolic succession (cf. PCS §39). That PCS is not explicit about what "apostolic succession" means is regrettable. The problem, as seen from a Lutheran perspec-

6. Let me make collective acknowledgment here of those readings of PCS, both critical and constructive, on which my interpretation in the foregoing in the main draws: Dalferth 1999: 29-35, Nørgaard-Højen 1996: 272-79, Tanner 1996: 119-25, and Tjørhom 1996.

tive, is not so much that the concept of apostolic succession in its undefined state might look suspiciously like a Trojan horse, slipping both *successio doctrinalis* and *succession in ministry* in between the lines. For both can find warrant in Lutheran theology. But the significance conferred on each, individually, is crucial. The relation between them is equally so. Within the framework of PCS's own theology is the theory that succession of bishops as a sign is operative. For the sign is the tie linking the apostolic succession as such and the succession of bishops. But the linking function is not unambiguous. As has been justly maintained in the discussion of PCS, there is lack of clarity in respect to the concept of sign, both because of the associations of sacramental theology that it evokes and which are not clarified in the text, and on account of the plurality of theological concepts and ecclesial functions and institutions that are bound together by the sign. There is the further fact that a clarification of the notion of sign does not in itself elucidate how apostolic succession as such is conceived of in the text.[7] That apostolic succession as such is not defined further leaves open for interpretation what understanding of the relation between apostolicity and succession is presupposed by PCS.

It is naturally not the intention of PCS explicitly to raise this as an open question and seek a clarification of it. For it is a question on another level than that of the overriding concern of the text, the issue of "communion" between the Anglican and Lutheran churches of northwestern Europe. In consequence, the text does not deliver an answer to the question — and due to the question's oblique nature, cannot do so. But this does not mean that there is no need for a full account.[8]

Before turning to that point, I interpose here a reflection on how I conceive of such an account.

7. On this see Dalferth 1999: 32f. as well as the chapters on episcopacy noted above. To keep issues separate I prescind in what follows from the fundamental question of the theology of ministry, including a consideration of the relation between the respective ministries of pastor and bishop.

8. Without an elucidation of this other question (the relation between apostolicity and succession) it is difficult to conduct a thoroughgoing analysis of the question of the theology of ministry, especially the issues of episcopal succession and the theology of sign in PCS. My omission of them in what follows should not be taken to indicate that I find them irrelevant. This applies equally to the relation between the ministries of pastor and bishop in relation to succession.

On Apostolicity and Succession after Porvoo — Methodico-Hermeneutic Remarks

What PCS has to say about apostolicity and succession definitely needs to be understood within a specific context. Such a context is required as a horizon of interpretation. However, that is not sufficient for the interpretation of PCS. Read in the light of its context, PCS leaves open a lot of questions about apostolicity and succession. This can be explained by the fact that the dual approach to apostolicity, which PCS has inherited from its predecessors, contains potential tensions and obscurities. The questions that PCS leaves open with respect to apostolicity and succession are related to this duality. These questions and obscurities are, then, — in part — a legacy.

Patently, such open questions must appear criticizable and infelicitous if the text is required to honor a standard of theological transparency that, for better or worse, lies beyond its terms of reference. Theologically, and from an ecclesial perspective, the open questions and obscurities may be disastrous. But so they are only if they remain obscurities unrecognized as such, for then they will paralyze and distort theological reflection and ecumenical dialogue. So it stands to reason that the open questions in PCS need to be addressed.

Whether it is this need that PCS's authors had in mind when, in the concluding Joint Declaration (cf. PCS §58b), they proposed that the signatory churches form a Porvoo Contact Group to follow up on the agreement entered into, I shall not attempt to determine. But the proposal, which has in fact been implemented, could be so interpreted. In any event, it sharpens the sense of PCS as a text that points beyond itself to a continuing practice of interpretation. Just as the interpretation of PCS in its current form as Common Statement and Joint Declaration and now endorsed by its signatories requires that its theological context be taken into account, it must by the same token be required regarding the interpretation of PCS that the exercise extend beyond PCS itself, so that the questions it leaves unanswered may be clarified — wholly or in part, under ecclesial or academic auspices, sooner or later. The question of how the various elucidative and continuing interpretations advanced will be received by the churches endorsing PCS is another matter.

My concluding observations in the following section about the relation between apostolicity and succession must be seen in the light of the need for such a continuing interpretation. They are supported by PCS inasmuch as they raise a crux that lies implicit in it: the relation between apostolicity and succession. But they are not, otherwise, in aim or method, constrained by PCS.

The Relation Between Apostolicity and Succession: Without Confusion, Without Separation

The concept of apostolicity proceeds — to explore the concept as I have understood it in the foregoing — on two levels: an ontological level where apostolicity is a predicate of the church's true nature, and a functional level where the normativity implicit in the predicative use of the concept on the first level is converted to an obligation that rests on the church in its actual life. Apostolicity is a necessary concept inasmuch as it concerns the true nature of the church and thus the criterion for what dogmatics specifies as necessary for salvation. Apostolicity is, categorically speaking, a qualitative matter, namely the church's objective congruence with the apostolic witness to Christ. Since apostolicity is a prism for the church's relation to time, the qualitative comprises a temporal dimension. Here the kairotic plays an important role in that the concept of apostolicity includes a strand that pertains to action and event. Where Christ in his Spirit is present here and now and the believer at once "believes himself/herself into" the church as the Body of Christ, apostolicity as retrospective connectedness and forward-looking missionary commitment interlock. The believer is traditionally spoken of in terms of conversion and reorientation. But these metaphors are aptly applicable to the church too in its coming into existence in apostolicity. Just as it is implicit in the notion of apostle that the apostle does not send himself but is, as a condition of mission, called by another, and turns towards the call and away from his own concerns, so too the notion of church — cf. the etymology of *ekklesia* — involves vocation and conversion and thus, abstractly expressed, contingency and a radical departure.[9]

9. The meaning of call and severance in Christian life has also been developed for the concept of church by the German theologian and priest Dietrich Bonhoeffer in a Lu-

To use the traditional locution, the church is not *of* this world, but is, with its message and its service, *in* the world and *for* the world. Equally, in a certain sense it is both *outside of* and *in* time. Summarily put, this is because both call and mission presuppose an agent that calls and sends — in time. And this other has, in turn, also been called and sent. That succession construed in terms of an ongoing transmission and reception of the gospel is indispensable hardly needs argument. Nor does the fact that succession can, in practice, assume all sorts of forms or that it can find manifold symbolic expressions.[10] But none of this specifies what succession is and is not. In order to capture that, we must bear in mind the nature of the continued transmission and reception. For in that too, as is easily overlooked, there are the marks of contingency and departure, inasmuch as he or she who receives the message from another in faith is converted, called out, and sent away from what is his or her own. But at the same time there remains a mark of continuity and identity within the process of transmission inasmuch as that which is passed on is what one has oneself received. It is *this* continuity that the concept of succession turns on: a continuity which is not unbroken but which proceeds via disjunctive steps. On that understanding of succession it is correct to say that the concept of apostolicity implies a notion of succession.

Apostolicity and succession, then, neither can nor should be separated. In that sense, and in a systematic perspective, apostolicity is a meaningful concept quite apart from its specific content in the history of dogmatics. But neither must apostolicity and succession be confused. That the relation between the two can be captured by what is in itself highly abstract, the Chalcedonian formula, derives from the fact that the necessity attaching to succession in its indispensability is of a different species than that attaching to apostolicity. This dichotomization of necessity is what the dogmatic tradition has sought to identify through the conception of *esse ecclesiae* as against *bene esse ecclesiae.*

---

theran critique of Lutheranism (cf. Bonhoeffer 1959). By so doing he highlights a central dimension of apostolicity.

10. Let me refer again to the theology of signs in PCS, which unquestionably registers — irrespective of how it be appraised — an awareness of the fact that succession can be expressed in various modes, and also suggests that succession may be a sign (or, we might say "mark," in the sense of "hallmark") of the belief in legitimate, i.e., apostolic, teaching and administration of the sacraments (PCS §§47ff.).

But the relation can be approached more nearly, in terms that do more than those of the classic theology of being or substance to exploit the relationality implicit in the concept of church. The dichotomization may be described in terms of the distinction drawn between the so-called ultimate and penultimate. This distinction concerns the divine justification of the sinner through faith as the ultimate against all that which, qua penultimate, has temporally preceded it. The point is that these two must not be separated. For the ultimate is not achievable in the absence of the penultimate. Moreover there is the difference between the two that the ultimate, i.e., divine justification which is likewise, in a qualitative sense, the ultimate, does not need — indeed controverts — the penultimate.[11] Given this distinction, the two must not be confused. Analogously, then, in the case of apostolicity and succession: the church's apostolicity is not realized in ecclesial life without succession, and the concept of apostolicity remains empty without a notion of succession. In that sense, apostolicity and succession must not be separated. But neither must they be confused.

The difference between apostolicity and succession resides in the fact that whereas apostolicity is fulfilled in that *kairos* in which Christ with his Spirit is present in, and for, the church here and now, in that the church in its hidden aspect becomes visible for faith, that other fulfillment is God's work alone — and as such is without "preconditions." Apostolicity in this latter sense interrupts succession in more ways than one. Either by succession being nullified in the eschatological fullness of apostolicity, or by its being judged, in the dogmatic sense, through the normativity that the notion of apostolicity also seeks to express, and whose content is given with the apostolic witness to Christ and so through Christ himself, the gospel.[12]

11. The distinction is Dietrich Bonhoeffer's. The relative necessity of the penultimate in relation to the ultimate's curtailment of the penultimate is described as follows: "A way must be traversed, even though, in fact, there is no way that leads to this goal; this way must be pursued to the end, that is to say, to the point at which God sets an end to it. The penultimate, therefore, remains, even though the ultimate entirely annuls and invalidates it" (Bonhoeffer 1983: 124-25).

12. On this, see Harding Meyer's account of the relation between the gospel, apostolicity, and succession: "[I]n the apostles' witness to Christ lies, so to speak, the point of intersection of the vertical line of God sending Christ, and the horizontal line of the historical process of transmitting the Christ event through the generations" (1996: 170).

Concluding Remarks

With the preceding reflections — representing an attempt to elucidate the question of the relation between apostolicity and succession that PCS, with its broad and narrow approach to apostolicity, leaves open — I have sought to hint at some of the issues that must be part of the continued process of interpretation and reception in any ongoing conversation about what the signatory churches of Porvoo understand by apostolicity and succession.

If it is kept in mind that apostolicity and succession must be neither separated nor confused, then the awareness that succession is — relative to perspective — at once both indispensable and dispensable, will be sharpened. This creates a space for solicitude and care on the part of the churches in relation to succession in the broadest sense.[13] But it also calls for the requisite precision in drawing the boundary of the theological function of succession. When the boundary is so drawn, apostolicity and succession share a criterion: consistency with the apostles' witness to Christ.

And, indeed, the entire discussion cannot but serve as a reminder of how frail and unpredictable both apostolicity and succession are to the extent that they are laid in human hands. When Jesus, according to Mark, sent the apostles "into all the world [to] . . . preach the good news to all creation," one of their number was missing (Mark 16:14f.). The betrayal of Christ lay in close proximity to the witness to him. In a sense, succession has been confused and uncertain from the outset. But the fact that the place vacated by the betrayer, according to Mark's (spurious?!) ending, went unfilled by any other did not render the

13. In this respect, not least Lutheran theologians can learn from PCS. When Eberhard Jüngel says that "[t]he successor of the Apostle is the Canon of the Holy Scriptures of the Old and the New Testament" (2000: 379, my translation, KBN), he articulates a decidedly "Reformational" standpoint. With such close interlocking of the *sola scriptura* and *solus Christus* — principles for which he could as well have invoked Luther as an authority, on the basis, for instance, of the identification of apostolicity with witness to Christ in the Preface to the Epistle of St. James: "Whatever does not teach Christ is not yet apostolic, even though St. Peter or St. Paul does the teaching. Again, whatever preaches Christ would be apostolic, even if Judas, Annas, Pilate, and Herod were doing it" (Luther 1960: 396). But the cost of Jüngel's orthodoxy in this area is that he omits to address the thornier issues relating to succession: that while not necessary, nor is it dispensable.

teaching of the remaining apostles non-apostolic. For what underlay the sending forth of the apostles into the world was Christ's promise to remain with them always.

Bibliography

Bonhoeffer, Dietrich. *Cost of Discipleship* (1937). Translated by Reginald H. Fuller. London: SCM Press, 1959.

Bonhoeffer, Dietrich. *Ethics* (1941-43). Translated by Neville Horton Smith (1965). Gloucester, Mass.: Peter Smith, 1983.

Dalferth, Ingolf. "Ministry and the Office of Bishop according to Meissen and Porvoo: Protestant Remarks about Several Unclarified Questions." In *Visible Unity and the Ministry of Oversight. The Second Theological Conference held under the Meissen Agreement between the Church of England and the Evangelical Church in Germany*, pp. 9-48. London: Church House Publishing, 1999.

Ebeling, Gerhard. *Dogmatik des christlichen Glaubens III* (1979). Tübingen: J. C. B. Mohr (Paul Siebeck), 1993.

Grundtvig, N. F. S. *A Grundtvig Anthology. Selections from the Writings of N. F. S. Grundtvig (1783-1872)*. Translated and edited by Niels Lyhne Jensen, William Michelsen, Gustav Albeck, Hellmut Toftdahl, and Chr. Thodberg. Cambridge/Aarhus: James Clarke & Co./Centrum, 1984.

Jüngel, Eberhard. "Thesen zum Amt der Kirche nach evangelischem Verständnis." In *Indikative der Gnade — Imperative der Freiheit*, pp. 373-80. Tübingen: J. C. B. Mohr (Paul Siebeck), 2000.

Luther, Martin. Prefaces to the Epistle of St. James and St. Jude (1522/46). In *Luther's Works* 35. Edited by E. Theodore Bachmann, pp. 395-98. Saint Louis: Concordia Publishing House, 1960.

Meyer, Harding. *Apostolic Continuity, Apostolic Succession and Ministry from a Reformation Perspective*. In Louvain Studies 21/2: *Apostolic Continuity of the Church and Apostolic Succession*. Edited by James E. Puglisi and Dennis J. Billy, pp. 169-82. Louvain: University of Louvain, 1996.

Nørgaard-Højen, Peder. "Kirken og kirkerne" (The Church and the Churches). In *Vinduer til Guds Rige. Seksten forelæsninger om kirken (Windows of the Kingdom of God. Sixteen Lectures about the Church)*. Edited by Hans Raun Iversen, pp. 249-68. Copenhagen: Anis, 1995.

Nørgaard-Højen, Peder. "Apostolsk succession og bispeembedet. Kritisk læsning af Fællesudtalelsen fra Porvoo" (Apostolic Succession and the Episcopal Ministry. Critical Interpretation of the Porvoo Common Statement). In *Verbum Dei — verba ecclasiae. Festskrift til Erik Kyndal.* Edited by Theodor Jørgensen and Peter Widmann, pp. 266-81. Århus: Århus Universitetsforlag, 1996.

Pannenberg, Wolfhart. *Systematische Theologie* 3. Göttingen: Vandenhoeck & Ruprecht, 1993.

Tanner, Mary. "The Anglican Position on Apostolic Continuity and Apostolic Succession in the Porvoo Common Statement." In *Louvain Studies 21/2: Apostolic Continuity of the Church and Apostolic Succession.* Edited by James E. Puglisi and Dennis J. Billy, pp. 114-25. Louvain: University of Louvain, 1996.

Tjørhom, Ola. "Apostolic Continuity and Apostolic Succession in the Porvoo Common Statement: A Challenge to the Nordic Lutheran Churches." In *Louvain Studies 21/2: Apostolic Continuity of the Church and Apostolic Succession.* Edited by James E. Puglisi and Dennis J. Billy, pp. 126-37. Louvain: University of Louvain, 1996.

The Sending and Mission of the Church in the Porvoo Common Statement

TORE FURBERG

There was a time when mission and unity were regarded as two different aspects of the life of the churches on the international scene. This was when mission was looked upon as a one-way street from the western so-called Christian countries to Africa, Asia, and Latin America, and when western churches were the only significant actors in the ecumenical movement.

In many parts of the world, however, there was quite early a movement of growing rapprochement between mission and unity. This was a key concern already at the World Missionary Conference in Edinburgh, 1910. Moreover, an important event in this respect took place in 1961 when the International Missionary Council joined two other main streams of the international ecumenical movement, namely Faith and Order and Life and Work, within the framework of the World Council of Churches. Since then it has been difficult to distinguish mission and unity from each other in both principle and practice.

One of the reasons for this integration was the idea that the diaconal aspect (the church as a servant to the world) would be much clearer and could be realized in a better way through this cooperation. This integration was not generally accepted from the beginning but has over time proven to be based on sound theology and strong Christian conviction. It has, therefore, played a very important role in the life of the churches everywhere.

Personally I am convinced that the Porvoo Common Statement

(PCS) to a considerable degree is the result of the growing emphasis on such an integration of "mission and unity." I think that without the input of a strong feeling of responsibility for our common call for mission, the long striving for unity between Anglicans and Lutherans would not have had the breakthrough it had in PCS. But a careful common study of the theological and sacramental basis of unity was also necessary for a positive outcome.

The importance of such a study is made clear in PCS. But at the same time, the document places heavy emphasis on the present call for joint action in mission and ministry. A short summary of PCS could then, in accordance with the main streams of international ecumenical work, be formulated like this: Having agreed on the basic fundamentals in faith and order, the churches should now direct their current efforts towards life and work for the world and do it together. In PCS, the churches also clearly state that one necessary instrument for establishing closer unity between them is common action.

Kairos

One of the most challenging ideas brought forward in the Porvoo Commission is the idea of *kairos:* now is the right time, God's time for mission and unity. The sending and mission of the church are related to *kairos*. Personally, I remember clearly how strongly we were seized by this vision. In a biblical perspective God is above time, he is the same yesterday, today, and tomorrow, and Christ has promised to be with us until the end of time. But we also know from biblical testimony and from our own experience that God sends periods of time to be received by us as gifts of grace from him and as a help to follow his will and further the kingdom of God — an opportunity given to take initiatives in his service. God's time is the right time and that time is now. We saw the signs of time both in the life of people in our part of the world and in our churches. It was the right time for our churches to take the opportunity for common action.

Those of us who worked together in the commission also felt that it was the *kairos* for us personally. If we did not meet God's challenge to us now, the opportunity for a closer community might never be given again. Both the situation in our churches — with a long history of negotiations and growing fellowship — and the situation in the world, especially in Europe, made it urgent for us to reflect upon the presence and demands of the *kairos*, God's time, our time to follow his call.

Apostolicity

Sending and mission also have to do with one outstanding theme in the commission dealing with the nature and life of the church of Christ, namely *apostolicity*. To try to define that central mark of the church was a delicate and important task. The urgency of this definition had to do with the burning issues of the historic episcopal order, apostolic succession, and related matters. Consideration of the total mission of Christ and the total mission of the church was decisive for the outcome of the discussion on the difficult subject of episcope.

The Greek word *apostello* means "to send" and *apostle* denotes "somebody who is sent." *Apostolicity* then must include as an important part of its meaning the aspect of sending. Apostolicity refers both to the origins of the church and to its continuing task and character. In PCS, we evidently agree that apostolicity is not only a question of continuity but also of mission. The apostolic succession is not primarily a technical matter but a sign of the Lord's faithfulness and the faithfulness of the church to its Lord. Apostolicity is, furthermore, primarily a characteristic of the whole church, the people of God. The role of the apostolic ministry is to be sent to the world in the framework of the whole church of Christ.

The Porvoo Commission could, in this respect, benefit from the work of the Niagara consultation, which took a new approach to episcope in light of the church's mission and of the ministry of the whole people of God.[1] This conception of apostolicity contributed to making an agreement possible between the representatives of both traditions by accepting apostolic succession as a sign and an instrument of the apostolicity of the church.

1. *The Niagara Report: Report of the Anglican-Lutheran Consultation on Episcope 1987* — especially chapter 1, "The Nature of the Church and Its Mission."

What World?

"Unity in and for the world": *What world?* After World Wars I and II, the world situation posed a strong challenge to the churches to work for unity. The ecumenical movement in its different forms was used by the churches in their work for peace and reconciliation and to help groups and individuals who had been hit by the devastating consequences of the wars. The relations between the churches were subsequently improved by this common effort to serve in a difficult situation.

The situation was somewhat similar for the Anglican and Lutheran churches which, in the late 1980s, tried to find a common road to unity through renewed negotiations. Several events and tendencies in the world convinced them that the *kairos* of unity had come. Their world was, of course, primarily Europe with an emphasis on the northern part.

Very important as a background to the Porvoo conversations were the political changes in Eastern Europe that took place just before and during the time of the commission's work (cf. PCS §§2, 3, and 10). Many efforts had earlier been made to strengthen the mutual relations between the Baltic churches, the Nordic Lutheran churches, and the Anglican churches in Great Britain and Ireland. Now a changed political situation opened completely new possibilities. It would, for instance, be possible for the Baltic churches to become part of a network of churches beyond their national boundaries.

But it was not only a matter of church relations. The churches were challenged to cooperate in addressing the problems of the secular world. The collapse of the earlier political system in Eastern Europe left a vacuum to which the churches felt called to respond. The problems of a spiritual vacuum could also be found in the Scandinavian countries and in Great Britain at this time as traditional Christian culture diminished. All the churches in the area had to meet the challenge of secularism and rapid changes in society and family life. The experience of the churches in the different situations could be of help to others — an exchange of ideas and strategies would be fruitful for the future. Especially valuable were the testimonies of churches that had been oppressed and more or less driven underground for a long time.

The changes in contemporary society were not only negative factors. There was and still is a moment of opportunity for Christian presence in the secular setting of present-day Europe, an indication of a spiritual and ethical recovery to which the churches could contribute together. There seems to be a growing awareness in our countries that spiritual values of some kind are needed as a basis for a sustainable society. For the churches and for the Christians it is time to enter into a constructive dialogue with all people of good will to try to find a solid basis for the future of our societies. PCS brings those matters to the forefront.

In our multicultural situation, many people are unaware of the fact that the general conception of many fundamental principles like love, justice, truth, and peace are based on the Christian gospel. This observation challenges the churches to work together for these values for the benefit of the people. The "national church" background in many of the Porvoo churches also makes them feel a responsibility towards the whole population — often in contact and cooperation with so-called "free churches." However, it should not be forgotten that within the Porvoo fellowship are some minority churches, both on the Anglican and Lutheran sides.

Many social problems came to the forefront as a result of the political changes in Europe. The lack of balance between the prosperous and the impoverished nations became clear. Because of the political conflicts, migrants, refugees, and ethnic minorities challenged the churches to serve them and to support their striving for a dignified life as human beings. This situation in Northern Europe became a strong challenge for pastoral care and mission for all the churches in the area.

The growing integration of Europe was also regarded as an evidence of the *kairos*. Even though not all the Porvoo churches are from member states of the European Union, there was a strong feeling that the churches in Northern Europe were called to work together in a common witness within the European society at large. The churches in the North wanted to support this step in a new direction in a Europe which — with grave consequences — had been fragmented for many centuries, not the least during the twentieth century. The split between the Christian churches of Europe had, it was understood, been part of the fragmentation and sometimes even contributed to it. The churches supported the idea of a more unified Europe that could take its place in a responsible way on the international scene. The churches especially emphasized that Europe ought not to be a "rich man's club," isolated from the rest of the world and mainly interested in protecting itself and its privileges and inherited benefits.

Such a position had certainly been taken earlier and advocated by European churches, including the Roman Catholic Church. As mentioned in PCS (§§11-12), these important problems are already being discussed by the churches in Europe in the Conference of European Churches (CEC) and in the Catholic Bishops' Conference in Europe (CCEE). On the international level, Anglican and Lutheran churches face the challenges and tasks related to these urgent needs in different parts of the Anglican Communion and the Lutheran World Federation.

The question is whether these world and regional organizations are able to take relevant action even on a basic level, where people live and work and where witness and service are needed. The Porvoo contribution to the debate was meant to support the existing efforts and not to be a separate Anglican-Lutheran voice. The perspective was broadening: the "world" in PCS is not just Northern Europe. Porvoo clearly takes a worldwide perspective.

PCS accentuates mission to the world. In §13 of Chapter C, "Our Common Task Today," there is a concentrated policy statement on this central perspective on the task of the churches. Quoted here, this is a central text for the theme of this essay:

> In the face of all the questions arising from our common mission today, our churches are called together to proclaim a duty of service to the wider world and to the societies in which they are set. Equally, they are called together to proclaim the Christian hope, arising from faith, which gives meaning in societies characterized by ambiguity. Again they are called together to proclaim the healing love of God and reconciliation in communities wounded by persecution, oppression and injustice. This common proclamation in word and sacrament manifests the mystery of God's love, God's presence and God's Kingdom.

How would this general aim be worked out in concrete terms? In PCS §10 this is done:

> Our churches and their nations are today facing new tasks and opportunities, in the context of many ideological, social and political changes in Europe. These include:
>
> a) a growing awareness by the European nations of their interdependence and mutual responsibility, and the need to rectify injustices resulting from the European wars of many centuries, but especially the twentieth century, which have affected the whole world;
>
> b) new opportunities — which are especially dramatic in the Baltic context — for evangelism, re-evangelism and pastoral work in all our countries, and the challenge to restate the Christian faith in response to both a prevalent practical materialism and a yearning among many people for spiritual values;
>
> c) a need to react to the vacuum arising from the collapse of a monolithic political system in Eastern Europe and to the increasingly pluriform character of society in Britain and Ireland and in the Nordic countries;
>
> d) opportunities to work for peace, justice and human rights, to diminish the imbalance between the prosperous nations and those impoverished and suffering from undue economic dependency, and to protect the rights and dignity of the poor and desolate — in particular, migrants, refugees and ethnic minorities;
>
> e) an ecological debate within and between the countries of Northern Europe, to which the churches have begun to bring a positive theology of creation and incarnation according permanent value to the earth and life in all its forms;
>
> f) a need for dialogue and understanding with people of other races, cultures and religious traditions as partners and fellow-citizens of a new Europe.

Diaconia

PCS deals thoroughly with episcope. It is possible that diaconia will be equally important for the continued cooperation and fellowship between the Porvoo churches. Diaconia is an essential part of the sending and mission of the church. Due to theological and structural differences, the diaconate was one of the factors considered, early on, to be a complication in the efforts to bring Anglican and Lutheran churches together. During the Porvoo Commission's negotiations, however, the question of the diaconate did not create any major difficulty. It was dealt with, not so much as a problem, but as a common challenge of renewal to the churches, both Anglican and Lutheran. Both are now making attempts to find new insight in the theology of diaconia and new ways for the work of the deacons.

In their conversations, church leaders have emphasized the need for a common study of the theology of diaconia in their churches. Great contributions in this area were made by the Anglican-Lutheran International Commission[2] and the Conference of European Churches.[3] Representatives of the Church of England and the Scandinavian churches are also studying this matter together. Some common practical diaconal projects have begun. There is, for instance, one promising cooperative project between the church in Wales and one of the most important diaconal institutions in Sweden — Ersta, in Stockholm.

The cooperating churches have agreed that diaconia is an indispensable part of Christianity, based in the central faith and life of the church. Its task is to engage the churches in support of human dignity, justice, and liberation. It is a wide perspective that also includes matters of peace and ecological welfare. Diaconia is a challenge to the churches to take part in the ideological and social debate, but it is also a matter of serving people in their daily life.

The increasing gap between rich and poor, unemployment, crime, broken families — all these troubles have political, ideological, and structural causes, and they affect people in their daily lives. Efforts to change the general situation must, therefore, include direct diaconal work with the oppressed groups and individuals, including support of their self-worth.

Diaconal work seems to be one of the most suitable areas for cooperation between the churches involved: common thinking, common

2. Cf. *The Diaconate as Ecumenical Opportunity: The Hanover Report of the Anglican-Lutheran International Commission,* 1996.

3. See, e.g., *The Bratislava Declaration: Towards a vision of diaconia in Europe, an invitation to take part in the action and reflection process,* by CEC.

planning, common training (part of the time), and even common action on the local level when it is suitable. Some areas of diaconal concern are especially appropriate as common ground, namely when there are aspects of transgressing boundaries involved, such as work among refugees, migrants, minority groups, etc. These might be areas in which Anglican and Lutheran churches, without a long delay, could engage in common diaconal work.

All the Porvoo churches seem to agree on the aims of diaconia: to work for justice, peace, freedom, health, human rights and dignity, and a sound ecology; to work against violence, poverty, and racism; and to support oppressed and minority groups. The method is to help, and try to prevent, but also to contribute constructively to necessary changes in the society. In some of the countries the social changes are more rapid than in others. The resources are also different in the different churches. The churches should consider the challenge of sharing, not only helping each other but really sharing their resources for these important purposes of diaconia.

Sharing of experience and information is important. Let me offer one example. I think that in the Church of Sweden there is a growing awareness of the necessity of renewing and improving the participation of lay people in the witness and service of the church. This insight is one of the results of the exchange of visitors and church workers that has recently taken place with the Church of England.

This experience is related to the discovery of Anglican diversity in the life of the church and in its relationships with society and with people of all kinds. This openness in attitude is a good starting point for the diaconal service. The active role of lay people in church life and on the ecumenical scene also presents a whole range of new questions that will have to be discussed. New possibilities and resources will certainly be found, which will be of great help for the future.

Mission and Unity

In PCS it is stated that the sending and the mission of the church are meant to be carried out not by the individual churches but as *a common task.* It was expressed in many ways during the negotiations and in PCS that the basis for and the subject of the mission is the fellowship in faith — the communion. Theologically this is grounded in the conviction that the mission of the church is Christ's mission and that only as fellow members of Christ's body are we truly able to serve in the mission. There is a double relationship between unity (*koinonia,* fellowship) on one hand and mission/service on the other. The unity in faith, which we have rediscovered, leads us towards a communion of love and of sharing our resources with one another: "This unity is also manifested as a communion of love, implying that Christians are bound together to one another in a committed relationship with mutual responsibilities, common spiritual goods and the obligation to share temporal resources" (PCS §24).

It leads further to a common responsibility for witness and service to the world. The unity is not aimed exclusively at the church. It is seen as "instrumental to God's ultimate purpose." The church is sent into the world "to serve, in obedience to the mission of Christ, the reconciliation of humankind and of all creation" (PCS §18). And this partaking in God's reconciliatory work binds the churches together and helps them penetrate even deeper in unity, not necessarily as a structure but as a spiritual *koinonia.*

This mutual relation between communion and witness is expressed in a strong and challenging way as one of the components of the vision of a church living in the light of the gospel: "it is a Church which manifests through its visible communion the healing and uniting power of God amidst the divisions of humankind; it is a Church in which the bonds of communion are strong enough to enable it to bear effective witness in the world, to guard and interpret the apostolic faith, to take decisions, to teach authoritatively, and share its goods with those in need" (PCS §20).

At the end of the document (§59), under the heading "Liturgical Celebration," there are recommendations concerning the inauguration and celebration of the agreement. Not only the joyful acceptance of one another and a joint commitment in faith and sacramental life, but also a "commitment to *engage in mission together*" should then be expressed. This is in line with and a consequence of the mission theology, which is developed in PCS. The churches and their members can find here a motivation for joining in the great effort to offer our own generation a living Christian faith in our own part of the world. This missionary approach of PCS will, hopefully, become one of Porvoo's greatest impacts on the thinking and life of Anglican and Lutheran churches in Europe and elsewhere.

Another matter of concern, when we think of the sending and mission of the church — unity in and for the world — is what earlier was called "foreign mission." I think that it is proper to discuss this matter in connection with PCS. As a matter of fact, the Scandinavian and British mission organizations for a long time were responsible for the theological and economic development in their so-called missionary churches, especially in Africa and Asia. The responsibility was gradually transferred to the "younger churches." Subsequently, mission was described as cooperation with sister-churches, emphasizing their mutual relationships.

In church history there are some examples of attempted cooperation between Anglicans and Lutherans in the field of mission (here taken in the more specific meaning of the word). One is mentioned by Christopher Hill in his introduction to *The Essays on Church and Ministry in Northern Europe,* published together with the Porvoo agreement.[4] He refers to the Danish Halle Mission in Trankebar, South India, between 1710 and 1725 when the Anglican Society for the Propagation of the Gospel supported and cooperated with Danish Lutheran missionaries.

Another example may also be taken from South India, but more than two hundred years later. The Tamil Evangelical Lutheran Church in South India was considering the possibility of joining the Church of South India, which was founded in 1947 by an Anglican and some other South Indian churches. It is likely that one of the reasons why the Lutheran church leaders hesitated was the fear that the continued strong support from German and Swedish Lutheran missions might be at risk if they joined the united church. Another reason was that the Lutherans in South India put their priority on the effort to create one Lutheran Church for all of India instead of working for regional ecumenical unity in the Church of South India.

Even if Jerusalem, naturally enough, did not belong to the conventional missionary areas, it reminds us of another example from history. It is the Anglican-Lutheran Jerusalem bishopric, which functioned between 1841 and 1886, based on an agreement between the

4. *Together in Mission and Ministry: The Porvoo Common Statement with Essays on Church and Ministry in Northern Europe,* 1993 — here pp. 45ff.

Archbishop of Canterbury and the church in Prussia. The aim was to establish an integrated Anglican-Lutheran Church in Jerusalem. Unfortunately, it did not succeed.

Behind these cases of attempted cooperation was the common call to mission and service for the purpose of establishing and supporting the church of Christ in places and areas where both Anglicans and Lutherans were present. One of the reasons why these and other similar ecumenical endeavors did not continue and did not develop into a common church life was, according to my understanding, that no sufficiently firm theological basis had been worked out for the planned unity. That was especially true about the question of episcopacy. When difficulties and conflicts occurred, as they usually do sooner or later, it was all too easy to refer to differences in theology and traditions and give up the attempts to work together.

There are also other, more or less non-theological, factors involved. Some churches were economically so dependent on the confessional world organizations, such as the Lutheran World Federation, that they did not want to take any chances by involving themselves in ecumenical ventures, even if they were assured that there would be no negative consequences for them if they did move in that direction. A similar attitude might be the result of a longstanding bilateral relation between a "rich" church in the West and a "poor" one in the so-called third world. There are several evidences of the fact that western missionary work in Africa and Asia through its structures and traditions has contributed to divisions and competition between Christians and churches in the areas concerned.

Nowadays, a substantial part of this "mission" is channeled through international or regional bodies, and the earlier one-sided bilateral relations are not so dominating as before. The situation on the "mission fields" in the nineteenth century, with competition and conflict between churches of different denominations, was once regarded as one of the main motivations for ecumenical work. Could we expect that the Porvoo agreement should influence the churches that have originated from Anglican and Lutheran missions related to the Porvoo churches to come together as PCS indicates? So far such a development does not seem to be emerging — even if a movement towards closer communion is going on, especially in Africa.

There are also several indications from all over the world that

Anglican and Lutheran churches are working well together in witness and service. One important area of cooperation is theological education, common training for the ministry, which hopefully will bring the churches closer to a united witness and service. Bishop David Tustin, Anglican co-chair of the Porvoo Commission, has reported that in Africa many Anglican-Lutheran consultations have been held and cooperation has begun. In the Johannesburg Declaration of 1993, for instance, Anglican and Lutheran churches pledged to undertake joint activity in certain fields — diaconia, pastoral work, and mission; youth and children's work; women's work; and addressing issues of poverty and injustice. I will continue to quote from a briefing given by Bishop Tustin at the annual conference of the Anglican-Lutheran Society in Virginia, USA:

> On the whole there is in Africa little interest in historical differences that originated in Europe or in abstract models of unity, but there are many positive signs in Tanzania, in Southern Africa (especially Namibia) and in Central Africa (especially Zimbabwe). On the ground there is co-operation over such issues as a common hymnal or liturgy, joint theological education and the pastoral care of refugees. There is widespread interconsecrations of bishops, often on an *ad hoc* and unregulated basis. There is little difficulty about episcopacy as such. Last year an interim committee began developing a pan-African agenda, and this is the level at which any formal agreement would need to be drafted. The immediate challenge is to secure the active support of all the bishops, but little has yet been done to involve key lay leaders. The two main obstacles are lack of resources and the complexity of jurisdictions.[5]

We cannot expect that our "sister churches" on other continents should always follow the examples of their partner churches in Europe. Such behavior may be looked upon as a kind of neo-colonialism. There are differences between the conditions for ecumenical cooperation in Africa and Asia and the situation in Europe. In many parts of Africa it seems that Anglican and Lutheran churches are maintaining

5. David Tustin, *Meissen, Porvoo and other Anglican-Lutheran Agreements*, unpublished manuscript.

good relationships and cooperating without raising some of the difficult questions of structures and historical traditions that have been problematic in Europe.

As for the present situation, I do not think that the Porvoo churches should put pressure on their partner churches in Africa, Asia, and Latin America to follow the example of the churches in Great Britain and Scandinavia by copying their way of uniting. But they should at least take measures to ensure that their structures of mission or church relief or mutual church interrelations are not a hindrance to a development towards Anglican-Lutheran unity. The same cautiousness should be required from international confessional bodies. And it is not only a question of structures but also of attitudes from the side of the stronger partner, which might function as hindrances to ecumenical development.

Most of the mission- and international-aid organizations in our churches have a basically ecumenical objective for their work, but their structures are not always moving in that direction. It is high time that these organizations, in light of PCS and its mission-oriented character, consider a renewal of their structures and functions and do it together. The Porvoo churches should take the initiative to support common reflection on the missionary task of the church in unity.

Looking Forward

It is clear that *koinonia* is the basis for the common mission of the churches. They have become and will continue to be partners in this mission. For the future it is important to remember that even if fellowship and partnership can be officially established through negotiations and agreements, it is necessary that unity is given time to grow, to be nourished and strengthened by reciprocal and mutual love and togetherness as a deep spiritual relation — a relation of trust, faithfulness, and communion on the personal and congregational level.

Relations of this kind are seldom without problems and frictions. In spite of all similarities, the churches, dioceses, and congregations involved are different in many ways. Some are big, others small; some are rich, others poor; some are relatively strong, others weak. Some are more influential in their own environment than others. It is vital that all can partake in the common mission as equal partners. This partnership should be founded on Christian ethical values like honesty, equality, openness, trust, respect, humility, and loyalty. This might seem to be self-evident but cannot be taken for granted. The most important issue for the common mission is not that of organization and structure but its spiritual character. The basic spiritual and sacramental unity is the necessary presupposition for the work.

According to PCS the idea of apostolicity refers both to the origins of the church and to its continuing task and character. That means that there should be a balance between preserving the apostolic heritage of faith and proclaiming the faith afresh in new situations. The aspect of "sending" in apostolicity does not only refer to geography. It has also to do with time: to witness to and serve every new generation. Apostolicity, therefore, also means a challenge to renewal. It is suggested in the agreement that a "Porvoo Contact Group" should nurture "our growth in communion and . . . coordinate the implementation of this agreement." This group should also be encouraged to take initiatives that could lead to renewal and development of fellowship. The content of a document like PCS cannot remain undisputed and unchanged forever. Take for instance §58b in the document, dealing with practical obligations of the churches. They will need to be revised from time to time.

It is also good to know that an Anglican-Lutheran international body of cooperation has been re-established under the name of The Anglican-Lutheran International Working Group, which has held its two first meetings in 2000 and 2001. The work of this group will most certainly be of inspiration to the regional and local work. But it is necessary to remember that other active church members of all kinds have a responsibility here. In order to facilitate development and renewal of the work for unity, the churches should keep and develop meeting places, even using new techniques, open for all kinds of common exchange and spiritual fellowship, and with a strategic priority on witness and service in our time.

III. The Significance of Porvoo Beyond the Signatory Churches — A Concluding Ecumenical Perspective

The Porvoo Common Statement from a Catholic Perspective

JAMES F. PUGLISI

Introduction

As we near the tenth anniversary of the process that terminated in the signing of the Porvoo Common Statement (PCS),[1] it is good to pause and reflect on where this process has led the Nordic and Baltic Lutheran churches and the British and Irish Anglican churches. I do this however from a Catholic perspective, as one even outside of the European church experience but as one who has followed closely the developments associated with this historic event.

The Catholic Church has been engaged in conversations with both of these ecclesial traditions for well over thirty years. Our conversations with them have been both bilateral and multilateral, especially in Faith and Order's *Baptism, Eucharist and Ministry* (BEM) project as well as in the joint efforts of the Conference of European Churches (CEC) and the Council of Catholic Bishops' Conferences in Europe (CCEE). It is precisely from this vantage point that a more fruitful "evaluation" of what has happened in Northern Europe can be framed.

1. We will refer to the Porvoo Common Statement as it is found with supporting essays and documentation in the volume entitled *Together in Mission and Ministry: The Porvoo Common Statement with Essays on Church and Ministry in Northern Europe* (London: Church House Publishing, 1993). The reference to pages and paragraphs will be numbered according to this edition of the statement and essays.

Ecumenical Relations

Both with the Anglican Communion and the Lutheran World Federation, the Catholic Church has elaborated substantial agreed statements on such issues as Eucharist, ministry and ordination, authority in the church, ethical living, ecclesiology and church structures, and most recently, on the meaning of the doctrine of justification — which has led to a major breakthrough in relation to Lutheran churches. It is important to note that the Catholic Church's relation to these two churches has been different in the past and in the dialogue process. One must likewise take note of the fact that the ecclesial relationships that have been carried out over the past fifty years with both of these churches runs the gamut from informal to formal and official status. This is one of the reasons why the Catholic Church follows with great interest the developments between these two church communions in Northern Europe. Another reason is that within both these traditions are the so-called "high church" and "low church" traditions, those that have a more "catholic" content and those with a more "evangelical" tendency. These categories are of course only a sociological "ideal-type" way of describing differing church traditions and cannot be rigidly held to.

The Porvoo Process

It should be noted that the real impulse that moved all of the churches engaged in what might be called the "Porvoo process" is the gospel. The very title of the collection of essays that was published together with the statement is *Together in Mission and Ministry.* Mission, namely the mission of spreading the good news of salvation, is the first focus of the Porvoo Common Statement. The second is ministry or service to the very gospel project. The realization of these two goals comes from a further observation on these communions' collaborative relationship in serving the gospel elsewhere in the world. However, their situation is more homogeneous in Northern Europe; hence the churches there were moved to take a courageous step together in witnessing to the world out of a common ground. The current secularization, especially in Western Europe, and the situation of the churches emerging from the grip of communism in Eastern Europe dictated that something further must be done to serve the gospel and answer the questions now being laid at the churches' feet. Another phenomenon was also confronting the churches: emigration. This is part of the new Europe that is coming to birth, with a new mix of religions and cultures and a whole new set of challenges in witnessing to the gospel. All of these factors prompted these two ecclesial traditions to take seriously their call to respond to new exigencies in a new context. They have boldly taken up this challenge in the Porvoo Common Statement.

How might one begin to evaluate this process designed to lead to a greater unity among baptized Christians? Is it enough to evaluate the achieved results of collaboration, sharing, and co-ministering, or is there another criterion that needs to be taken into account? Have all of the churches involved really agreed to this process and have they fully participated in the realization of this program? It might be possible to answer all of these questions from within the Porvoo experience. Clearly though, this author cannot do so, as the Catholic Church is not part of the agreement or the experience. This does not mean, of course, that we are uninterested. Quite the contrary! We are very much involved with both traditions, especially in a dialogue that has borne much fruit in terms of theological convergence, pastoral practice, and mission. What happens between these two traditions interests us very much as it will also impact our relationship with both of these communions.

Several dimensions of this agreement interest us: the doctrinal position of the churches that enables them to arrive at the solution proposed by PCS; the concrete experience of ministering together in each other's tradition; and the results, difficulties, and challenges that presented themselves on the road. Obviously it is not possible to treat all of these dimensions here and from my vantage point; I will leave this to those within the Porvoo experience. Instead, I will attempt here to look at the doctrinal results of this agreement, especially as they touch on the ministry and apostolicity of the church.

Doctrinal Results

First, the Porvoo Common Statement speaks of the nature of communion that is desired by Jesus for his disciples. This communion is one that is identified as being joyful and rooted in the mysterious relationship of the Trinity (§21). There is furthermore the correct understanding that this is not a human-made product but rather a gift that comes from God. The proper stance from which to begin, it seems to me, is a full realization that the communion of the church is not something we ourselves can bring about, but rather is something we receive. This has ramifications, however, for what we must do in receiving this gift and putting it into practice. It is interesting that when the document speaks about this dimension of the communion of the church it cites the work of the Catholic-Lutheran dialogue.[2] It is precisely in this dialogue that there is an awareness, in the relationship of our two churches, of appropriating the gift in stages and finding ways for implementing it. This seems to be exactly what Anglicans and Lutherans have tried to do through the Porvoo process.

There is a full realization that the visible unity the gospel requires is not that of uniformity. Here the scriptural images of unity and diversity come into play in the understanding of how this gift of God through the Spirit is to be received in the life of the churches. Both unity and diversity are seen as rooted in the Trinity itself. This is fine on a spiritual level, but we all know that the pinch comes in realizing it on the human level. For some reason we have trouble seeing the same, identical reality expressed in different forms, with different words and expressions. We prefer to see the identical expression — which obviously leads to uniformity and the suppression of diversity. It is important to be able to identify this tendency on the human level and to combat it, since ultimately this will destroy communion. From the Catholic experience we already have an interesting precedent or model, from our bilateral dialogues with the Ancient Church of the East and the Christological declarations signed between the Oriental Orthodox churches (the pre-Chalcedonian churches) and the Catholic Church. It is sufficient to note that in the former case we have already established eucharistic hospitality between our two churches even though we do not have the same canon of Scripture or the same sacramental system. This shows that there can be communion even though

2. See *Ways to Community* (Geneva: The Lutheran World Federation, 1981) and *Facing Unity: Models, Forms and Phases of Catholic-Lutheran Church Fellowship* (Geneva: The Lutheran World Federation, 1985).

there is diversity of expression and form, as long as the same apostolic faith is recognized. In the case just cited full communion between the two churches has not been realized, but there is a mutual recognition of each other as church. This is the beginning of the road that leads to full ecclesiastical and canonical communion. What is required is a new way of thinking and acting toward one another that is dictated by the Scriptures themselves. This is the position the Porvoo Common Statement takes in stating its understanding of unity and communion (§§26-28).

It is clearly stated that the basis of communion and unity is first a relation with God and with fellow believers, manifested in baptism, in the response to apostolic preaching, in the common confession of the apostolic faith, in the united celebration of the Eucharist, and in a single ministry (§24). All of these demand therefore a new way of acting toward the other and of being together in the world. This section of the document thus concludes that "for the fullness of communion all these visible aspects of the life of the Church require to be permeated by a profound spiritual communion, a growing together in a common mind, mutual concern and a care for unity (Phil. 2:2)" (§28). In short, it is the putting on the mind of Christ that will enable the churches to render visible the reality of a spiritual communion. Another (unofficial) dialogue, the Groupe des Dombes, has spoken about this same process in a document published several years ago, *For the Conversion of the Churches*.[3] In a certain way, then, we are witnessing this process of conversion in the Porvoo agreement. It is a matter of conversion on several levels: the level of Christian identity, of confessional identity, and of ecclesial identity. One factor in the Porvoo process that renders this more easily realizable is that in the history of the relationships between the two churches there has been no serious animosity between them and therefore no need for the healing of memories because of past wounds inflicted by the other. In fact, the history of Anglican-Lutheran conversations has helped facilitate the possibility of moving in the direction that the Northern European churches have gone. We need to look, then, at the doctrinal basis that has enabled these conversations to become a reality in fact.

3. Groupe des Dombes, *Pour la conversion des Églises* (Paris: Centurion, 1991); English translation *For the Conversion of the Churches* (Geneva: WCC Publications, 1993).

At the heart of the declaration are chapters three and four, treating what is the common faith of the churches and dealing with the question of episcopacy, a central issue that is at the core of most ecumenical discussions concerning the structuring of the church.

From a Catholic perspective these two traditions came into existence for two different reasons. The Lutheran tradition was born out of a strong desire to reform the church because of abuses in the life of the church and what were considered doctrinal errors, while the Anglican tradition rose out of a more historical-political situation that was less concerned with the doctrinal reform of the church than with who is ultimate head of the church and who had the ultimate say over what happens in the church. In both cases, however, an Erastian solution seems to have been arrived at: in both cases state churches quickly evolved.[4] In many aspects the Reformation in the Nordic countries was also less radical than was that of the Continental Reformation. What some might find surprising in both of these regional contexts is that the doctrinal basis of what has traditionally been represented as the Lutheran teaching or the Anglican teaching is far less radical. This becomes clear from PCS's summary of the principal beliefs held in common by the two traditions (§32).

In this list of twelve sub-paragraphs we find expressed a sort of consensus of faith, which is further substantiated in the appendix by both the proper canonical and/or confessional writings of each of the churches. It is reflected too in the agreed statements produced by the various dialogues held not only between these two traditions but from Faith and Order's BEM document, and from each tradition's dialogues with the Catholic Church.[5] This doctrinal summary contains elements ranging from the symbols of faith accepted in each tradition to the question of the practice of the celebration of the sacraments of initiation, in particular the question of the different ways of doing and understanding confirmation. The chapter realistically considers the lack of uniformity in the practice of these two traditions, but recognizes unity in the way that both traditions express the same faith through

4. I have dealt with this in another setting that is pertinent for our discussion here. See my *The Process of Admission to Ordained Ministry: A Comparative Study*, vol. 2, *The First Lutheran, Reformed, Anglican and Wesleyan Rites* (Collegeville, Minn.: The Liturgical Press, 1998).

5. See *Together in Mission . . .*, pp. 195-218.

their different practices. What can still be bothersome from a Catholic perspective is the verification of what is professed together here and what is practiced in fact. It is sufficient to recall a problem in Catholic-Anglican understanding by the fact of the affirmation in a joint statement by the Anglican–Roman Catholic International Commission (ARCIC), that the liturgical president of the eucharistic celebration is always an ordained minister — in contrast to the recent proposal of an Anglican province (Sydney, Australia) that it could have "lay presidency." The question arises as to the veracity of the statements of the agreed documents and what the churches actually do.

The same difficulties could arise in the context of the Porvoo Common Statement and what the churches actually practice. What will be interesting to observe is whether the practice will change and confirm the statement, or whether the practice is the actual belief of a particular "province" of the church. This fact likewise points up a crucial question within each church as to the "tolerance of deviation" from the norm. How much deviation is allowed for a church to remain part of the communion, and what mechanism will ultimately have authority to confirm the existence of a church-dividing abuse or deviation from the "orthodox faith," and to deal with and correct it? We may already see some shift in the way each tradition deals with difficulties such as the case cited above, or even in the context of the recently signed Joint Declaration on the Doctrine of Justification between the Catholic and Lutheran churches. One of the ways of reading the conflict arose in this process on the Lutheran side: Who, it was asked, could authorize the signing of this declaration when a certain number of Lutheran theologians were raising objections to its contents? It might be possible to see here a conflict in magisterial authority. Who had the authority to say that this was in conformity with authentic Lutheran teaching on justification — the traditional teaching magisterium of university theologians, or the bishops together with their synods? From my perspective it seems that the principle of episcopal supervision and leadership as well as the pastoral care for the right teaching of the church — as exercised in synodically taken decisions — represents a return to a more orthodox understanding of how *episkope* should function in the church, according to a model that is at the same time personal, collegial, and communal. For Catholics this instance should also be a challenge to our way of dealing with important issues in the church that far too frequently are resolved in a far less participatory way. It is interesting that John Paul II called for all local churches to hold synods in preparation of the new millennium. In this we might be able to see how a synodical understanding is being added to Vatican II's collegial understanding of the exercise of authority in the church. We can likewise make reference to the most recent ARCIC statement, *The Gift of Authority* (1999), which points in the same direction. It should be noted that most of what is affirmed in chapter three of the Porvoo Common Statement would not surprise Catholics except maybe to dispel some misconceptions commonly held about the beliefs of our Lutheran and Anglican brethren, for example, concerning the presence of the Lord in the Eucharist or the necessity of the ordained ministry.

Ministry and Apostolicity

It is concerning the last question, namely the ministry, that I would like to make some observations, since obviously the concern of the mutual recognition of each other's ministry is an essential element on the road to full, visible unity. PCS's paragraph 32j takes up the issue of the ordained ministry only after considering the ministeriality of the whole people of God. This approach should not be unfamiliar to Catholics, since *Lumen Gentium* treats the question in similar fashion, as does BEM and several bilateral statements on ministry. There is agreement on the question of the divine institution of the ordained ministry at the service of the ministry of the whole people of God, and in locating it among the charisms God gives to the church for its mission of preaching the gospel in the world. Missing is a clear statement of the necessity of the threefold ministry at the service of the church, and of its divine institution. We can say that the discussion at Vatican II likewise talks about a historical evolution of the tripartite forms of ministry *(ab antiquo)* while maintaining the classical position of the divine institution of the ministry itself and affirming the necessity of the episcopacy for the church's mission of safeguarding the deposit of faith. Even though it seems that there is a difference of position regarding both the necessity of the episcopal office and its mode of functioning in each tradition, there is nevertheless an important statement made in

§32k: "We retain and employ the episcopal office as a sign of our intention, under God, to ensure the continuity of the Church in apostolic life and witness." This statement is not expanded or explained any further in this context, but is treated later in the next chapter on "Episcopacy in the service of the apostolicity of the church" (§§34-57).

It is important to understand the relationship between the apostolic continuity of the church and apostolic succession in ministry. It appears that the Porvoo Common Statement has adopted BEM's understanding of the issue as common ground rather than the position of one or the other of the churches. It further appears to me that PCS has adopted a more historical, linear approach that conceives apostolicity as rooted in the understanding of "apostle" as one who is sent as a missionary,[6] rather than seeing the body of the Twelve as an eschatological reality that gathers the dispersed people of God. This later position is to be seen in the meaning attributed to the substitution of Matthias for Judas — a substitution that bears witness to and establishes the apostolic succession. The principle it points to is not so much that of the *historical continuity* of witnesses succeeding the Twelve, but rather the *eschatological mission* of the Twelve, the unique and lasting event that assumes decisive importance for the history of salvation. The reality of the Twelve indicates the beginning of the realization of the promise: in eschatological times all of Israel will once again be reunited. This eschatological link could have been made very easily if the eschatological realization of the kingdom was seen as being realized in the permanent characteristics of the church of the apostles that are listed in §36 ("witness to the apostolic faith, proclamation and fresh interpretation of the Gospel, celebration of baptism and the eucharist, the transmission of ministerial responsibilities, communion in prayer, love, joy and suffering, service to the sick and needy, unity among the local churches and sharing the gifts which the Lord has given to each"[7]).

This eschatological dimension is very important in that it helps avoid an overly materialistic sense of succession but sees first the qualities of each eucharistic community in continuity with the communi-

6. See PCS: "Apostolicity means that the Church is sent by Jesus . . ." in §37, citing in note the reference taken from the Niagara Report from the Anglican-Lutheran International Consultation on Episcope, 1987.

7. All these points are taken from the Lima document's section on Ministry, §34.

ties of the apostles in relationship to their fulfillment in the kingdom. It is correctly observed that each community needs to be seen in the continuity of the mission that Christ entrusted to the church. Once again the Porvoo Common Statement follows very closely the work of BEM when it speaks about the relationship of the succession in ministry to the apostolic continuity of the church. The tendency here is to understand the englobing reality first (apostolic continuity of the church) and then to see the relation of the particular in the service of the wider reality (succession in ministry).

A Catholic concern would be to see clearly the fact that the office of bishop is truly a pastoral ministry and not merely a function of coordination.[8] Since at least the second century and probably even earlier, the church was considered realized in her fullness whenever and wherever the faithful of a certain place, following their bishop as Christ himself, were united under his presidency in one eucharistic community.[9] The role of the bishop was considered to be fundamental; in the ecclesiology of Ignatius of Antioch there is a Christological role attributed to the bishop, though not in relation to a particular apostle, as the college of the apostles was represented by the college of presbyters. For him it is a succession of *communities* and not of individuals. If the bishop is crucial in this kind of succession it is because he is head of a community imaging the eschatological gathering of the church around Christ, and not because he has received apostolic authority as an individual. This role is clearly seen both in the role of the neighboring bishops at the ordination of a bishop and the action of the community concerned in the election of their bishop. In both cases their involvement signifies theologically the activity of the Holy Spirit. This pneumatological dimension to ordination is rooted in the concept of witnessing, thereby demonstrating the confessional dimension of the process of access to the ordained ministry of bishop.[10]

8. I have tried to show in another context how the recovery of a truly pastoral office of leadership of the bishop for Lutheranism was one of the factors that helped save German Lutheranism from being manipulated by a national socialist interpretation. See J. Puglisi, "50th Anniversary of the Barmen Synod," *Ecumenical Trends* 13, no. 8 (1984): 120-22.

9. J. Zizioulas, *L'eucharistie, l'évêque et l'église durant les trois premiers siècles* (Paris: Desclée de Brouwer, 1994).

10. These ideas have been developed in more detail in my *The Process of Admission*

While the Porvoo Common Statement takes into account much of the progress that has been expressed by the BEM document and the real progress this document has led to in the theological reflection of many churches, there still seems to be a hesitation in expressing the necessity of the episcopal ministry — for reasons that go beyond the practical level of "coordination." There seems to be much concern about establishing the "historical" continuity and not enough about the Christological and pneumatological dimensions of the episcopal ministry. In a symposium held at the Centro Pro Unione in Rome, Metropolitan John of Pergamon provided a very extensive analysis of different theological approaches to the question of apostolicity. Particularly interesting was his comparison of all the Patristic sources — Latin, Greek, and Syriac — to the question at hand.[11] It seems to me that a reflection by all the churches (not just those engaged in the Porvoo process) would be helpful in avoiding what has traditionally been an overly historical and material understanding of the question of apostolic continuity and apostolic succession in ministry. The Metropolitan's approach takes much more into consideration the continuity of eucharistic communities. If this were taken more seriously into consideration, the question of in or out of succession might be more easily resolved; the question would not end up by trying to trace the unbroken chain of imposition of hands with a search for a valid pedigree. Apostolicity depends on other elements that have to do with the community's faith and practice and not just that of the holder of an office, even though the latter is important.

Conclusion

Taking a look at the Porvoo Common Statement from a distance of ten years is an important move. Looking at Porvoo as an outsider can be dangerous but sometimes helpful. I have tried to offer reflections more

to Ordained Ministry: A Comparative Study, vol. 1, *Epistemological Principles and Roman Catholic Rites* (Collegeville, Minn.: The Liturgical Press, 1996), pp. 27ff.

11. John (Zizioulas) of Pergamon, *Apostolic Continuity of the Church and Apostolic Succession in the First Five Centuries,* Louvain Studies 21, no. 2 (Louvain: University of Louvain, 1996), pp. 153-68.

on the text and the process as I have come to understand it, not as one from within — something that really needs to be done by those who have lived the experience for ten years. I believe the experience has proven helpful for all, even those outside the process. All have been challenged to reconsider their paradigms and to begin to think through, with a fresh interpretation, important issues such as apostolicity. However, this does not mean abandoning one's theological positions but rather looking at them again with a different ecclesiology based on rediscoveries from the past that do not always fit our old schemas. We can only hope that the experience of Porvoo will indeed serve the purpose of ecumenism in the future and the mission and ministry of the church in this new millennium.

The Porvoo Common Statement: An Orthodox Response

PETER C. BOUTENEFF

Inaugurating what would become something of a tradition within twentieth-century ecumenism, the Orthodox delegates at the first World Conference on Faith and Order (Lausanne, 1927) felt compelled to issue a separate statement. They wished to make two points: one was to explain why their conscience did not permit them to vote — the underlying principles of ecclesiology (both "faith" and "order") were foreign to them. But the other was to say that they participated in the conference with "love, and [the] desire to achieve an understanding." The ambivalent experience of these early Orthodox ecumenists to a certain degree describes the character of the Orthodox participation throughout the modern ecumenical movement. Alternately engaged and aloof, the Orthodox seem to say at every step, "This terrain seems foreign to us, and some of it even looks 'wrong' to us, but there is too much that is precious here, too much that is of profound meaning, for us to leave, to dissociate ourselves from this reality."

I am asked to respond, as an Orthodox, to the Porvoo Common Statement (PCS) — the central text of an agreement process between Anglican and Lutheran churches in Northern Europe. But my response cannot help being also a reaction, a series of impressions, which in fact come in line with the ambivalence I am ascribing to the Orthodox in their ecumenical participation as a whole — the fascination and excitement blended with the sense that something of the terrain is foreign.

The Orthodox contingent at Lausanne addressed our present

theme more specifically when they noted a sincere delight at witnessing "reunions" of other churches:

> . . . as Orthodox delegates we should view a partial reunion of those churches which share the same principles with satisfaction as a precedent to general union, inasmuch as it would thus be easier for our Orthodox Church to discuss reunion with the Church which had so united into a single Church and had a single faith, than with many Churches with different faiths.[1]

Precisely the same sentiment is echoed at the second World Conference (Edinburgh, 1937), with reference to Lausanne.[2] The simple principle is that multilateral dialogue becomes more manageable with each merger experienced on the "other side": the array of dialogue partners is less daunting the smaller it is.

One step beyond this rather basic level of interpretation, church unions (and the processes on the way) can have definite repercussions on the other churches who are not immediately involved. Even when they pertain to only two churches or church families, such agreements are never merely a bilateral affair. This is why church union conversations do well to include observers from other churches.

Orthodox were not among the formal observers in the Porvoo process. But what does the Porvoo Common Statement, and the church union process it represents, mean for the Orthodox? How might it affect Orthodox relations with Anglicans and Lutherans in general, and with the British, Irish, and Nordic and Baltic churches involved in specifics? And how would the Orthodox interpret Porvoo theologically? This essay will attempt an Orthodox response — and reaction — to the phenomenon of Porvoo and its theology.

A. Church Relations

Within the region affected by Porvoo, the Orthodox have their strongest numerical presence in the Baltics. In Finland they constitute a mi-

1. Reprinted in Gennadios Limouris, ed., *Orthodox Visions of Ecumenism* (Geneva: WCC, 1994), p. 14.

2. Cf. Limouris, ed., *Orthodox Visions,* p. 17.

nority, but a very visible one, with strong and positive relations with the Lutheran Church. Outside this, the Orthodox in England have included some very notable figures, but the imprint of Orthodox churches on the church scene in England is not of great significance. As to the rest of the Porvoo countries, the Orthodox presence is limited.

All the more then, on the diplomatic level at any rate, the Orthodox bilateral dialogues with either Anglicans or Lutherans will remain largely unaffected by the relationships advanced through Porvoo.

Another quite basic and evident factor concerning the church-relation repercussions of Porvoo is that this process does not constitute the creation of a united church. The full implementation of Porvoo would not result in an Orthodox bilateral relationship with a united Anglo-Nordic-Baltic Church that is somehow Anglico-Lutheran in its faith and order. Porvoo describes a communion of church families on the local level, church families that will each retain their own character and history, and therefore ecclesiastical integrity.

While Porvoo and other agreements serve to show the many things that Anglicans and Lutherans can say together on matters of faith and order, there are still enough classical particularities to each communion. Doctrinal particularities (such as the doctrine of justification for the Lutherans) remain, as inevitably do the historical realities that have led to differences in character and self-perception. And finally, the differences on the level of *episcope*, which rightly take up the major portion of Porvoo, are real. It is neither realistic, nor is it perceived to be urgently necessary, to try to erase such specificities, and Porvoo itself serves to illustrate that the differences on these levels can remain even as the communions are drawn ever-closer together.

Let us follow these fundamental observations with a broader analysis of the evolving ecumenical scene involving Orthodox, Anglicans, and Lutherans. It has been suggested above that while the particularities of Anglicans and Lutherans are shown to be separating them less and less, they continue to insure the discrete character of Orthodox bilateral relations with each. Two conclusions might be drawn. One is that the bilateral dialogues that Anglicans and Lutherans continue to have on their own with the Orthodox and Roman Catholic churches constitute one of the increasingly few places where Anglican-Lutheran distinctions are in effect lifted up. The dialogues provide an opportunity for these two communions to define themselves with a greater doctrinal specificity. The other is that one could almost suggest, at the risk of sounding absurd, that the doctrinal differences between Anglicans and Lutherans are in some way more important to the Orthodox than they are to the Anglicans and Lutherans themselves.

If this last statement deserves any credence whatsoever, it might be better understood against the backdrop of the observation, made with ever-increasing frequency, that the main divisions one perceives in the churches stemming from the Reformation are now *within* the churches, rather than between them. Especially to the outside (e.g., Orthodox) observer, the range of doctrinal, moral, and ethical positions taken within most churches outside Roman Catholicism and Orthodoxy is at least comparable to, if not greater than, many of the differences that allegedly divide the churches from each other. The Anglican communion, which has historically and quite consciously managed to hold together a broad spectrum of views in communion, is a particular example of how liberal and conservative theological positions, high-church and low-church liturgical practice, can diverge within a church more than in many bilateral church relationships.

The Orthodox are not monolithic, neither on moral/ethical matters (where we strive for a balance of the absolute and the situational), nor even on theological matters (where a certain degree of diversity is also in evidence). But the diversity in each case is on a smaller scale. Ask any Orthodox bishop or teacher what is meant by any of the articles of the Nicene Creed, and the response will be unified to a great degree. Attend an Orthodox liturgy in Kyoto, Minsk, Damascus, or Detroit, and the core experience is likely to be one of a remarkable consistency. For the Orthodox, unity is not uniformity, it always (and necessarily) involves diversity. But as it happens, the diversity is of a quite different character and a different scale than what we behold elsewhere.

I assert the above with the sole purpose of helping to explain Orthodox reactions to the evolving ecumenical scene, for these parameters of diversity indicate that the Orthodox radar is finely tuned to differences on the theological, liturgical, and ministerial levels. To the Orthodox perception, the analogous Anglican and Lutheran radar is tuned more broadly. This is evidenced not only by the positions taken within these churches, but also by the kind of agreements that Lutherans and Anglicans are able to achieve with each other. (Not only Anglicans and Lutherans, but at the same time Lutherans and Reformed: one must take note of the fact, e.g., that there are signatories of Porvoo who also participate in the Leuenberg agreement from 1973 — so that some of the Lutheran churches are in communion with both episcopally ordered and non-episcopally ordered churches.)

Thus, to the Orthodox, Anglican-Lutheran agreements not only testify to broader limits to diversity, but also appear to a degree to be *enabled* by these broader parameters.

Evidently, the present situation provides a fertile ground for important church agreements, such as Porvoo and the Meissen Common Statement from the dialogue between the British and Irish Anglican churches and the German Evangelical churches (1988/1991). Admitting a degree of diversity in matters of faith and order that is wider than that of the Orthodox, or finding ways to "reconciled diversity," is surely a part of what — to Orthodox eyes — enables the Anglican communion to hold together in the first place, and enables Anglicans and Lutherans to come to a common statement such as Porvoo.[3]

This does not imply that Porvoo was formed simply on the basis of doctrinal diversity, or that it was enabled by a doctrinal *laissez faire.* It rather means that church union is evidently a far more viable task among the churches coming from the Reformation than it is for the Orthodox. (This situation helps explain the chronically awkward character of Orthodox membership in the World Council of Churches.) Wider limits to diversity are definitely a part of the reason for this viability, but there are other important factors: the divisions between these churches were not as profound as those that split the Christian West from the Christian East. And finally, the churches coming from the Reformation view themselves in relation to the *una sancta* differently than do the Orthodox — on this, more below.

Ultimately, the achievement of Porvoo is obviously more than the natural result of a climate I have described in quite broad and simplistic terms. As is clear from the statement and its process, Porvoo is a

3. If their understanding of diversity is beneficial for Anglican-Lutheran relations, it is potentially harmful for Orthodox relations with either. Aside from describing, in itself a theological difference, a difference of *measure* or *canon,* the enlarged diversity makes it increasingly difficult for Orthodox to know precisely with whom one is in dialogue: the more variety a church embraces, the more difficult it is to find a representative dialogue partner.

hard-earned accomplishment arising out of a deep and prayerful thirst for unity and out of significant and refined theological work. We now turn to an Orthodox analytical response (and again, reaction) to the theology that undergirds Porvoo.

B. Theological Underpinnings and Repercussions of Porvoo

There are two main categories of theological thinking that are of interest — both in and of themselves and also as enabling the agreement at Porvoo. One is the way in which Anglicans and Lutherans perceive their relationship to the *una sancta* — the one, holy, catholic, and apostolic church. The other is the way in which the agreement speaks about the nature of the episcopal ministry and apostolicity, which in turn also stems from ecclesiological understanding.

i. The Universal Church

The "branch theory of the church" has been caricaturized, sometimes by Orthodox and sometimes by conservative Protestants, as holding that the one church of Christ, the *una sancta* of the Nicene Creed, is simply coextensive with world Christianity. In such an understanding, anyone calling himself "Christian" (or, if one is to be more specific, anyone who is baptized) is *ipso facto* as much a member of the church as anyone else. However, if one traces the branch theory to its Anglican origins in the Oxford Movement of the mid-nineteenth century, it is more specific, more limiting. It stipulates that churches, if they are to be construed as "branches" of the *una sancta,* must continue to hold the faith of the original "undivided" church, and that they maintain "apostolic succession" of their bishops. These are quite significant qualifiers.

Of a necessity, Porvoo devotes considerable energy to this latter question of apostolic succession. And in the confidence of finding a resolution to this question Porvoo rests on the understanding that the participating churches of both families all belong to the *una sancta.* This is expressed early on in the statement that each church involved in the agreement understands *itself* to be "a part of the One, Holy, Catholic Church of Jesus Christ" (PCS §7). Later on, with reference to earlier agreements (affirmed subsequently at Lambeth 1988, and similarly by the Lutheran World Federation), there is expressed recognition by the Anglicans of "the presence of the Church of Jesus Christ in the Lutheran Communion as in our own" (§31). Finally, the closing Joint Declaration makes it fully clear:

> we acknowledge one another's churches as churches belonging to the One, Holy, Catholic and Apostolic Church of Jesus Christ and truly participating in the apostolic mission of the whole people of God. (§58a.i)[4]

Porvoo would not have been possible, or it would certainly have taken a radically different form, had either of the communions held to an ecclesiological self-understanding such as that of the Orthodox. What we witness in Porvoo is the convergence of sister churches who are already in some way very near one another, and who do not perceive their claim to be "church" as exclusive of one another.

This observation might be self-evident to the churches involved, but not for the Orthodox, who would not recognize with doctrinal certitude a church other than their own as a "part" of the one holy catholic and apostolic church. Officially, the Orthodox understand the Orthodox Church to *be the church*, and the other churches to be, in some way and to different extents, separated from the fullness of the church.

The question then becomes: Does the mutual recognition among the Porvoo churches of each other as parts of the church constitute an ecclesiological rift with the Orthodox? Not in itself. But, together with other bilateral agreements of the Porvoo churches, Porvoo itself does testify to a "branch"-type of ecclesiology.

It is interesting to note in this context some of the consequences of the terms *koinonia* and "visible unity," popular in ecumenical texts and prominent also in Porvoo. The term and concept of *koinonia* was introduced (or if not introduced then certainly promoted) by Orthodox participants in Faith and Order, most notably Metropolitan John (Zizioulas) of Pergamon. It came primarily to denote the communion we perceive, experience, and know in each other as (baptized) believers in Jesus Christ, and in the one God — Father, Son, and Holy Spirit.

4. Cf. also the Niagara Report, paragraph 80.

The introduction of Greek words into the multilinguistic and multiconfessional ecumenical sphere is sometimes a blessing in that they are absent, initially, of preconceptions, and are malleable enough to support a variety of applications according to need. But the term *koinonia,* after an initial nearly universal popularity, has begun to be treated with concern (ironically, often by the Orthodox). The trouble begins when one defines *koinonia* as "communion," and makes the mental leap to "eucharistic communion" or "full communion." From there begin all the qualifiers such as "real-but-imperfect" or "real-but-imperfectly-realized," which are also of use, but limited use.

The concern is not fully understood until brought into relation with another potentially important concept, that of "visible unity." This too was seemingly a neutral term that meant to describe the unity we seek — a unity that is not experienced only at some official level, or only at certain local levels, but one that is expressed visibly in a common sacramental life, a common mission, a common life — everything listed in the World Council of Churches' Canberra Statement, §2.1.[5] More recently, to some people the idea of "visible unity" has appeared to imply certain specific ecclesiological presuppositions. Once you invoke the idea of "visible unity," it is asserted, you are assuming that an *invisible* unity already exists among all Christians (here is the link with *koinonia,* and with the "branch theory," broadly understood). This invisible unity only needs to be uncovered, made visible, through "denominational adjustments" (not through the renunciation or alteration of doctrine or practice), or through simply opening one's eyes to *recognize* the church outside one's own ecclesiastical borders.

An emphasis, therefore, on describing the church itself as *koinonia,* and seeing interchurch relationships in terms of *koinonia,* goes hand-in-hand with seeing churches as already being in a kind of unity that only needs to be made visible. To the extent that this presupposition is normative, doctrinal differences become less divisive. One can move with greater ease through the steps of recognition, to reconciliation and ultimately to full communion.

Koinonia and "visible unity" language is neutral, and can emerge from a variety of ecclesiological self-understandings. In Porvoo, it appears however to draw on the concepts sketched quite broadly above.

5. Cf. http://www.wcc-coe.org/wcc/what/faith/canb.html.

For example, Porvoo sees unity both as something to which the churches are "summoned" (§22), and something that already exists and needs to be made visible, speaking of a visible unity that needs to be recovered (§27). In this spirit, Porvoo asserts that in some sense "all existing denominational traditions are provisional" (§22). For the Porvoo churches, who at any rate treat one another as fully equal partners, this means that one must find creative ways to make the walls that separate them no longer separate them. Such a perspective, at face value, is more conducive to a mutual coming together than the mainstream Orthodox perspective: there, the same assertions might be made about the provisionality of denominations and to the invisible unity, but only if by visible unity and by the dissolution of the denominations one understands return to apostolic origins in both doctrine and ministry, which are preserved inviolate in the Orthodox Church.

ii. Episcopal Ministry and Apostolicity

The area of the episcopal ministry, and in specific how apostolicity relates to historic (and even "tactile") succession, is the major obstacle that Porvoo sets out to overcome. It is an obstacle that touches on theology and practice, on history and the present experience of the churches. In fact, however, the obstacles faced by the Porvoo churches in this area are nowhere near as great as those in church agreements between episcopally ordered and non-episcopally ordered churches. Therefore Porvoo, while an ecumenical landmark, is not as thorny as are, e.g., Lutheran-Reformed agreements.

Part of Porvoo's importance, and the particular difficulty it sets out to resolve, lies in the fact that Anglicans, who retain the historic succession of bishops, are entering into communion not only with those Lutheran churches who have consciously done so as well, but also with some who have broken that historic succession. The Porvoo churches had two options before them. One was to insist on the normative character of the historic episcopate and tactile apostolic succession, and find ways of re-establishing this succession in those churches that had severed it. The other was to uphold the different approaches of the participating churches as regards the episcopate, and so focus priorities in such a way as to de-absolutize the historic episcopal succession. Porvoo has chosen the second option.

The approach taken by Porvoo follows the basic methodology found in Faith and Order's document *Baptism, Eucharist and Ministry* (BEM) from 1982.[6] The so-called Lima document tends to treat substantial matters of disagreement by (a) defusing absolute interpretations, (b) validating both viewpoints, and (c) encouraging each to try to recognize the validity of the other view. This useful tactic has been widely influential in bilateral church relations in general, and in many specific church agreements. Logically, it is the only conceivable way forward other than the assimilation of one church's views into another, or the "repentance" of one church and subsequent change of practice.

It can be argued that the Orthodox Church has not been part of any fully realized bilateral church union agreement in modern history, including between the Chalcedonian and non-Chalcedonian churches, precisely because of a conscious unwillingness to adopt a BEM-like methodology in any matter that touches on theology. History may show, and indeed the Lord will judge, whether (or where) such thinking was a holy fidelity or mere human obstinacy. But here again, the Orthodox reaction on witnessing others' willingness to adopt the way of mutual recognition promulgated by BEM is one of both bewilderment (as to how matters of theology can be apparently "compromised") and deep respect (at the apparent kenotic openness that is engendered by the serious commitment to unity).

Within the basic BEM methodology, then, Porvoo finds its way to an agreement on apostolicity and episcopal ordering through a series of steps.

Presuming Right Intention As Porvoo states explicitly, in those churches where episcopal succession was interrupted, this was done (a) in accordance with "what was believed to be the precedent of the early Church," and (b) in every case "accompanied by the intention and measures to secure the apostolic continuity of the Church . . ." (§34). Presuming the right intention of the other is a vital feature of

6. Indeed, as footnote references attest, Porvoo paragraphs 36-45 on Apostolicity and Apostolic Ministry draw frequently and explicitly on the relevant sections of the Ministry portion of BEM.

constructive dialogue. But here specifically, and also more widely in the case of the entire Protestant Reformation, it is indeed important to be reminded of the intentions behind what were commonly perceived as divisive actions — intentions that had to do with the preservation or re-establishment of a theology and practice commensurate with that of the apostolic age.

Apostolicity Without Absolutes Porvoo's definition of the nature of apostolicity accounts for both senses that are generally given, i.e., having origins and norm in the apostolic era (§36), and being sent by God into and for the world (§37). As far as *apostolic succession* is concerned, that expression is expanded out of its more traditional definition and location in the historic (tactile) succession, and defined in terms of "the apostolic tradition of the Church as a whole" (§39), with special reference to the "continuity of the Church in its life in Christ . . ." (§40). This expanded definition is in line with most of the recent ecumenical reflection on the question of *episcope* and apostolicity.[7]

Criteria for apostolic continuity are not specified. Rather, a description is given of the special coordinating role of oversight in preserving this continuity. An account of the historic threefold ministry of bishops, priests, and deacons constitutes a part of the exposition on ministry and apostolicity, but emphasis is placed on the unfixed nature of this ministry, and its continuing evolution today (§41).

The Porvoo Common Statement subsequently addresses the relationship between apostolicity/apostolic succession and the historic episcopal succession. There is recognition that "Apostolic succession in the episcopal office is a visible and personal way of focusing the apostolicity of the whole Church" (§46). The multivalent significance of the laying on of hands is helpfully and carefully set out, in terms of God's own faithfulness, the church's intention of faithfulness, the catholicity testified by the presence of a group of bishops, and transmission of ministerial office (§48). Naturally, the laying on of hands is not in itself a guarantee in the technical or commercial sense of that word.

7. Cf., e.g., Peter C. Bouteneff and Alan Falconer, eds., *Episkopé and Episcopacy and the Quest for Visible Unity: Two Consultations,* Faith and Order Paper No. 183 (Geneva: WCC, 1999), pp. 57-62; also *Apostolicity and Succession,* Occasional Paper of the House of Bishops of the Church of England (London, 1994).

Sign Language This last point is emphasized and developed further in the section in Porvoo on "The Historic Episcopal Succession as Sign." Ordination in historic succession is a sign (indication) of continuity, just as the church itself is a sign of the kingdom of God. It indicates or "reinforces [the Church's] determination to manifest the permanent characteristics of the Church of the apostles" (§50).

Here follows a salutary reminder: ". . . the historic episcopal succession does not by itself guarantee the fidelity of a church to every aspect of apostolic faith, life and mission" (§51). (Indeed and of course, as we Orthodox like also to recall, most if not all of the great heresiarchs in the early centuries of the church were bishops and archbishops ordained squarely in apostolic succession.) "The retention of the sign remains a permanent challenge to fidelity and to unity, a summons . . . and a commission. . . ."

What follows is more of a breach with Orthodox thinking. First, there is a logical problem. Porvoo notes that "Faithfulness to the apostolic calling of the whole Church is carried by more than one means of continuity" (§52). It *follows,* says Porvoo, that authentic episcopal ministry can be recognized also in churches that have not retained the historic succession. The historic succession appears here, by implication, to be elevated from mere sign to being a *means* of continuity. This may well be deliberate, for it strengthens the following assertion: if there are indeed multiple means of continuity, it would ensue that any one of these means could be invoked as a way of maintaining apostolicity.

But to my reading, the logic is faulty in either case: the existence of multiple signs or even *means* of continuity does not *ipso facto* enable one to lessen the absolute or indispensable character of any one of these means. Nevertheless, it is this assumption underlying the statement which is subsequently presented as fact: "The mutual acknowledgment of our churches and ministries is theologically prior to the use of the sign of the laying on of hands in the historic succession" (§53).

Here then is the break with Orthodox thought. For the Porvoo churches, apostolic succession is understood in terms of any of the signs, either symbolic or phenomenological, of continuity with the apostolic era. The historic succession of bishops is a special sign of this continuity. For the Orthodox Church, to speak of apostolic succession is to speak of the historic episcopal succession. As with Porvoo, that historic succession is not seen as a guarantee in itself of fidelity, but the absence of the historic succession is the absence of an essential element of the being of the church. There can be historic episcopal succession without apostolic fidelity, but there can be no full apostolic fidelity without the historic episcopal succession. To the Orthodox the historic succession is more than a sign that "reinforces [the Church's] determination to manifest the permanent characteristics of the Church of the apostles" (§50). The historic succession is in fact one of those permanent characteristics. It is on the level of *esse* and not *bene esse.*

The interpretation of our different confessions of the four classical "marks" of the church is drawn on similar lines. Oneness, holiness, catholicity, and apostolicity: all of our churches recognize in these characteristics the two dimensions of "gift" and "calling." Nobody is saying that they are magic; rather they are in some way both inherent and also require a responsible "living-out," or realization by us. But the Orthodox do not divide between an invisible church in heaven that naturally espouses these qualities and an earthly church that fails to. This is why the Orthodox will always have a different answer to the questions of how sin affects the church, whether and how the church can be divided in itself, whether the church is lacking something. This is also why the Orthodox will respond differently to the very real problem of fallible and even sinful bishops. The episcopacy is, together with the church's apostolic doctrine and its sacramental structure, an inalienable part of what the church is. The Orthodox understanding of the church's holiness (and thus sinlessness) in the face of obvious breaches of morality, the Orthodox assertion of the church's oneness in the face of even intra-Orthodox schisms, will continue to puzzle the Reformation mind — as will the Orthodox insistence that their ecclesiology is not Platonic!

C. Conclusions

To any observer, regardless of confessional status, Porvoo is a remarkable achievement. Its ultimate significance will be revealed over the course of time, and is already evident to those closely involved with the participating churches. What the present essay has attempted to show is that, to the Orthodox eye and Orthodox sensibility, Porvoo was made theologically and even psychologically possible by three factors.

One is a generally greater tolerance of diversity both within and between the churches. This is not to say that Porvoo was easy going, or that it does away with or trivializes doctrinal differences. The celebration of diversity, as the text says, should not be "a mere concession to theological pluralism" (§23), and this is not what brings Porvoo about. But naturally the habit of an increased internal diversity makes it less difficult for the churches to imagine drawing their perimeters wider than before.

A second is the fact of the churches seeing themselves and each other as parts of the one church of Christ, seeing that church (which in some way presumably embraces all the Christian communions) to be defined in terms of a *koinonia,* an existing unity, which needs only to be realized and made visible — enacted, as it were.

And the third factor is its agreement on the nature of apostolicity, one within which the historic episcopal succession is both respected and at the same time not absolutized.

The Orthodox reaction to Porvoo — or mine, at least, as it has been made explicit above — is twofold. There is, on the one hand, a degree of puzzlement, or in any event a reminder of some of the differences in matters of faith and order between our churches. A part of this disorientation lies in the fact of the awkwardness of the different interim stages that the various intra-Reformation churches must pass through, and the acknowledged anomalies involved as local churches progress at necessarily different paces.

But there is a concomitant sense of respect for what is able to go on between these churches, an awe at the ability to let go of some of the enshrined distinctions and particularities and allow a healing of memories. Together with that respect, there is also for some of us a certain envy, when we look at the kind of freedom that has made Porvoo and other bilateral and local agreements possible. These agreements were by no means easy, but in our own most hopeful bilateral dialogue, between Eastern (Chalcedonian) and Oriental (non-Chalcedonian) Orthodox churches, the evident slow pace of the dialogue and the immense difficulty of reception testify to some of the obstacles we face in our own attempts at being faithful to apostolic truth.

Bewilderment and awe — it is the Orthodox at Lausanne all over again.

The Porvoo Common Statement: A Methodist Response

BRIAN E. BECK

Internationally Methodism is very diverse. Not all Methodist churches are episcopally ordered. In those that are, episcopal ministry has evolved in different ways, sometimes in response to external political pressure. While in most such churches the episcopal office is held for life, in some it is for a limited term only. Behind this diversity, however, lie two main streams of tradition, the one, episcopally ordered, deriving from the formation in the United States of the Methodist Episcopal Church in 1784; the other, without personal episcopacy, having evolved in Britain directly from John Wesley's connection of Methodist societies. It is impossible to reflect all this variety in this response. These pages are written from a British perspective, although the implications of Porvoo for the United Methodist Church, the main representative of the American tradition, will also be briefly considered.

On several occasions the Methodist Church in Britain has declared itself willing to accept episcopacy in the historic succession, most recently in 2000. Previously it had done so in the context of unity proposals, the South and North India Schemes, the Anglican-Methodist Conversations of 1955-72, and the Covenant proposals a decade later. It needs to be remembered, however, that there were many who opposed those decisions on the grounds that they required of Methodism a willingness to accept a condition for union which they saw as alien to their tradition and extraneous to the gospel, and who would now have sympathy with the reservations of Danish and other Lutherans about the Porvoo agreement. Communities that have laid great stress on justification by grace through faith do not easily accept an emphasis on church order, which seems to them to limit the free availability of that grace. The theological basis offered for the emphasis on historic episcopal succession is thus of paramount importance.

How then should one respond to the Porvoo Common Statement and its Declaration? First of all, naturally, to welcome any forward step taken on the long and painful road toward the unity that is God's calling and gift to the church. That some of the impulse for this has come from the political and secularizing situation in which the churches find themselves is only to say that the Spirit employs many means to make his voice heard. The fact remains, the Porvoo agreement and its acceptance are steps forward made possible by the grace of God.

Secondly, to welcome the fact that unity and mission are held so firmly together. Ecumenists have often been accused of neglecting mission and diverting energies from it, and indeed ecumenical texts have sometimes done little to dispel the notion. That accusation cannot be made against Porvoo. By addressing the issues in the context of apostolicity, rather than, say, catholicity, the report has kept mission in the center of the discussion.

Thirdly, one must warmly welcome the clear recognition that apostolic continuity in the church is carried along all streams of its life, in its theology, liturgy, spirituality, pastoral care, missionary outreach and witness, as well as in its order. That recognition is applied to achieve a breakthrough in establishing communion between Anglican and Lutheran churches that had previously proved elusive. I shall return to this point later, but for the moment draw attention to its importance and the fact that it is a fruit of the widespread appreciation of the concept of *koinonia* as one that releases us from excessively static and structural approaches to church relations.

Welcome too is the recognition of diversity as the prerequisite of any significant unity. It is so often stated these days as to be almost an ecumenical commonplace, but it is often not wholly believed by those who are suspicious of where the ecumenical movement may lead. Equally welcome, especially to Methodists with their particular history, is the candid acknowledgment, following Faith and Order's document *Baptism, Eucharist and Ministry* (1982), that the historic episcopal succession, though a sign, cannot be a guarantee of apostolicity. Given the part played by the shortcomings of eighteenth-century English bishops (for reasons, be it said, not wholly of their own making) in the separation of Methodism from the Church of England, Methodists cannot ask for less.

Important as the breakthrough is, it is not a union. The churches remain distinct and autonomous. They have much in common and will now be free to develop common structures and initiatives. To that extent the autonomy may begin to break down. Territorially, however, the Anglican and Lutheran participants in the Porvoo process overlap only in the presence of scattered expatriate chaplaincies. These will now be brought into canonical relationship with the host church, but in other respects the churches will co-exist in communion. The comment of the House of Bishops of the Church of England is significant: "The House can only imagine entering into a relationship of union with another church in England if that entailed a unity in faith, sacramental life, a single presbyteral ministry with a common episcopate in the historic succession and common structures: in short a single Church for the sake of strengthening a common mission and service to all."[1]

So, of course, Methodists will be asking: What is there in this for us? Does Porvoo offer a way forward that can fruitfully be followed in other contexts? That is the question this chapter seeks to explore, and effectively that means: Does Porvoo offer a way to resolve the difficulties that confront Methodists and Anglicans? Numerically the Lutheran churches are not strongly represented in Britain although they are active in ecumenical councils. Elsewhere in the world Methodists and Lutherans are to be found side by side, Lutherans often being the majority. The Methodist churches in Britain and Ireland and on the European continent have entered into agreement with the churches of the Leuenberg Fellowship, which involves fellowship of word and sacrament including mutual recognition of ordination. The World Methodist-Lutheran dialogue has opened up bilateral agreements for pulpit and table fellowship in a number of places. Communion between Lutheran and Methodist churches, therefore, does not present insuperable problems. What then does Porvoo offer to Methodists and Anglicans, who in many parts of the world share the same territory but are still separated by the issue of the historic succession?

1. See GS 1156, House of Bishops' Report to the General Synod, June 1995, p. 14.

The detail of the Porvoo agreement needs to be noted carefully. The temptation on a superficial reading of concluding that historic episcopal succession is seen as but one sign of apostolicity among many so that, if the succession is broken, apostolicity can be carried by the others until it is restored, like a broken bone being supported by a splint, is one to be resisted. Each of the churches in the agreement claims to be the continuation of the mediaeval church in the country concerned. They are described as national churches (although the picture in Scotland in particular is rather more complex). Each is now episcopally ordered. Moreover, the justification offered for disregarding the interruptions in the episcopal succession is not simply that the churches are truly apostolic in other respects, but rests on a combination of factors: first, the interruptions were not deliberate or dogmatically based (there was no intention to embrace a presbyterian polity), but were forced upon the churches by political circumstances; secondly, when in 1536 consecrations in Denmark were performed, not by bishops but by Johannes Bugenhagen, a presbyter, they were performed nevertheless by one whose ministry can be regarded as episcopal in all but name; thirdly, although there was not a succession in consecration there was a succession in historic sees.[2] No Methodist church matches that combination of characteristics. Nevertheless the movement beyond the simple insistence on continuity in episcopal consecration characteristic of earlier conversations is striking and welcome. Apostolicity is a multiple cord, not a single thread.

Equally striking are other allowances made. Episcopal ordination of presbyters is not invariably required practice in all the Lutheran churches concerned. In certain circumstances deans of cathedrals may ordain. But the Anglican churches have been willing to judge by the norm rather than the exception. Similarly striking is the degree of difference accepted in the interpretation of episcopacy. In the supporting essays published with the Porvoo Common Statement it is made unambiguously clear that for some at least in the Lutheran churches the episcopate, although requiring a further act of consecration, is an extension of the presbyterate. The presbyterate is *jure divino*, the episcopate *jure humano*. The episcopate is not seen as a dis-

2. See the essay by John Halliburton in *Together in Mission and Ministry* (London, 1993), pp. 155ff.

tinct order.[3] Moreover, the Lutheran churches remain free to be in communion with non-episcopal churches, thus taking a different view from Anglicans of the significance of episcopal succession. From a Methodist point of view these are hopeful signs.

Methodism cannot claim direct evolution from the mediaeval church. Its roots lie in the Church of England of the eighteenth century. Its development into separate churches was prolonged and messy. Many political and sociological factors were involved. In Britain it is impossible to name a date at which Wesley's Methodist societies became a church, although there are many landmarks along the way. In the United States it is clearer: at the Christmas Conference of 1784 they declared themselves to be The Methodist Episcopal Church in America and soon replaced Wesley's term "superintendent" by "bishop." The critical point of no return for both sides of the Atlantic was Wesley's ordinations in September 1784.[4]

The precipitating factor was the situation created in America by the end of the War of Independence and the absence of any ordained clergy to minister to the Methodist societies there. It needs to be remembered that one reason for Wesley's action was to prevent the development of lay eucharistic presidency or the creation of a presbyterate *de novo* from the laity, for some of the lay preachers in America had already attempted to take matters into their own hands. It is also important that he took this step only after the bishop of London and others had refused to act. He was thus attempting, not only to provide pastoral oversight of the American Societies but to preserve some semblance of catholic order. He claimed theological justification in the thesis of Baron Peter King and Bishop Edward Stillingfleet, that in the primitive church bishops and presbyters were of one order, and he therefore, as a presbyter, considered himself to be "as real a Christian bishop as the Archbishop of Canterbury," though he vehemently refused the title.[5]

3. See for example the statement on behalf of the Lutheran Church of Norway by Gunnar Lislerud, *Together in Mission and Ministry*, p. 96.

4. For what follows see especially the discussion by A. R. George in *A History of the Methodist Church in Great Britain*, vol. 2 (London, 1978), pp. 143ff.

5. *Letters*, ed. J. Telford (London, 1931), vol. 7, p. 262, vol. 8, p. 91. Wesley is sometimes quoted as dismissing the historic succession as a fable. His actual words were "The *uninterrupted succession* I know to be a fable, which no man ever did or can prove" (*Letters*, vol. 7, p. 284, italics original).

That he had no canonical authority for this was for him set aside by the precedent of Scripture and the primitive church and his sense that God had set him apart for the oversight of the developing revival.

Wesley not only ordained lay preachers as deacons and presbyters, he also ordained Thomas Coke, already a presbyter, as "superintendent" for the American Methodist Church, with authority similarly to ordain Francis Asbury who was already resident there. Although he later fiercely resisted the conclusion, the Americans instantly recognized the implications of this action and the service-book he sent them, which contained with few adaptations the threefold ordinal of the *Book of Common Prayer.* Coke and Asbury were bishops, and the church was episcopally ordered.

There has been much debate about Wesley's thinking on this issue, and it is difficult to excuse him from some element of inconsistency. One could reasonably argue on the King-Stillingfleet principle that Coke was already invested with the same episcopal authority as Wesley claimed for himself and needed no further ordination. On the other hand, in using the term "superintendent" it seems that Wesley was recognizing that Coke needed to receive from him a share for the American church in the authority he himself exercised over the whole connection of Methodist societies and preachers. Wesley was an episcopal figure in all but name. To assert that bishops and presbyters were one order was not to deny the possibility of a wider ministry of oversight within it. To this day the United Methodist Church affirms only two orders of ministry, deacon and elder (presbyter), but consecrates elders to the (lifelong) office of bishop, to exercise collegially the "general superintendency" of the whole church.

The American Methodist situation thus bears resemblance in many respects to that of the Nordic and Baltic Lutheran churches. The United Methodist Church is not a national church, nor is there a succession in historic sees (how could either be the case?), but it is an episcopally ordered church, whose orders were received by presbyteral ordination at the hands of a man who exercised (albeit not by formal appointment) an effectively episcopal ministry, at a time when external constraints (and the reluctance of the established church) made canonical observance impossible. That the episcopate is seen as an extension of presbyteral ministry is no different from the position of some Lutheran churches. There is substantial agreement on general matters of faith and doctrine, as the Anglican-Methodist International Commission has observed.[6] One asks, what more is required to bring Methodists and Anglicans together, not just in the United States but wherever the United Methodist Church and the Anglican Communion are represented?

The British situation is different. Although Wesley continued to ordain after 1784, most were for ministry outside the jurisdiction of the Church of England, in Scotland and overseas. Only at the very end of his life did he ordain men for England, apparently to provide for the situation after his death. In fact these ordinations were ignored, and ordination by the imposition of hands was not generally introduced until 1836. No attempt was made to continue the succession from those ordained by Wesley, rather the reverse.[7] The reasons were complex. There was still a strong desire after Wesley's death not to make a formal separation from the Church of England, and an equally strong desire not to perpetuate distinctions among the traveling preachers between ordained and unordained, all of whom in time came to exercise a ministry of Word and Sacraments. The result was that when ordination by the imposition of hands was introduced it was to a single presbyteral order.[8] Until then it was held that the formal act of reception into full connection with the Conference was "virtual ordination," and it has continued to be held that *episcope* over the whole church is exercised corporately by the annual Conference. British Methodism is not in any other sense episcopally ordered, although there are ministers (not least the President of the Conference) who exercise many episcopal functions.[9]

Methodists in the British tradition cannot therefore expect some sudden breakthrough as a result of Porvoo in the difficulties that have always beset formal relations with Anglicans. The most that could be asked is a generous recognition, in the spirit of Porvoo, that a *presbyteral* succession in ministry has been continued even though the accom-

6. See *Sharing in the Apostolic Communion: Report of the Anglican-Methodist International Commission to the World Methodist Council and the Lambeth Conference* (1996) §68.

7. There had earlier been sporadic cases mostly for service overseas; see A. R. George, *A History*, pp. 153ff.

8. A diaconate was not introduced until the last decade of the nineteenth century and not formally acknowledged to be an order of ministry until 1988.

9. None, however, has authority to ordain by virtue of office alone.

panying *sign,* ordination by the imposition of hands, was lacking for some decades. It is unrealistic to expect that more should have been done in the circumstances of the 1790s and early 1800s.

But that brings us to the heart of the matter, the longstanding Anglican stipulation, articulated in the Chicago-Lambeth Quadrilateral of 1886/88, that the historic episcopal succession must be a part of any reconciliation of the churches. If the goal is indeed, in the words of the House of Bishops, "a single church," it is difficult to see how anything less could be required. If the succession is a valued sign of apostolicity and a gift that Anglicans bring, then clearly it should be preserved, unbroken, in any future united church. Provided that its acceptance does not imply an adverse judgment on the apostolic continuity (to use Porvoo's phrase) of the receiving church, there is no reason why Methodists should resist it. Indeed there would be positive gain. The ministry of bishops whose consecration witnessed to the long continuity of the church from apostolic times would help to rescue Methodism from its delusion that "everything began with John Wesley." There is little awareness in the corporate consciousness of Methodism (on either side of the Atlantic) of being heir to a living church tradition in the interval between the Bible and the eighteenth century.[10] British Methodism, as noted above, is already on record as being willing to receive the gift. The careful statement in Porvoo on apostolicity and its relation to the sign of historic episcopal succession, building as it does on earlier statements, is very helpful in this regard.

But a single church may not always be the goal. Geographical distance between churches or differences between them in inessential matters may make a structural union undesirable or not yet attainable. Yet each may recognize in the other elements of doctrine, order, and spiritual life that it believes to be the essential marks of the church of Jesus Christ, and on that basis a relationship of communion between autonomous churches may be declared to exist. Here the Anglican communion does not appear to be speaking with a clear voice.

In August 1999 and July 2000 respectively the Evangelical Lutheran Church in America and the Episcopal Church in the United States agreed on the statement *Called to Common Mission* (CCM), in

10. Official statements of course say otherwise; I am referring here to popular perceptions.

which the two churches become interdependent but remain autonomous. The agreement provides that from the date of adoption the ministry of bishops in the historic succession will be the future pattern in both churches, seen as a sign, though not a guarantee, of the unity and apostolic continuity of the whole church. In the context of Lutheran commitment to receive this, the Episcopal Church has resolved to suspend its rules so as to permit "the full interchangeability and reciprocity of all [Lutheran] pastors as priests or presbyters within the Episcopal Church, without any further ordination or re-ordination or supplemental ordination whatsoever."[11] The contrast with Porvoo is striking. There the commitment is "to welcome persons episcopally ordained in any of our churches to the office of bishop, priest or deacon to serve . . . in that ministry in the receiving church without re-ordination."[12] Both agreements contain provisos about invitation and observance of regulations, but Porvoo is based on recognition that all the churches already possess the historic succession, the American statement on a commitment by Lutherans to introduce it. Porvoo explicitly excludes presbyters who have not been episcopally ordained (as, for instance, those ordained by a cathedral dean, or presumably any received by transfer from another, non-episcopal, church); CCM does not.

One therefore has to ask what does the phrase "a sign of the apostolicity of the church" really mean? Paragraphs 52f. of Porvoo are crucial: "Faithfulness to the apostolic calling of the whole Church is carried by more than one means of continuity. . . . The mutual acknowledgement of our churches and ministries is theologically prior to the use of the sign of the laying on of hands in the historic succession. Resumption of the use of the sign does not imply an adverse judgement on the ministries of those churches that did not previously make use of the sign. It is rather a means of making more visible the unity and continuity of the Church at all times and in all places." I take it that "sign" here means more than a mere emblem of something that is independently the case. The sign does not simply represent apostolicity, it contributes something to it.[13] Nevertheless although it is one of

11. See *Called to Common Mission: A Lutheran Proposal for a Revision of the Concordat of Agreement* (1999) §16. This is effectively the approach adopted in the Church of South India, which encountered such difficulties elsewhere in the Anglican Communion.

12. *Porvoo,* Joint Declaration §58b.v.

13. See the Porvoo Common Statement §48.

the many elements that constitute apostolicity, it is not determinative. Churches that have not preserved the succession without interruption can be recognized as apostolic. One may think of other elements in the church's life, whose presence enhances, but whose absence does not deny, its apostolic character.

When therefore one finds stipulations that presbyters are interchangeable between autonomous churches that are in communion with each other only if they are episcopally ordained, one is driven to ask whether the same understanding of sign is operating. In this context it does not look like one among many signs, whose presence makes apostolicity more visible but whose absence does not deny it. It begins to look like a *necessary* sign, whose absence is a serious impairment of apostolicity and an impediment to communion. It appears that it is not the apostolicity of churches that is at issue but the apostolicity of individual ministers. But in dealing with the interrupted episcopal succession, that was precisely where Porvoo represented a breakthrough. Apostolicity is not carried by the individual but by the church, which the individual represents. That is the view, evidently, that the Episcopal Church in the United States has taken.

One can understand the reluctance of British and Irish Anglicans. The Eucharist is at the center of the church's life. It represents visibly the continuity of the church from the disciples at the Last Supper and the unity of all Christians in their dependence on the grace of the crucified and risen Jesus. As the sacrament is a sign of unity and catholicity so also is the one who presides at it. But when two churches have reached the point of recognizing each other as truly apostolic, one has to ask whether a bar on the presidency by the minister of one church at the Eucharist of another endorses the fact that the Eucharist is a sign of unity or denies it.

Yet the logic is not entirely with *Called to Common Mission*. Both parties to it are already episcopally ordered. A formal union is not contemplated. Yet full communion has been achieved only because the Lutherans have agreed to accept the sign of the historic succession. Here too the sign appears, not as a gift to be shared in common life but more as a condition of mutual recognition.[14]

14. A similar ambiguity lurks in the international Anglican-Methodist dialogue. It calls for "Methodist and Anglican Churches everywhere . . . to recognise formally the

This stance is all the harder to understand when one remembers that both in Porvoo and in CCM wide differences in the diaconate are set on one side. Historically a formal diaconal ministry is at least as ancient a feature of the life of the church as personal episcopacy. In the skein of apostolic continuity the absence of a diaconal thread might be considered a more serious, though still not fatal, deficiency than the absence of the sign of episcopal succession. Its contemporary forms and ordering are very diverse, but while, clearly, a person ordained to one form of diaconate could not be appointed to serve in a diaconate of a different form, the lack of a common diaconate has not been seen as an impediment to communion.[15]

It seems therefore that, in addition to the ambiguity inherent in the word "sign" there is an ambiguity or tension in the concept of apostolicity. Does the recognition of the apostolicity of a church really take us as far as we think and hope, or does it mask a reservation about ministerial orders still to be resolved, and if that is the case, is "recognition of apostolicity" appropriate language to use?

In making this point I do not wish to minimize the immense progress that has been made over the last half-century in Anglican-Methodist relations in many parts of the world. In England there is now canonical provision for non-Anglicans to receive communion in Anglican churches, and for non-episcopal ministers to preside over the Eucharist celebrated in their own tradition in an Anglican church building in an ecumenical partnership. Relationships in very many places are excellent. Over a hundred ministers of the Church of England are officially authorized by the Methodist Church to minister to Methodist congregations. Formal conversations are taking place with the hope of further progress. At the time of writing the outcome is not known, although a proposal for a full union is unlikely. In Wales and Scotland also conversations are proceeding. All this is real gain. But the less than full recognition of Methodist orders is already hard for many Methodists to understand and would be even harder if there

---

apostolicity of each other's churches and our common intention to maintain the apostolic faith. Following this mutual recognition the churches together may institute a united ministry which includes the historic succession. . . ." But it leaves unclear whether agreement to the former will be conditional upon a declared intention to adopt the latter (*Sharing in the Apostolic Communion* §85).

15. See *Called to Common Mission* §§8-9.

were a more formal recognition of communion between the two churches. Indeed it is hard to see how Methodists could concur in a declaration of communion that excluded it.

As already noted, Methodist churches in the British tradition are not episcopally ordered, although they do exercise *episcope* in various forms in personal, collegial, and communal ways. It would be appropriate for Methodism to accept episcopal ministry in the historic succession at the point of a union. Conceivably, as the outcome of present conversations or at some time in the future, there may be a proposal for an interim situation of parallel churches in communion, in which case there would be occasions when a Methodist minister is authorized to serve as vicar of an Anglican parish or is transferred permanently into the Anglican priesthood. Whether in a union or in an interim situation, the standing of Methodist ministers already ordained would need to be resolved. What one would look for would be some liturgical act that would receive them into the fellowship of those who stand in the historic succession and into the jurisdiction of a bishop, but fell short of a reordination or supplemental ordination implying that the minister's existing orders and previous ministry (or the apostolic character of the church to which he or she belongs) are somehow defective. But that is exactly what we have been looking for over the last fifty years, and so far the search has not borne fruit. Does Porvoo really represent, as *Called to Common Mission* clearly does, a movement towards affirming the theological priority of church over ministry that would unlock the door?

There is a further question that might perhaps be added. It ought at least to be noted for the agenda of future discussions. As observed above, under the Porvoo agreement Anglicans recognize the apostolic character of the Lutheran churches, even though they do not invariably practice episcopal ordination to the presbyterate. Exceptions to the norm are tolerated, even though ministry of the individuals concerned is not recognized. Since 1932 British Methodism has affirmed the right of the Conference, exercising *episcope* over the church, to authorize named lay persons to preside over the Eucharist in specified places in cases of pastoral need. They are seen as exceptional, the norm being presbyteral presidency. The custom presents difficulties in formal unity conversations. Can Porvoo's attitude to non-episcopal ordinations be seen as providing a precedent by which, without committing Anglicans to accepting the ministry of such a lay person, the practice could be accepted as not constituting an obstacle to communion? Such toleration might not be envisaged in a full union, but might offer a way forward if an interim stage of two parallel churches in communion were envisaged.[16]

16. It would mark an advance on the Anglican-Methodist Scheme, 1968, which recommended that the practice should cease as soon as possible.

The Porvoo Common Statement and the Leuenberg Concord — Are They Compatible?

RISTO SAARINEN

The Nordic Background

During the 1970s the Nordic European Lutheran churches discussed intensively whether they should sign the Leuenberg Concord, a continental European theological agreement that declares church fellowship among various churches coming from Lutheran, United, and Reformed traditions. After long considerations the Nordic churches did not sign the Concord, although they continued to participate in the so-called Leuenberg doctrinal discussions. Reasons for this decision have largely remained unexplored. It is sometimes claimed that while the negative answer in Denmark and possibly also in Norway was based on the assumption that the national church order does not easily allow for binding ecumenical agreements, the Finnish and Swedish churches had serious doubts in regard to the theology found in the Leuenberg Concord.[1]

At least in the Evangelical Lutheran Church of Finland this was clearly the case. In May 1977 the Finnish Synod decided not to sign the Concord, although many prominent Finnish theologians, such as the

1. See, e.g., the various Nordic contributions in the volume *Leuenberg, Meissen and Porvoo,* Leuenberger Texte 4 (henceforth LMP), ed. Wilhelm Hüffmeier and Colin Podmore (Frankfurt: Lembeck, 1996) and materials available at the Leuenberg internet site http://www.leuenberg.net/. A note on language: Leuenberg Concord (or Agreement) is the text; the Leuenberg Church Fellowship is the organization or communion that the signatory churches form together.

Lutheran World Federation (LWF) President Mikko Juva, were among its supporters. The majority of the synod found that the theological method of the Concord was not acceptable; they also argued that the eucharistic articles of the Concord were not in agreement with Lutheran theology.[2]

The Finnish doubts concerning Leuenberg found elaborate theological expression in a monograph by Tuomo Mannermaa that appeared in Finnish in 1978 and in German in 1981. This book had a profound and long-lasting effect on Finnish ecumenism. Mannermaa argues that the Leuenberg Concord grows out of a Barthian actualistic theology that was made compatible with an existential interpretation of Protestantism. As a result, the Concord often replaces doctrinal issues and quantitative unity statements with experiential and qualitative expressions. Thus the unity statements of the Concord relate rather to the individual prerequisites of doctrine than to its factual content.[3]

The new millennium has, however, changed the Nordic Lutheran ecumenical scene. In 1999 the Church of Norway decided to join the Leuenberg Church Fellowship, and in 2001 the Church of Denmark also signed the Leuenberg Concord. Although we are not yet in a position to evaluate the changes in church history that brought about this new development, I am convinced that the Porvoo Common Statement has given some impetus to the churches also in this respect.

In the Finnish church newspaper *Kotimaa* the editorial of 1 June 2001 claimed that after the decisions in Norway and Denmark, Leuenberg should be re-examined in Finland also. Two weeks later Juhani Forsberg wrote in *Kotimaa* that Finnish Lutherans should not rush to Leuenberg. If any re-examination occurs, it should be based on two considerations: (1) whether the teaching of the Finnish church has changed in some way since the 1970s; and (2) whether the work of the Leuenberg Church Fellowship has undergone such developments that would speak for the signing of the Concord today.

These two considerations of Juhani Forsberg are highly relevant

2. Mikko Juva's autobiography, *Seurasin nuoruuteni näkyä* (Helsinki: Otava, 1994), pp. 271-74.

3. Tuomo Mannermaa, *Von Preussen nach Leuenberg. Hintergrund und Entwicklung der theologischen Methode der Leuenberger Konkordie* (Hamburg: Lutherisches Verlagshaus, 1981).

not only for the Finnish church situation today but also for our general topic. In the following I will address these two issues in order to highlight the compatibility between Porvoo and Leuenberg. I will use the situation of the Finnish church as an example which, I hope, sheds light on the difficult but important issue of the compatibility of various ecumenical agreements.

Is There a New Situation after Porvoo?

In view of Juhani Forsberg's first consideration I think that we must answer positively: yes, the teaching of the Finnish church has changed as a result of various synodal decisions and binding ecumenical agreements between 1977 and 2001. In 1984 and 1990 the LWF decided that all member churches, including the Evangelical Lutheran Church of Finland, are in pulpit and altar fellowship and that they belong to one Lutheran communion. In November 1995 the Finnish synod adopted the Porvoo Common Statement. Domestic doctrinal decisions include, for example, the decision to ordain women in 1986.

Of course there is a deeper sense in which the doctrine of the church does not and should not change. But at the concrete level of agreements things have clearly changed and some anomalous situations have emerged as a result. For instance, seeing the LWF as a communion implies that the Finnish church is in communion with the Lutheran territorial churches of the German Evangelical Church (EKD), but not with the United territorial churches in Germany. When the Finnish church sends pastors to Germany, special arrangements are needed — while some theological matters must be ignored — in order that they can work in the United territories also. A common European Protestant church fellowship would regularize this anomaly.

More interesting and more difficult is the issue whether the Porvoo Common Statement has changed the teaching of the Finnish church. One can argue that the ability to tolerate existing differences within one communion has clearly grown as a result of the Porvoo communion. The Church of England embraces doctrines and practices that derive from many traditions, including Roman Catholic and Reformed. A communion with this pluriformity necessarily brings about an awareness of existing differences and a certain tolerance of them.

In view of the compatibility of Porvoo and Leuenberg, the Reformed wing of Anglicanism is particularly interesting but much neglected in today's ecumenical evaluation of Porvoo. Since the Nordic Lutheran churches have a long tradition of dealing with the Reformed features of Anglicanism, an awareness of this history can be helpful. The Finnish historian Tuija Laine, for instance, has identified more than 100 English devotional books that were translated and read in Finland already before 1809. Concerning the theology of this literature Tuija Laine writes:

> From an orthodox Lutheran point of view, the original English books were heretical. Therefore, the translations had to be revised and molded according to Lutheran doctrine before the censorship officials were satisfied. Without exception, the Calvinist teachings on Communion and predestination were rejected. . . . Puritan books were considered especially harmful. However, not even the clergy could always distinguish between the books of the Puritans and the High Church Anglicans, so both were equally rejected.[4]

Tuija Laine shows that in Finland, Anglicanism was largely considered a type of Calvinism. In spite of active censorship English devotional books were translated and read intensively. Many English books had a significant and lasting impact on Finnish Pietist and revivalist leaders. For instance, *A choice drop of honey from the rock Christ* by the Puritan preacher Thomas Wilcox (1690) has been read in Finnish Pietism from the eighteenth century until today.[5] Finns have thus been well aware of the Reformed elements of English and Anglican theology.

In keeping with this history one may argue that the Porvoo communion means not only a reception of episcopal succession or other High Church elements, but also an appreciation of those Reformed elements of Anglicanism that have fertilized Scandinavian Pietism for

4. Tuija Laine, *Ylösherätys suruttomille* [English Devotional Literature in Finland During the Swedish Era] (Helsinki: Suomalaisen kirjallisuuden seura, 2000), pp. 5-6.

5. Laine, *Ylösherätys suruttomille,* pp. 221-29. The first Finnish translation was printed 1779; until 1852 there were six printings, and the book is still today available in Finnish! For a different evaluation of Reformed influence in Finland, see Eero Huovinen, "Safeguarding Classical Christianity: Ecumenical Relations of the Evangelical Lutheran Church of Finland," *Ecumenical Review* (1996): 69-78, esp. 75.

three hundred years and continue to do so today in the form of various evangelical movements. This side of Porvoo has, however, not been discussed much, either in Finland or elsewhere.

On the contrary, Porvoo has been regarded by many as "quasi-Catholic" and "anti-Presbyterian" because of its emphasis on episcopacy. I have some fears that even the present collection of essays may strengthen this prejudice if continental Protestantism remains neglected. We know that in Germany many theologians have found Porvoo to be theologically problematic. Likewise the Church of Denmark could not sign the Porvoo Common Statement because Danish theologians criticized it heavily.[6]

But if the comprehensive nature of Anglicanism can be grasped and received, the Porvoo communion might open the doors for a positive reception of Reformed theology and church life. A comprehensive reception of Porvoo could then bring about a reconsideration that might well lead to the signing of Leuenberg. In this context the English-German Meissen Agreement (1988/91) and the English-French Reuilly Agreement (1997) can provide the Nordic churches with instructive examples. If the Church of England is ready to enter an altar and pulpit fellowship with the EKD and with the French Protestants, why should another member church of the Porvoo communion limit its contacts to the Lutheran territorial churches only?

But can Porvoo be a real resource in Lutheran-Reformed relations? Or is it rather the case that Porvoo is and should remain an Episcopalian counterweight to the Presbyterian-minded Leuenberg Church Fellowship? This counterweight view is, in my opinion, both historically and ecumenically problematic. It is historically false since it ignores the pluriformity of Anglicanism, and it is ecumenically problematic since it ignores the strong presence of episcopal churches within the Leuenberg Church Fellowship. We have today two churches that are members of both Porvoo and Leuenberg. These churches, the Estonian Evangelical Lutheran Church and the Church of Norway, are quite typical "Northern" churches.

The counterweight view is even more untenable when we study

6. Reinhard Frieling, "Kritische Anfragen an Porvoo aus der Sicht der Leuenberger Konkordie," LMP, pp. 163-72. Danish criticisms are collected in the 2/1995 issue of the journal *Fönix*.

the Leuenberg, Meissen, and Porvoo texts together. This was done by a comprehensive theological group in a trilateral consultation in Liebfrauenberg in 1995. In his Liebfrauenberg presentation the French Lutheran theologian André Birmelé draws the conclusion that in the three documents a basic consensus can be found with regard to the following topics:

- the authority of Scripture
- the authority of the Creeds of the Early Church
- the understanding of the gospel as the message of the justifying action of God
- baptism and the Eucharist
- the understanding of the church as the community of the faithful which lives from word and sacrament
- the eschatological completion.[7]

Birmelé further argues that most items of this basic consensus have been dealt with in the international dialogues and other doctrinal discussions of the ecumenical movement such as Faith and Order's statement *Baptism, Eucharist and Ministry* (BEM, 1982).[8] The ecumenical contributions that have emerged since the 1970s thus contribute constructively to the new openness of which the Porvoo communion is one prominent witness.

In this sense the teaching of the Finnish church, as well as of many other churches, has changed or developed since the 1970s as a result of various ecumenical processes. This development, of which Porvoo is an especially rich resource and milestone, enables a re-evaluation of our earlier decisions. One may note that since Porvoo draws many items and conclusions immediately from BEM and since the Reformed and the United churches have embraced BEM, a member church of Porvoo can now employ the BEM text as a resource in approaching the Leuenberg Church Fellowship. As a common metatext of many different ecumenical agreements, BEM is especially helpful in defining the compatibility issues.

7. André Birmelé, "Leuenberg — Meissen — Porvoo: On the Fellowship of the Anglican, Lutheran, Reformed and United Churches of Europe," LMP, pp. 56-78, here p. 66.

8. Birmelé, "Leuenberg — Meissen — Porvoo," pp. 57-65.

What Is Leuenberg Like Today?

Concerning the second question put forward by Juhani Forsberg, the Leuenberg Church Fellowship has also changed since the 1970s. One of the criticisms made by Mannermaa and other Nordic theologians during the 1970s was that the Leuenberg Concord offers only a "proleptic" consensus, i.e., a view that we already now agree in faith, although many doctrinal issues, such as ecclesiology and the theology of the ministry, remain unsolved. A critic can easily argue that this simply shows a lack of consensus in the quantitative content of church doctrine.[9]

The Leuenberg Church Fellowship has, however, continued its doctrinal talks for thirty years and produced many new documents that explain the consensus achieved. In view of the Porvoo communion, the most important Leuenberg document is the ecclesiological text "The Church of Jesus Christ" (1995), which extensively spells out the understanding of the church and its ministry in the Leuenberg Fellowship. This text also includes the so-called "Tampere theses," which aim at explaining the nature of ministry and episkopé within the Leuenberg Church Fellowship. They state, for example, that

> The Lutheran as well as the Reformed and the United churches recognize pastoral care and episkopé as belonging to the ordained ministry both in the individual congregation and also at a level . . . going beyond the congregation. . . . The Lutheran churches, especially in Scandinavia, put more stress on continuity with the historical office of the bishop whereas the Reformed churches are committed in principle to a presbyterial-synodical order. Nonetheless, the churches participating in the Leuenberg Agreement concur in regarding the service of episkopé as a service of the Word for the unity of the church and that in all churches the non-ordained members of the church also participate in the leadership of the church.[10]

9. Mannermaa, *Von Preussen nach Leuenberg.*

10. Wilhelm Hüffmeier, ed., *The Church of Jesus Christ: The Contribution of the Reformation towards Ecumenical Dialogue on Church Unity,* Leuenberger Texte 1 (Frankfurt: Lembeck, 1995), here pp. 98-99 (also available from http://www.leuenberg.net/english/en-documents.html).

The subsequent developments in the Leuenberg doctrinal talks have been reviewed, for example, in the Liebfrauenberg consultation in 1995. In his contribution at Liebfrauenberg the Swedish Lutheran theologian Ragnar Persenius observes that the document entitled "The Church of Jesus Christ" shows "real progress," but concludes that the original Leuenberg Concord offers only a minimal consensus that leaves the ecclesiological issues unsolved.[11] Since the churches have only signed the original Leuenberg Concord text of 1973, this critical observation is well founded. It remains an issue of trust whether the subsequent doctrinal talks really have achieved something or whether they only present opinions prevailing in some parts of the Leuenberg Fellowship.

On the other hand, if there is trust and willingness to say that "The Church of Jesus Christ" and other documents are genuine expressions of a Leuenberg theology, one can find them very helpful in the evaluation of the Concord itself. In its common report the Liebfrauenberg consultation explicitly states:

> The Nordic Lutheran churches should examine whether, especially in view of the recent Leuenberg document "The Church of Jesus Christ," their existing participation in the Leuenberg Church Fellowship could not be extended and deepened.[12]

In the light of this recommendation, I made already in 1996 a proposal that the Finnish church should seriously consider negotiating a "Leuenberg variata" agreement, i.e., a document in which a preamble or an annex to the Leuenberg Concord of 1973 would state the achieved convergence in ecclesiology, ministry, and perhaps sacramental theology. As a technical model the churches could employ the "Joint Declaration of Church Fellowship" agreement between the Leuenberg Church Fellowship and the European Methodists. This agreement declares church fellowship between the Leuenberg churches and the Methodist churches in Europe — employing the Leuenberg Concord as its basis.[13]

11. Ragnar Persenius, "Critical Questions from a Nordic Lutheran Perspective," LMP, pp. 100-108.

12. LMP, p. 13.

13. Risto Saarinen, "Voiko Pohjolan luterilaisuus edetä Porvoosta Leuenbergiin?" [Can Nordic Lutheranism Proceed from Porvoo to Leuenberg?], *Teologinen Aikakauskirja*

In Finland my proposal passed more or less unnoticed, but I still think that this kind of "Leuenberg variata" would be a useful model for the Finnish and Swedish churches in defining their relationship to the United and Reformed churches on the European continent. Such an agreement would also give more weight to "The Church of Jesus Christ" text within the Leuenberg Church Fellowship. The Meissen and Reuilly agreements and the recent agreement between American Lutheran and Reformed churches should also be consulted in this process.[14]

In my 1996 proposal I also discussed the big stumbling block of the 1970s, i.e., the methodology of the Leuenberg Concord. It is true that the idea of a "proleptic" consensus is not unproblematic. The achievements of subsequent doctrinal talks have, however, given more credibility to the Concord. Moreover, other texts such as BEM and many bilateral statements have been able to show that important doctrinal convergences really exist.

My main criticism of Mannermaa's book is that he overemphasizes the genesis of the Leuenberg Concord. He succeeds in showing that some earlier versions of the Concord gravely neglect quantitative consensus in doctrine. But I argue that the final Concord to a great extent corrects this problem through employing important quantitative statements that give the final document credibility and theological weight. Moreover, I agree with Harding Meyer and disagree with Mannermaa in the interpretation of the German concept of "Kirchengemeinschaft" (church fellowship or communion). Mannermaa finds this concept existentialistic and rather empty of content, but Meyer has shown that the Leuenberg Concord has taken it from German doctrinal discussions in which it relates closely to the biblical and patristic concept of koinonia. Thus there is a much stronger link between Leuenberg and the classical theology of the ecumenical movement than Mannermaa believes.[15]

(1995): 289-301, here 301 (Leuenberger Kirchengemeinschaft und Evangelisch-Methodistische Kirchen in Europa: Gemeinsame Erklärung zur Kirchengemeinschaft, Basel 1993).

14. The American document "A Formula of Agreement" is available at http://www.elca.org/ea/Relationships/formula.html. For Meissen, Reuilly, and various compatibility issues see the excellent book of André Birmelé, *La communion ecclesiale* (Paris: Cerf, 2000).

15. Saarinen, "Voiko Pohjolan luterilaisuus edetä Porvoosta Leuenbergiin?" See

Here again subsequent developments in the ecumenical movement are highly important. Since the 1970s the concept of koinonia/communion has become prominent, and we have a new wave of ecumenical ecclesiology in which this concept has been fruitful. The LWF, the Porvoo communion, and the World Council of Churches have employed the biblical and patristic concept of koinonia in order to describe their self-understanding. If we can see that the German and Leuenberg idea of "Kirchengemeinschaft" belongs to this same discussion, we can approach Leuenberg with less suspicion.[16]

A Caution: Leuenberg and Porvoo as Instruments of Church Politics

Thus far I have argued that (a) I agree with André Birmelé that there is a basic doctrinal consensus among the Leuenberg, Meissen, and Porvoo agreements and that they are in that sense mutually compatible, and (b) that for historical and theological reasons, the Porvoo communion can help the Nordic Lutheran churches define their relationship to Reformed and United churches. I am, of course, aware that the issues of ecclesiology and ordained ministry are not yet solved between the churches. The ministry of the bishop still causes problems between the Episcopal and Presbyterian branches of Protestantism.

One reason why I have not dealt with the disputes between episcopal and presbyterial church order is that they have not been a stumbling block among Nordic Lutherans. In Finland we are critical of Reformed theology for reasons other than church order and the nature of the ordained ministry. We tolerate and even embrace presbyterial attitudes in our congregations and revivalist movements. It is hard to explain to Continental European or American Lutherans why Finnish theologians and pastors generally find Porvoo a solid agreement but Leuenberg problematic. We know, for example, that in the Evangelical

---

Harding Meyer, "Zur Entstehung und Bedeutung des Konzepts 'Kirchengemeinschaft,'" in *Communio Sanctorum: Festschrift für P.-W. Scheele* (Würzburg: Echter, 1988), pp. 204-30.

16. See Risto Saarinen, "The Concept of Communion in Ecumenical Dialogues," in *The Church as Communion: Lutheran Contributions to Ecclesiology*, LWF Documentation 42, ed. Heinrich Holze (Geneva: LWF, 1997), pp. 287-316.

Lutheran Church of America the situation is a different one: whereas the altar and pulpit fellowship with the Reformed churches was passed in 1997 without much controversy, the agreement with the Episcopal Church continues to draw heated debate.

Theological factors play here an important role that should not be neglected. In addition, some non-theological factors need to be mentioned. The Leuenberg Church Fellowship is, at least in Finland, often regarded as an instrument of the EKD and related to the idea of building a European Protestant Forum that could and should become a counterweight to Roman Catholicism. Nordic Lutherans are very suspicious of splitting Christianity into two competing confessions or streams. Our folk church tradition presupposes that the majority church represents the whole of Christianity, not a particular confession.

These non-theological or semi-theological factors became visible in the context of the recent "Joint Declaration on the Doctrine of Justification" (JD, 1999), a global Lutheran–Roman Catholic agreement in which the mutual condemnations from the time of the Reformation concerning the doctrine of justification were declared to be non-applicable to today's churches. The JD was much debated in Germany, where only the Lutheran territorial churches participated in the JD process. Some of the United territorial churches felt that they were neglected. Thus the EKD, the Leuenberg Church Fellowship, and in particular many German university theologians became active in debating the Joint Declaration.[17]

In the Nordic countries many theologians felt that the German United churches and the Leuenberg Church Fellowship were acting as an external pressure group concerning the JD debate in an inappropriate manner. The Leuenberg Concord was highlighted by some as the ecumenical agreement par excellence to which loyalty must be shown before any other agreements can be made.[18] Such voices caused a lot of

17. See the 24(!) special issues on the JD debate of *epd-Dokumentation* between 1997 and 1999. For the position of the United churches and Leuenberg, cf., e.g., Wilhelm Hüffmeier, "Die Gemeinsame Erklärung zur Rechtfertigungslehre — Beobachtungen aus ev.-unierter Sicht," *epd-Dokumentation* 23 (1998): 23-30.

18. In a position paper of 141 theology professors (*epd-Dokumentation* 7 [1998]: 1) it was stated that with the JD "ist zugleich die Gemeinschaft mit den nicht zum Lutherischen Weltbund gehörenden evangelischen Kirchen Deutschlands in Frage gestellt. Das gilt auch für die Leuenberger Gemeinschaft."

indignation in Northern Europe since they were often interpreted as expressions of arrogance and hegemony.

One must add that in the final rounds of the JD process the churches of the Leuenberg Church Fellowship acted fairly. But my experience is that, at least in Finland today, most theologians who support Porvoo and the JD are very consciously against joining the Leuenberg Church Fellowship. This attitude got stronger during the German debates around the Joint Declaration. The JD process is thus an instructive example of how a third party can influence the behavior of ecumenical partners and how theological voices are interpreted in terms of non-theological factors. Much remains to be learned here, and we cannot predict how churches and individual theologians will behave in complex ecumenical situations.

We must also study whether the Porvoo communion is a product of abstract theological wisdom alone. Perhaps future church historians will evaluate it rather as one aspect of a general English cultural orientation. Non-theological factors, such as the predominance of English language and cultural orientation in all the Nordic countries, certainly contribute to the popularity of Porvoo today. Church historians in Finland are beginning to point out that the traditional low-church and lay-centered Finnish Pietism is currently being replaced by a more episcopal view of the church. The ministry of the bishop has also been strengthened by the mass media, which have lifted some bishops to act as the spokesmen and public "faces" of their communities. When Porvoo is being applied to the concrete life of the churches, caution and skill are needed to distinguish between theological and contextual matters. Ecumenical texts are useful tools for guiding the church, but they can also be used in a manner that is not appropriate.

Contributors

The Rt. Revd. Dr. Sebastian Bakare, Anglican Bishop of Manicaland, Zimbabwe.

The Revd. Dr. Brian E. Beck, British Methodist minister (now retired), former tutor and Principal of Wesley House, Cambridge, UK.

Prof. Dr. Peter C. Bouteneff, Assistant Professor of Dogmatic Theology and Spirituality at St. Vladimir's Orthodox Theological Seminary, Crestwood, N.Y., USA.

Prof. Dr. Kirsten Busch Nielsen, Associate Professor of Systematic Theology, University of Copenhagen, Denmark.

The Revd. Dr. Juhani Forsberg, Executive Secretary for Theology (now retired), Department of International Relations, The Evangelical-Lutheran Church of Finland.

The Rt. Revd. Dr. Tore Furberg, Bishop of Visby, Church of Sweden (now retired), Lutheran co-chair of the Porvoo Commission.

The Revd. Dr. Charles Hill, European Secretary, the Council for Christian Unity, Church of England.

The Rt. Revd. John Hind, The Bishop of Chichester, Church of England.

Prof. Dr. Heinrich Holze, Professor of Church History, University of Rostock, Germany.

Prof. Dr. Peter Lodberg, Associate Professor of Systematic Theology, University of Aarhus, Denmark, now General Secretary of Danish Church Relief.

Prof. Dr. Harding Meyer, former Research Professor and Director of the Institute for Ecumenical Research, Strasbourg, France.

The Rt. Revd. John Neill, the Bishop of Cashel and Ossory, Church of Ireland.

The Rev. Tiit Pädam, Rector of the Theological Institute of the Estonian Evangelical Lutheran Church in Tallinn.

Prof. Dr. James F. Puglisi, S.A., Director of Centro Pro Unione in Rome, Italy — also teaching ecumenical theology at several Pontifical universities in Rome.

Prof. Dr. Michael Root, Edward C. Fendt Professor of Systematic Theology, Trinity Lutheran Seminary, Columbus, Ohio, USA.

Prof. Dr. Risto Saarinen, Professor of Ecumenical Theology, University of Helsinki, Finland.

Prof. Jan Schumacher, Associate Professor of Church History at the Norwegian Lutheran School of Theology, Oslo.

The Rt. Revd. Prof. Stephen W. Sykes, Principal of St. John's College, University of Durham, UK, former Bishop of Ely, Church of England.

Dr. Mary Tanner, General Secretary of the Council for Christian Unity, Church of England (now retired) and former Moderator of Faith and Order.

Prof. Dr. Ola Tjørhom, Professor of Dogmatics and Ecumenical Theology at the School of Mission and Theology in Stavanger, Norway, from 1999-2001 Research Professor at the Institute for Ecumenical Research in Strasbourg, France.

The Rt. Revd. Dr. David Tustin, Bishop of Grimsby, Church of England (now retired), Anglican co-chair of the Porvoo Commission.

Furberg, Hind, Neill, Pädam, Sykes, Tanner, Tjørhom, and Tustin were all directly involved in the work of the Porvoo Commission.